W9-CHS-288

AUTISM AND THE MYTH OF THE PERSON ALONE

QUALITATIVE STUDIES IN PSYCHOLOGY

This series showcases the power and possibility of qualitative work in psychology. Books feature detailed and vivid accounts of qualitative psychology research using a variety of methods, including participant observation and fieldwork, discursive and textual analyses, and critical cultural history. They probe vital issues of theory, implementation, interpretation, representation, and ethics that qualitative workers confront. The series mission is to enlarge and refine the repertoire of qualitative approaches to psychology.

GENERAL EDITORS
Michelle Fine and Jeanne Marecek

Everyday Courage: The Lives and Stories of Urban Teenagers
Niobe Way

Negotiating Consent in Psychotherapy
Patrick O'Neill

Flirting with Danger: Young Women's Reflections on Sexuality
and Domination
Lynn M. Phillips

Voted Out: The Psychological Consequences of Anti-Gay Politics
Glenda M. Russell

Inner City Kids: Adolescents Confront Life and Violence
in an Urban Community
Alice McIntyre

From Subjects to Subjectivities: A Handbook of Interpretive and
Participatory Methods
Edited by Deborah L. Tolman and Mary Brydon-Miller

Growing Up Girl: Psychosocial Explorations of Gender and Class
Valerie Walkerdine, Helen Lucey, and June Melody

Voicing Chicana Feminisms: Young Women Speak Out on
Sexuality and Identity
Aída Hurtado

Situating Sadness: Women and Depression in Social Context
Edited by Janet M. Stoppard and Linda M. McMullen

Living Outside Mental Illness: Qualitative Studies of Recovery
in Schizophrenia
Larry Davidson

Autism and the Myth of the Person Alone
Douglas Biklen
With Richard Attfield, Larry Bissonnette, Lucy Blackman, Jamie Burke,
Alberto Frugone, Tito Rajarshi Mukhopadhyay, and Sue Rubin

AUTISM AND THE MYTH OF THE PERSON ALONE

DOUGLAS BIKLEN

With Richard Attfield, Larry Bissonnette,
Lucy Blackman, Jamie Burke, Alberto Frugone,
Tito Rajarshi Mukhopadhyay, and Sue Rubin

New York University Press
New York and London

NEW YORK UNIVERSITY PRESS
New York and London
www.nyupress.org

Library of Congress Cataloging-in-Publication Data
Autism and the myth of the person alone / [edited] by
Douglas Biklen, with Richard Attfield . . . [et al.].
p. ; cm. — (Qualitative studies in psychology)
Includes bibliographical references and index.
ISBN 0-8147-9927-2 (cloth : alk. paper) —
ISBN 0-8147-9928-0 (pbk. : alk. paper)
1. Autism. 2. Autism—Patients—Language.
3. Autism—Patients—Biography.
[DNLM: 1. Autistic Disorder—Personal Narratives.]
I. Biklen, Douglas. II. Series.
RC553.A88A835 2005
616.85'882—dc22 2005003691

New York University Press books are printed on acid-free paper, and their bind-
ing materials are chosen for strength and durability.

Manufactured in the United States of America
c 10 9 8 7 6 5 4 3 2 1
p 10 9 8 7 6 5 4 3 2 1

■　　■　　■　　■　　■　　■　　■　　■　　■

To Sari Knopp Biklen

Contents

■　　■　　■　　■

Acknowledgments

The Nancy Lurie Marks Foundation provided a grant that enabled me to travel to meet with the contributing authors and to put aside teaching for a semester while working on the manuscript. For the analysis and editing stages of the project, Syracuse University gave me a research leave for another semester. I am most grateful to both institutions for their support in this project, as well as for their support of my earlier work that led to this project. I want to thank Debbie Freund, Nancy Cantor, Kenneth Shaw, Steven Bossert, Corinne Smith, Emily Robertson, and Louise Wilkinson of Syracuse University for using their administrative positions to give me the opportunity to engage in work that has been exciting and sometimes controversial. I thank Nancy Lurie Marks for her personal support for my work and Cathy Lurie and Eric Cushing for their encouragement of this project. Thanks, too, to Clarence Schutt and Ken Farber for their advice about the project.

I am grateful to my colleagues who have worked with me on issues of communication and autism, especially Marilyn Chadwick, Mayer Shevin, Christi Kasa-Hendrickson, Chris Kliewer, Maho Kasahara, Julia White, Christy Ashby, Keonhee Kim, Amanda Musolino, Valerie Smith, David Smukler, Alicia Broderick, Katrina Arndt, Pat English-Sand, Eugene

Marcus, Zach Rossetti, Zhaoyang Chi, Qing Shen, and Paula Kluth. Thanks to Dani Weinstein and MaryAnn Barker for their secretarial support. Thanks to my colleagues at the Center on Disability Studies, Law and Human Policy, especially to Bob Bogdan, Steve Taylor, Beth Ferri, Arlene Kanter, Michael Schwartz, and Nancy Mudrick.

Thanks to Michael Gray for photographing Larry Bissonnette's paintings and drawings and to Pascal Cravedi-Cheng for assisting me in contacting and meeting with Larry on so many occasions. I want to express special thanks to Anne Donnellan for introducing me to Tito Mukhopadhyay. Thanks to Gilola Sisera and Patrizia Cadei for their assistance in translating Alberto's chapter. Thanks also to each of the relatives of the contributing authors for the support they gave me and the contributing authors during the process of preparing this book; you did so much to make this book possible, including providing me with sleeping accommodations; meeting me at hotels, train stations, and airports; driving me to interviews with your sons and daughters; providing me with countless meals; searching out diagnostic documents from years past; and welcoming me into your family lives.

I thank Robert and Janet Bogdan for discussing this project with me, Sari Knopp Biklen for her constant support and willingness to talk to me about the book, and Gerardine Wurzburg for her willingness to create a documentary about Sue Rubin, one of the contributing authors.

Thanks to Michelle Fine and Jeanne Marecek, general editors for the Qualitative Studies in Psychology series at New York University Press; to my editor, Jennifer Hammer, who provided encouragement and editing suggestions; as well as to the external reviewers for New York University Press, who provided many comments and helpful suggestions on the draft manuscript.

Douglas Biklen
Syracuse, New York

■　■　　■　　　■　　　■　　　■　　　■　　　■　　　■

Introduction

A Discussion of Methods

Autism and the Myth of the Person Alone is a qualitative study in which people classified as autistic are primary, contributing authors. Unlike any prior research, it draws on the perspectives of people who have previously been perceived as both autistic and retarded and is written from a critical disability studies framework. A basic premise of the book is that people classified as autistic, even those who cannot speak, are thinking people with ideas about their lives and their relationship to the world. I call this orientation the *presumption of competence.* The wisdom of this lens will become clear with the contributed chapters, for each of the authors describes autism as a social construct behind which lie complex and layered relationships between individuals and society. *Autism and the Myth of the Person Alone* is an optimistic exploration of the multiple meanings of autism and both the possibility and the reality of inclusion for people classified as autistic. It challenges one of the most basic tenets of autism, the one implied by the root of its name; that the person classified as autistic is, and perhaps is content to be, alone.

The book is based on more than two years of qualitative research that included solicitation of autobiographical accounts, interviews and conversations, e-mail correspondence, and participant observation (Spradley

1980; Bogdan and Biklen 2003). Two of the eight chapters are constructed directly from interviews. Four of the chapters are narrative accounts that reflect on themes that the editor and the contributors discussed over many months and, in several cases, years. Although there are ethnographic elements to these works—the authors reflect on the classification of autism as well as on their own experiences within cultural contexts (e.g., national contexts such as India, England, Italy, Australia, and America, and institutional locations such as residential institutions and public schools)—they are not presented as *the* culture of autism or even *the* meaning of autism in particular cultures. While it is true that these works focus on "experience and the everyday," what Willis refers to as "the bread and butter of ethnography," these works were not written with an eye to formulating full-blown ethnographies (Willis 2000, p. viii). Instead this book is a collection of first-person accounts that examine everyday life as well as watershed events and that draw on the authors' critical awareness and interpretations of culturally constructed concepts such as autism, disability, normal and abnormal, inclusion and exclusion.

In addition to the contributed chapters, which were conceptualized collaboratively between the editor and the authors but wholly written by the contributing authors—in several instances the authors draw on materials written prior to this project—the book includes a review essay (Chapter 1) on meanings of autism, taking in both its public and professional representations. Preceding each contributed chapter, I provide an introduction with an explanation of the process that led to the chapter being written, as well as of the editing process. A concluding chapter explores practical implications of the contributors' perspectives on autism.

Prevailing modes of research in autism are quasi-experimental and biomedical/neurological. Given that this book presents firsthand narratives, it differs significantly from the dominant literature on autism. Yet readers will find that a number of the themes—for example, motor planning difficulties, intellectual activity, obsessions and compulsions, anxiety, and extreme sensory sensitivities—relate to (and may confirm, extend, or contradict) issues being addressed through the prevailing research methods. Perhaps more important, however, *Autism and the Myth of the Person Alone* brings a new dimension to the literature, including the existing autobiographical literature in autism, by focusing specifically on the perspectives of individuals who traditionally have not been published, if mainly because they were seen as being unable to say more than individual words and phrases or short sentences and to participate in free-flowing conversation, and who all need support from other people in order to participate in everyday social situations.

I began the research for this book with the phenomenologist's assumption that autism, like any topic, is not knowable in a definitively objective sense. If, for example, I observe a thirty-year-old clutching a stack of books and then leafing through them at a rapid pace, all the time humming and seemingly not responding to the people and happenings around her, what am I to conclude from this about autism? Is the person nervous? Is the person involved in a repetitive and meaningless exercise? Is the stack of books the equivalent of a favorite blanket? Is the person reading or scanning the magazines, or perhaps listening to the sound of the pages turning? Is the humming a way to block out distractions that may cause anxiety? Is the clutching of books akin to a smoker chain-smoking or a professor tapping his leg nervously during a faculty meeting? The point is that autism is a list of symptoms or behaviors or representations that can be studied and discussed, but it is not knowable as a truth. It must always be interpreted. Qualitative researchers speak of seeking multiple truths. That is, I can study what autism means at this time, to particular people, in given contexts, knowing that my understanding may change as I become aware of other perspectives and am affected by new experiences and contexts. I am obliged to welcome complexity, even contradictions, as they arise. In sum, I want to consider autism's layered, subjective identities. And most of all, I want to know how people who have been classified with autism interpret themselves and the world.

Most studies and representations of autism are based on deductive analysis. This book represents a different tradition, inductive research using qualitative inquiry. It involves spending time in the field; collecting data (e.g., interviews, documents) systematically; interacting with people; seeking multiple interpretations of events; coding, sorting, and analyzing data; interpreting data in relation to cultural ideas; and formulating hypotheses, interrogating hypotheses during the research process, and developing theoretical understandings. It emphasizes meanings that people give to concepts and events (e.g., autism, competence, independence and dependence, sensory awareness, communication). While contributors' narratives raise issues that touch on and may resonate with research in the fields of psychology and medicine, my focus is on autobiographical narratives themselves, others' interpretations of previously published autobiographical accounts, and cultural representations/perceptions of autism. From this analysis, I then consider, in a concluding chapter, possible implications for educational, therapeutic, or other human service practice as well as for general social interactions. The intent is not to privilege the narratives of people classed as autistic—except that I do put them in the foreground, which is important inasmuch as they are most affected by the classification and since their voices have been so often absent in professional narratives—but to hear firsthand perspectives, to examine them in the context of prevailing ideas about autism, and to derive lessons for practice.

Early in its development as a method of social science, qualitative research was characterized by Glaser and Strauss (1967) as "grounded research" in the book *The Discovery of Grounded Theory*. This referred to the notion that the research involved collecting data in everyday, naturalistic environments; analyzing data in the context of others' accounts; developing hypotheses; seeking new data to challenge or adjust hypotheses; and developing theory. It suggested that researchers could build understanding from the ground up (Strauss and Corbin 1998). Recent investigations that have relied on the grounded-theory approach have addressed such diverse issues as perinatal crack cocaine use (Prusley-Crotteau 2001), the effects of civil war on social networks in El Salvadoran neighborhoods (Oakes and Lucas 2001), women's caregiving with patients who have AIDS (Bunting 2001), resettlement of Bosnian refugees in the United States (Matsuo, Garrow, and Koric 2002), and stepfathers' experiences with claiming stepchildren as their own (Marsiglio 2004). Kliewer has spoken about the method's focus on "local knowledge" (see, for example, Kliewer 1998) in reference to voices that are often absent in deductive research. To the extent that the grounded-theory method may also capture cultural contexts and everyday practices within its lens, it is often also referred to as ethnography (Atkinson 1990; Willis 2000). Often researchers participate in settings as they observe and record, thus giving rise to yet another term for this kind of inquiry: participant observation (Bogdan and Biklen 2003). As I have suggested above, this book comprises elements of these traditions, though most obviously it is a collection of first-person accounts, where each contributing author interprets the disability category known as autism. The authors do so in the context of everyday situations, within institutional constraints of human service systems and public policy, under the shadow of popular and professional scientific representations of autism and disability, through their social relations with family and friends as well as with strangers, and by reflecting on their own personalities. In these ways, their accounts also contribute to the literature on identity (Vryan, Adler, and Adler 2003).

Doing qualitative research requires practitioners to acknowledge the difficulty of *describing and interpreting without objectifying or speaking for* others. On the surface, at least, this book might seem to avoid that problem inasmuch as it creates a venue for people to speak for themselves, through their own narratives. But it is not so simple. This book invites all the same challenges that attend any qualitative research. First, I do not assume that the perspectives of a person classified as autistic are especially "authentic," for this person, like anyone, lives in the world, is affected by available ideas and language, and is not any more context-free than the next person. The fact that an account is personal and based on lived experience does not make it "true" in the sense of being objective (i.e., not subjective) or wholly divorced from "public" understandings, "the interior" in contrast to "the exterior" (Atkinson, Coffey, and Delamont 2003, p. 139). As Atkinson, Coffey, and Delamont note, "The expression of 'experience' never escapes the shared cultural frameworks" (2003, p. 140). So it is important not to treat the voice of the labeled person as uniquely "valid," or as the essential experience. Yet, at the same time, hearing perspectives that have been less available is imperative from the standpoint that it allows for an expanded dialogue with prevailing ideas, and as a matter of equality. This is the meaning of the disability-rights community's clarion call "nothing about us without us" (Charlton 1998).

Similarly, in Chapters 1 and 8 and in the introductions to contributing authors' chapters, I do not assume that my writing is in some way neutral. I, too, am *situated.* I must ask, for example, what is my relationship to the contributing authors? Can I examine the concept of autism without recreating the unequal, clinical relationship of doctor to client, teacher to student, or researcher to subject? I hope so, and I certainly try to, but I know that I must continually question how I may have taken up particular culturally dominant ideas about autism as if they were truths. How do I interpret the contributors' words? What context do I provide in terms of the literature I cite, the issues I choose to highlight, and the conclusions I draw? What devices do I employ to establish authority for my arguments? There is also the question of how I decided whom to include in this book. Then there is the matter of what form authors' narratives take. Who decided about the authors' topics? What was the editing process between contributing authors and me, the editor? Moreover, how will readers interpret these works? These are all questions that followed me around as I planned and worked on this manuscript, and I suspect they are questions that readers will ask as well. For this reason, I want to briefly describe the process I used—"method," if you will.

An obvious issue is "Who do the contributing authors represent?" I will not make the case that they are typical of all people on the autistic spectrum or even of a particular subgroup within those so labeled. At the same time, I do not believe that these authors are necessarily fundamentally different from other people I could have interviewed. Yet they do fit a certain profile I had in mind when I recruited them to this project. I introduce them more fully in Chapter 1 and then again in introductions to their chapters. They, in turn, introduce themselves through their accounts. But even before I met them I had identified certain qualities that led me to them. I knew, for example, that I wanted to interview people who self-identified as autistic and/or who had been formally diagnosed as autistic, and who had at one time or another been thought of as significantly impaired, to the point of having been given poor prognoses for education and participation in intellectual life; it is noteworthy, however, that a few professionals and certainly some parents did see intellectual ability even if many professionals did not. The particular background experience of the authors is revealed in their chapters. As I describe later, I also sought participants who had already established themselves creatively (e.g., as writers, public speakers, or artists). At the same time, all the authors still struggle in many aspects of their daily lives, even though in other ways they are seen as very accomplished. My expectation was not that I would discover a particular "truth" about the concept of autism, but that through my interactions with the contributors and through their writing this book would suggest ways that people classified as autistic negotiate their place in the world, and that this analysis would suggest new or adjusted ideas about autism, inclusion, and representation.

The contributing authors were not drawn randomly to this project. They are, instead, a purposeful sample. My criteria for inclusion in the book were stringent, and hence the group from which I invited the contributors was relatively small. Several of the authors are people I had met previously at conferences, and in one case while pursuing another research project. Others I learned about from colleagues in the field of autism.

The contributing authors, like any authors, occupy a particular historical moment and traditions, and thus readers cannot expect that their accounts are definitive. As Gallagher (1999) has explained, "the contextual complexity of the discursive community is invisible" (1999, p. 76), so the role of critical inquiry is to make it visible. True, the contributing authors' narratives are accounts of living with disability and disability labels, but they are also their understandings about living where they do, amid social forces they encounter, embedded in culture, and about whatever histories they have had. Several of the authors, for example, developed the ability to communicate through typing just as they were entering their teen years. Presumably their accounts would have been different had they been able to converse earlier in life. All but one of the authors were denied entrance to academic instruction with their nondisabled peers in typical schools during the time that they were of primary school age. Thus they and we might ask, how different would their accounts be if they had been welcomed into and supported in inclusive schooling? The social justice elements of their narratives are more surely a reflection of their experiences with prejudice, discrimination, and stereotyping than they are a reflection of particular aspects of disability.

Explaining who the contributors are gives me reason to pause, for while I have images of each that I can rerun in my mind as I introduce his or her chapter (e.g., moments we shared), my dilemma is to convey pictures of the contributors without objectifying them.

A significant criterion in selecting contributors was that they had to be individuals who had developed an independent way to communicate, either through speech or through writing and typing; I wanted readers to be confident that the words they would be reading were those of the individuals classified as autistic and not my or other people's interpretations of them.[1] Two of the authors could do some handwriting in their early years to form both words and short sentences and could also point to letters on demand and could say and read words aloud. One reports that he could move plastic letters around to form words, move word cards to form sentences, and answer questions for assignments by pointing to letters and numbers as well as to words. All the other authors could eventually communicate by pointing at words and letters or by typing on computers and other communication devices. Their use of *augmentative and alternative communication* (AAC, sometimes referred to simply as augmentative communication; Beukelman and Mirenda 1998; Crossley 1994) allowed them to convey complex messages that they were unable to convey or have understood through their speech alone. Some of the authors describe having learned *facilitated communication,* a method that involves using physical support to aid individuals with autism and other developmental disabilities who have unreliable pointing skills to communicate by pointing. Others learned through informal methods that their parents and teachers developed, such as pointing at letters and words on cards; they remember being able to point and to make choices or to select letters and words on communication boards and then later becoming proficient at typing on a computer or communication device (e.g., a Lightwriter) or at independent handwriting.

Controversy has swirled around the method of facilitated communication because it has been shown that a facilitator's physical touch of the typist's hand or arm could influence the person's pointing, and because a number of studies failed to validate authorship (Bebko, Perry, and Bryson 1996; Bomba et al. 1996; Cabay 1994; Crews et al. 1995; Eberlin et al. 1993; Klewe 1993; Montee, Miltenberger, and Wittrock 1995; Moore et al. 1993; Regal, Rooney, and Wandas 1994; Shane and Kearns 1994; Smith and Belcher 1993; Szempruch and Jacobson 1993; Wheeler et al. 1993).[2] Each of the above studies used one basic type of assessment, namely, message passing; the person being assessed was asked to convey information that could not be known to the facilitator. Other studies, using a range of test situations as well as linguistic analysis and documentation of physical, independent-of-facilitator typing, have successfully demonstrated authorship (Broderick and Kasa-Hendrickson 2001; Calculator and Singer 1992; Cardinal, Hanson, and Wakeham 1996; Emerson, Grayson, and Griffiths 2001; Janzen-Wilde, Duchan, and Higginbotham 1995; Niemi and Kärnä-Lin 2002; Rubin et al. 2001; Sheehan and Matuozzi 1996; Tuzzi, Cemin, and Castagna 2004; Weiss, Wagner, and Bauman 1996; and Zanobini and Scopesi 2001). The studies by Cardinal and his colleagues (1996), Sheehan and Matuozzi (1996), and Weiss, Wagner, and Bauman (1996) all involved message-passing experiments, but unlike many of the assessments in which individuals failed to demonstrate authorship, these involved extensive testing sessions, with the possible effect of desensitizing the subjects to test anxiety. The other studies noted above in which individuals have successfully demonstrated authorship involved unobtrusive assessments such as linguistic analysis, statistical analysis of word selection, and independent typing after a period of facilitated typing. Controversy over the facilitated communication method has continued, with some reviewers claiming it has no benefit and may be harmful (e.g., Mostert 2001); others arguing that criticisms of the method are reflective of a tendency within disability fields to equate problems of speech with intellect (Borthwick and Crossley 1999; Mirenda 2003); and others suggesting how parents and practitioners should address any contested methods of education or communication training (Duchan et al. 2001). In light of the controversy, this book includes individuals who can type without physical support or who can speak the words they type, before and as they type them and after they have typed them. Beukelman and Mirenda (1998) state that "in regard to a small group of people around the world who began communicating through FC (facilitated communication) and are now able to type either independently or with minimal, hand-on-shoulder support . . . there can be no doubt that, for them, [facilitated communication] 'worked,' in that it opened the door to communication for the first time. . . . For them, the controversy has ended" (p. 327). Several of the authors included in this book have published accounts of their emergence into independent typing (Blackman 1999; Mukhopadhyay 2000; Rubin et al. 2001), and one is featured in a research article on learning to speak after first learning to type (Broderick and Kasa-Hendrickson 2001). The one exception to this independent-typing-or-speaking criterion is the artist Larry Bissonnette, who at the time of writing for this book could type with a facilitator's hand on his shoulder and lifting off the shoulder—giving him confidence and focus. He does, however, paint without any physical support, and his artwork is the core of his chapter; his writing consists of titles and brief, autobiographical commentary to the pictures.

Another criterion for selecting authors was location. I wanted to include people from different countries, in part to expand the social and cultural contexts in which to see autism but also to acknowledge that autism discourses are not circumscribed by national borders. The contributors are from Australia, England, India, Italy, and the United States. They include two college students, one student who is waiting to enter a university, a secondary school student, one student who has been home-schooled due to the fact that he was not accepted at traditional schools, a university alumna who is a graduate student, and an adult who is an artist. I was interested in including people who had published other work to which the contributions in this book could be related. Four of the authors, including Bissonnette, have been featured in documentary films (Wurzburg 2004; Kasa-Hendrickson, Broderick, and Biklen 2002; Terrill 2000; Mabrey 2003; and Biklen and Rossetti 2005), and so their ability to communicate can be observed. And all the contributors have given addresses to professional and other conferences and will presumably continue to do so; thus readers may have opportunities to view and hear their presentations. Beyond being purposeful in selecting contributing authors, I followed what has been described as the "optimistic approach" (Bogdan and Biklen 1998, pp. 220–221.) This involves the researcher deciding to look at situations that others have identified as "successful" and then learning from them. Whereas many researchers might ask, "Can all people classified as autistic learn?" or "Is inclusion in school and society a good idea?" the optimistic approach assumes that such questions cannot be answered empirically, and even if they might be addressed in the light of empirical evidence, these are "not the right one[s] to ask" (Bogdan and Biklen 1998, p. 220). They are doubting questions. More optimistic questions would be "How do people classified as autistic achieve inclusion, and what does it look like?" or "How do people classified as autistic experience learning to read or to converse?" My main question was quite broad. I asked simply: What can I learn about autism and about the participation in schools and other social settings from people who by all accounts have done well in this regard? By selecting contributing authors who have achieved a great deal, I hoped they might explain or at least hint at new ways of understanding autism.

Having recruited the authors, I turned to what qualitative researchers do: participant observation and extensive interviewing, transcribing, and interpreting. I systematically explored themes that they raised in their earlier writings and in their correspondence with me, or that had appeared in autobiographical accounts by others and in observational accounts by earlier researchers who were the first to describe autism as a clinical category (e.g., Kanner 1943/1985 and Asperger 1944/1991). The nature of this work is not to impose particular understandings but rather to have topics or themes emerge from the contributing authors' accounts and then to interpret these ideas in relation to other ideas (e.g., other research, particular theories of autism, cultural representations).

It is inherently challenging to do qualitative inquiry in a field as highly medicalized as autism, for most of the language of the field assumes a shared, normative perspective of an observable reality. It is common in scientific accounts of autism to treat autism more or less as a relatively stable concept. For example, researchers will describe it as comprised of a triad of deficits, for instance, involving social interaction, communication, and imagination (Frith 1989). Or they may point to the American Psychiatric Association's definition in DSM-IV to say what autism *is:* "(1) qualitative impairment in social interaction" evidenced by impairments in such nonverbal forms of communication as facial expression, eye gaze, social give-and-take, and sharing of interests or enjoyment; "(2) qualitative impairments in communication" evidenced by delays in or lack of spoken communication, problems initiating conversation, stereotyped language, absence of or unusual "make believe play or social imitative play" suited to the person's age; and "(3) restricted repetitive and stereotyped patterns of behavior, interests, and activities," as seen through preoccupations in one or several seeming stereotyped actions, seeming inflexibility with regard to routines, adherence to seemingly nonsensical routines or ritualistic actions, stereotyped behavior such as hand flapping, and "persistent preoccupation with parts of the body" (American Psychiatric Association 2000, p. 75). Here, words that may have been intended as descriptive are judgmental. Calling an action "ritualistic" is different from calling it "consistent," and labeling an action a "persistent preoccupation" is different from "strong interest." Referring to an absence of or impaired "imagination" is more problematic still, for it implies the author's ability to know what the other person is thinking. Even saying that a person "is autistic" could be problematic if the person does not chose the label and if the labeling implies that autism is a tangible reality. So, from an ethnographic inquiry point of view, even talking about autism becomes difficult.

I learned that lesson during the course of writing this book when one of the contributing authors objected vigorously to my using phrases such as "people with autism" or "autistic persons," preferring instead phrases such as "classified autistic" or "diagnosed as being on the autistic spectrum," thus keeping in the foreground recognition that autism is a concept *developed and applied, not discovered.* Consequently, I found myself, in the latter stages of manuscript editing, scouring the parts of the book that I wrote to make this change. I know other people who embrace the term *autistic* or *autie,* just as some individuals with physical disabilities have embraced the term *crip,* and so I know there is no agreement about best language. Again, I decided in favor of not labeling people myself but instead referring to labels that others had applied, feeling that anyone should have the right to decide to self-name, especially if a label might be interpreted pejoratively. Throughout this research, I found I had to remind myself not to interpret events or actions as indicative of autism, though such deterministic reductionism seemed ever available in the medicalized field of autism. As Gallagher (1999) explains, a critical perspective recognizes that "mainstream texts of a discourse community" are "social artifacts," and as such are part of the "meaning-making system" that we inherit. Our role is to see these texts not as *natural* but as *social constructions.* The ethnographer's obligation is to try to understand lives and ascribed meanings "within their respective and collective contexts" and to theorize this understanding (Cole and Knowles 2001, p. 11). The qualitative researcher's role as inquirer about the other person's perspective and the other person's understandings proved to be a workable protective strategy against imposing my own or, worse yet, the autism field's dominant interpretations on events or actions; I will not claim to have avoided this entirely, but it was a constant goal.

Take the example, for instance, of an interaction I had with Tito Mukhopadhyay about his fear of riding in cars. As hard as I tried to imagine what it was that frightened him—possibly the change of routines of moving from walking to riding, or the speed of the car, or the fear of oncoming traffic—I could not know unless he could figure it out and tell me. I was especially at a loss on this matter of riding in an automobile, because in contrast to his apparent fear of cars, he seemed perfectly comfortable when he and I and his mother rode through the city of Bangalore in motorscooter-powered, open-air, three-wheeled transports; these seemed to me far more flimsy and potentially dangerous than riding in a car. But any hypothesizing on my part about what Tito experienced or felt would be just that: hypothesizing. Even worse, as Gallagher explains in her analysis of student behavior, the tendency of the outside observer may be to impose explanations that originate in the dominant narrative of the discourse community, for example, among school psychologists and their research literature. Gallagher explains that "what a behavior may mean to a student is ignored or marginalized as unimportant" (p. 79); this is reminiscent of Fine's (1991) analysis of school "dropouts," where she found students' explanations of why they left high school were widely at odds with school officials' understandings, with students often feeling unwanted and pushed out, "discharged coercively" (p. 79). Equally worrisome, Fine notes that the students who stay in school and are defined as behaving, or as one teacher in Fine's study put it, "quiet" (p. 137), may have reached a point where they "dare not speak on behalf of their own collective interests" (p. 137). In the case of Tito's fear of car travel, he eventually explained that when traffic flowed from the opposite direction, at a rapid rate of speed, his sense of depth perception failed him; also, he said that the rushing sound of the air from outside the car bothered him.

The ethnographer's role by definition is to focus on gathering, not suppressing or ignoring, the other person's interpretation of events. Duchan (1998) explains how this would work in regard to autism when she writes that "in no case should a behavioral description be seen as the only possible 'true' rendition of a behavior" (p. 108). Even descriptions are not "objective reports," she warns, for here too the observer has "selected and interpreted in light of a prevailing theoretical paradigm or discourse agenda" (p. 102). Autism, Duchan reminds us, "like other categories of disability, is based on a particular and fluctuating construction of reality, varying with one's goals, audience, frame of reference, and point of view" (p. 108).

To set the context for discussing autism, the book includes analysis of prevailing theories of autism. It acknowledges the historical roots of the concept as well as autobiographical accounts by people with autism whose speech is relatively unimpaired. It references quasi-experimental as well as ethnographic narratives and notes varying official definitions of autism, including diagnostic information generated by official bureaucracies. Drawing on these traditions, however, I attempt to approach them critically by examining their embedded assumptions. Not only did I want to explore how the idea of autism was formulated and used; I wanted to know what metaphors had arisen in relation to it, and how and why ideas about autism have shifted. I want not to presume the correctness of current language or definitions or to treat them as having objectively captured reality. Thus I read texts about autism with a critical eye to the adjectives that authors use, asking myself the meaning of an expert saying that "knowing seems beyond most children with autism" (Baron-Cohen 1996, p. 77) or that "mental state terms" are "tragically" missing in children with the autism label (p. 84). As I reviewed various accounts, it became obvious that in speaking about the idea of autism, researchers often lapsed into speaking *for* the labeled person. This is evident even in the first attempt to define autism, when Kanner (1943/1985) declared that a student "does not observe the fact that anyone comes or goes" (p. 12), that a student "paid no attention to persons," that a student's remarks were not "meant to have communicative value" (p. 24), that a student had "no affective tie to people" (p. 24), that a student could not "associate his misconduct with his punishment" (p. 12), and that a child dreaded "noise or motion that intrudes itself, or threatens to intrude itself, upon the child's aloneness" (p. 44). Similarly, Asperger (1944/1991) said of one of his clients, Fritz, that he "was not interested in" other children, that he "had no real love for anybody," and that he did not "know the meaning of respect" (p. 40). Speaking more generally about people he classified as autistic, Asperger concluded, "They have a genuine defect in their understanding of the other person" (p. 81). Acknowledging that no person can know what another is feeling or thinking unless the other person can express his or her inner experience, this book asks people with the autism label to name and describe their own experiences and perceptions. These insider accounts (i.e., autobiographical accounts of people who have been classified as autistic or as autistic and with another disability) are thus juxtapositioned to professional explanations of autism. This is a standard approach in much ethnographic research, where the researcher seeks insider perspectives and holds them up to official narratives, in effect exposing the contradictions, even fictions, that inevitably surface.

Collecting and reporting interviews and autobiographical accounts involves composing narratives that follow particular traditions and may challenge or shift others. At times the narrative may feel intimate, at others removed and more obviously observational, as from an outsider viewpoint. At points, the text may follow an expected course, for example, a chronology of events over time, or familiar topics related to autism that seemingly match often-discussed topics in the field. In short, there is no avoiding the fact that while the book may deliver new insights, it will certainly reproduce some formats or conform to certain conventions in existing literature. Yet, throughout, following Atkinson's advice in *The Ethnographic Imagination,* I attempt to live the phenomenologist's appointed role of looking critically, of asking what assumptions underlie the tendency to follow certain formats or to visit particular topics.

Naturally, in those instances where the chapters take the form of interviews, I had to create a context within which the authors might share their perspectives. In these, I tried to reference my questions either to issues the contributors had raised in their own, prior writing or to other autobiographical narratives. As the authors provided their accounts, I pursued specific themes through follow-up questions. For instance, if an author said she often failed to accomplish certain tasks because of motor difficulties, I asked for examples of the tasks and a description of what she meant by "motor difficulties." Much of my editorial role was to ask clarifying questions, usually to secure more specific, illustrative examples. This is a typical role for the qualitative investigator; the researcher seeks as much as possible not to assume what people mean but to have them provide enough detail that the reader can be confident about the meaning the researcher might ascribe in his or her interpretations.

As I describe in the introductions to particular autobiographical chapters, my role as editor was in some instances very limited. That is, I requested few additional explanations or changes in phrasing. With other contributions, my involvement as an editor .vas much more elaborate. I had many questions and the actual writing and rewriting by the authors occurred over a two-and-a-half-year period. I describe this in the introduction to the narratives. In every instance, however, the authors have written and edited their own work. For all the chapters, I met with the authors in their own communities and conversed with them about the book project and about their contributions. In addition, I emailed back and forth with each author during the editing process.

As the project progressed, I asked myself whether readers would think these accounts a valid picture of people classified as autistic. On one level, this is to say: Are we seeing what we think we are seeing? To this question, readers are likely not to have many doubts. The contributors raise so many issues that resonate with what others have observed that there will likely be no uncertainty as to whether these are people who have been classified as autistic, and little debate as to whether their descriptions are informative. Beyond this initial consideration lie other criteria that are more reflective of the phenomenologist's idea of validity. Specifically, as Kvale (1995) has explained, the qualitative researcher might think of validity in terms of whether it is pragmatic, by which he or she means "Does it lead to useful understanding?" and whether it is communicative, intelligible, open (i.e., transparent to the reader), and nonsectarian.

Ideally, the investigator admits to his or her assumptions, endeavors to avoid imposing an ideological agenda, and seeks instead to see and hear others' perspectives. Cherryholmes (1988) describes this as "looking", where the researcher's "*looking* shifts locus of control and power from researchers to subjects" (p. 109). In this type of inquiry, researchers are "proscribed" even "from imposing categories of observation" and instead learn to listen to how people, in this case the contributing authors, refer to their "sense and understanding of the world" (Cherryholmes 1988, p. 108). Another term for this kind of research is *critical research,* where the researcher questions his or her own ideas at the same time that he or she reflects on, and may even argue with, the ideas of others. If there is one thing that I hope for this book, it is that people classified as autistic who not so many years ago were believed unable to say how they perceived the world, and who were often spoken for and explained by others, are seen speaking loudly, poignantly, and with wisdom. It is not my role to "equalize the relationship" (Shakespeare 1996, p. 116) between the contributing authors and myself; rather, their words do this of their own accord. The contributing authors establish their own authority to be read and appreciated.

Notes

1. Historically, the possibility that people with autism could communicate through typing has been controversial, particularly if they required physical support to type their words. Physical independence in typing and/or the ability to speak words as they are being typed are two criteria that the field has identified as evidence that the person is indeed producing the typed words. For examples of research and AAC texts that address this question, see Beukelman and Mirenda (1998) and Wing (2000).
2. None of the authors in this book participated in any of these studies.

References

American Psychiatric Association (2000). Diagnostic and statistical manual of mental disorders. 4th ed. Washington, D.C.: APA.

Asperger, H. (1944/1991). "Autistic psychopathy" in childhood. In U. Frith (ed. and trans.), *Autism and Asperger syndrome* (pp. 37–92). Cambridge: Cambridge University Press. Originally Asperger, Hans (1944). Die autistischen Psychopathen. In *Kindesalter, archiv. fur psychiatrie und nervenkrankheiten, 117,* pp. 76–136.

Atkinson, P. (1990). *The ethnographic imagination: Textual constructions of reality.* London: Routledge.

Atkinson, P., Coffey, A., and Delamont, S. (2003). *Key themes in qualitative research.* New York: AltaMira.

Baron-Cohen, S. (1996). *Mindblindness: An essay on autism and theory of mind.* Cambridge: MIT Press.

Bebko, J., Perry, A., and Bryson, S. (1996). Multiple method validation study of facilitated communication: Individual differences and subgroup results. *Journal of autism and developmental disabilities, 26,* pp. 43–58.

Beukelman, D., and Mirenda, P. (1998). *Augmentative and alternative communication: Management of severe communication disorders in children and adults.* Baltimore: Paul H. Brookes.

Biklen, D., and Rosetti, Z. (producers) (2005). *My classic life as an artist: A por-*

trait of Larry Bissonnette. Video documentary. Available from Syracuse University, 370 Huntington Hall, Syracuse, New York.

Blackman, L. (1999). *Lucy's story: Autism and other adventures*. Redcliffe, Queensland, Australia: Book in Hand.

Bogdan, R. and Biklen, S. (1998). *Introduction to qualitative research in education*. Boston: Allyn and Bacon.

———— (2003). *Qualitative research for education*. 4th ed. Boston: Allyn and Bacon.

Bomba, C., O'Donnell, L., Markowitz, C., and Holmes, D. (1996). Evaluating the impact of facilitated communication on the communicative competence of fourteen students with autism. *Journal of autism and developmental disorders, 26*, pp. 43–58.

Borthwick, C., and Crossley, R. (1999). Language and retardation. *Psycholoquy, 10*, #38. Viewed on July 13, 2004, http://psycprints.ecs.soton.ac.uk/archive/00000673/.

Broderick, A., and Kasa-Hendrickson, C. (2001). "Say just one word at first": The emergence of reliable speech in a student labelled with autism. *Journal of the association for persons with severe handicaps, 26*, pp. 13–24.

Bunting, S. M. (2001). Sustaining the relationship: Women's caregiving in the context of HIV disease. *Health care for women international, 22*, pp. 131–148.

Cabay, M. (1994). A controlled evaluation of facilitated communication with four autistic children. *Journal of autism and developmental disorders, 24*, pp. 517–527.

Calculator, S., and Singer, K. (1992). Preliminary validation of facilitated communication. *Topics in language disorders, 12*, p. ix.

Cardinal D. N., Hanson, D., and Wakeham, J. (1996). An investigation of authorship in facilitated communication. *Mental retardation, 34*, pp. 231–242.

Charlton, J. I. (1998). *Nothing about us without us*. Berkeley: University of California Press.

Cherryholmes, C. (1988). *Power and criticism*. New York: Teachers College Press.

Cole, A. L., and Knowles, J. G. (2001). *Lives in context: The art of life history research*. Walnut Creek, CA: AltaMira Press.

Crews, W., Sanders, E., Hensley, L., Johnson, Y., Bonaventura, S., and Rhodes, R. (1995). An evaluation of facilitated communication in a group of nonverbal individuals with mental retardation. *Journal of autism and developmental disorders, 25*, pp. 205–213.

Crossley, R. (1994). *Facilitated communication training*. New York: Teachers College Press.

Duchan, J. F. (1998). Describing the unusual behavior of children with autism. *Journal of communication disorders, 31*, pp. 93–112.

Duchan, J., Calculator, S., Sonnenmeier, R., Diehl, S., and Cumley, G. (2001). A framework for managing controversial practices. *Language speech and hearing services in schools, 32*, pp. 133–141.

Eberlin, M., McConnachie, G., Ibel, S., and Volpe, L. (1993). "Facilitated communication": A failure to replicate the phenomenon. *Journal of autism and developmental disorders, 23,* pp. 507–529

Emerson, A., Grayson, A., and Griffiths, A. (2001). Can't or won't? Evidence relating to authorship in facilitated communication. *International journal of language and communication disorders, 36* (suppl.), pp. 98–103.

Fine, M. (1991). *Framing dropouts.* Albany: State University of New York Press.

Frith, U. (1989). *Autism: Explaining the enigma.* Cambridge, MA: Blackwell Publishers.

Gallagher, S. (1999). An exchange of gazes. In J. L. Kincheloe, S. R. Steinberg, and L. E. Villaverde (eds.), *Rethinking intelligence* (pp. 69–83). New York: Routledge.

Glaser, B., and Strauss, A. L. (1967). *The discovery of grounded theory.* Chicago: Aldine.

Janzen-Wilde, M., Duchan, J., and Higginbotham, D. (1995). Successful use of facilitated communication with an oral child. *Journal of speech and hearing research, 38,* pp. 658–676.

Kanner, L. (1943/1985). Autistic disturbances of affective contact. In A. M. Donnellan (ed.), *Classic readings in autism* (pp. 11–50). New York: Teachers College Press.

Kasa-Hendrickson, C., Broderick, A., Biklen, D. (producers), and Gambell, J. (director) (2002). *Inside the edge.* Video documentary. Available from Syracuse University, 370 Huntington Hall, Syracuse, New York.

Klewe, L. (1993). An empirical evaluation of spelling boards as a means of communication for the multihandicapped. *Journal of Autism and developmental disorders, 23,* pp. 559–566.

Kliewer, C. (1998). *Schooling children with Down syndrome.* New York: Teachers College Press.

Kvale, S. (1995). The social construction of validity. *Qualitative Inquiry, 1,* pp. 19–40.

Mabrey, V. (producer/director) (2003). *Breaking the silence.* Documentary. *60 Minutes II* (United States).

Marsiglio, W. (2004). When stepfathers claim stepchildren: A conceptual analysis. *Journal of marriage and family, 66,* pp. 22–39.

Matsuo, H. Garrow, S., and Koric, A. (2002). Resettlement process of refugee immigrants from Bosnia and Herzegovina in St. Louis: Finding material and emotional niches. Conference paper, International Sociological Association (ISA), Brisbane, Australia.

Mirenda, P. (2003). "He's not really a reader . . . ": Perspectives on supporting literacy development in individuals with autism. *Topics in language disorders, 23,* pp. 271–282.

Montee, B., Miltenberger, R., and Wittrock, D. (1995). An experimental analysis of facilitated communication. *Journal of applied behaviour analysis, 28,* pp. 189–200.

Moore, S., Donovan, B., Hudson, A., Dykstra, J., and Lawrence, J. (1993). Brief report: Evaluation of eight case studies of facilitated communication. *Journal of autism and developmental disorders, 23,* pp. 541–552.

Mostert, M. P. (2001). Facilitated communication since 1995: A review of published studies. *Journal of autism and developmental disorders, 31,* pp. 287–313.

Mukhopadhyay, T. R. (2000). *Beyond the silence: My life, the world and autism.* London: National Autistic Society.

Niemi, J., and Kärnä-Lin, E. (2002). Grammar and lexicon in facilitated communication: A linguistic authorship analysis of a Finnish case. *Mental retardation 40,* pp. 347–357.

Oakes, M., and Lucas, F. (2001). How war affects daily life: Adjustments in Salvadoran social networks. *Journal of social work research and evaluation, 2,* pp. 143–155.

Prusley-Crotteau, S. (2001). Perinatal crack users becoming temperant: The social psychological processes. *Health care for women international, 22,* pp. 1–2.

Regal, R., Rooney, J., and Wandas, T. (1994). Facilitated communication: An experimental evaluation. *Journal of autism and developmental disorders, 24,* pp. 345–355.

Rubin, S., Biklen, D., Kasa-Hendrickson, C., Kluth, P., Cardinal, D. N., and Broderick, A. (2001). Independence, participation, and the meaning of intellectual ability. *Disability and society, 16,* pp. 425–429.

Shakespeare, T. (1996). Rules of engagement. *Disability and society, 11,* pp. 115–119.

Shane, H., and Kearns, K. (1994). An examination of the role of the facilitator in "facilitated communication," *American journal of speechlanguage pathology,* September, pp. 48–54.

Sheehan, C., and Matuozzi, R. (1996). Investigation of the validity of facilitated communication through the disclosure of unknown information. *Mental retardation, 34,* pp. 94–107.

Smith, M., and Belcher, R. (1993). Brief report: Facilitated communication with adults with autism. *Journal of autism and developmental disorders, 23,* p. 175.

Spradley, J. P. (1980). *Participant observation.* Orlando, FL: Harcourt.

Strauss, A., and Corbin, J. (1998). *Basics of qualitative research techniques and procedures for developing grounded theory.* 2nd ed. London: Sage Publications.

Szempruch, J., and Jacobson, J. (1993). Evaluating facilitated communications of people with developmental disabilities. *Research in developmental disabilities, 14,* pp. 253–264.

Terrill, C. (producer/director) (2000). *Inside story: Tito's story.* Documentary. London: BBC.

Tuzzi, A., Cemin, M., and Castagna, M. (2004). "Moved deeply I am." Autistic language in texts produced with FC. *Journées internationals d'analyse statistique des données textuelles, 7,* pp. 1–9.

Vryan, K. D., Adler, P. A., and Adler, P. (2003). In L. T. Reynolds and N. J. Herman-Kinney (eds.), *Handbook of symbolic interactionism* (pp. 367–390). Walnut Creek, CA: AltaMira Press.

Weiss, M., Wagner, S., and Bauman, M. (1996). A validated case study of facilitated communication. *Mental retardation, 34,* pp. 220–230.

Wheeler, D., Jacobson, J., Paglieri, R., and Schwartz, A. (1993). An experimental assessment of facilitated communication. *Mental retardation, 31,* pp. 49–60.

Willis, P. (2000). *The ethnographic imagination.* Malden, MA: Blackwell Publishers.

Wing, L. (2000). Foreword. In T. R. Mukhopadhyay, *Beyond the silence: My life, the world and autism,* pp. 1–3. London: National Autistic Society.

Wurzburg, G. (producer/director) (2004). *Autism is a world.* Documentary. Atlanta: CNN.

Zanobini, M., and Scopesi, A. (2001). La comunicazione facilitata in un bambino autistico. *Psicologia clinica dello Sviluppo, 5,* pp. 395–421.

1

■　　■　　■　　■　　■　　■　　■　　■　　■

Framing Autism

Douglas Biklen

The Person inside the Body

Alberto Frugone lives with his mother and stepfather in a house far above the town of Zoagli in northern Italy, on the coast of the Mediterranean. Until 2003, when he was twenty-four years old, he attended secondary school. He has taken Italy's postsecondary qualifying exams, and so he may become the first nonspeaking Italian classified as autistic to attend a university.

I first met Alberto several years ago when he had just begun learning to communicate by typing. He still communicates in this way, typing slowly, letter by letter. Alberto is blind in one eye. He squints with his left eye as he types with the index finger of his right hand. When he first began this way of expressing himself, he needed someone to stabilize his arm as he typed, prompting him to pull back after each letter selection. Now, however, he can type without any physical support, though he requires his mother or a teacher to sit beside him as he types; he says the presence of his mother or teacher helps him maintain attention. The words come slowly but clearly.

On a late June day when we met—I had come to discuss his contribution to this book of seven narratives by people classified as autistic—it was exceptionally hot. Alberto is small in stature and has deep brown, shortly cropped hair and a square chin. On this summer day he had a brilliant tan and was wearing a white T-shirt, blue shorts, and sandals. We had met many times before over the preceding eight years, so I knew that he was not a person who could walk up to me and shake my hand. Instead, it was left to me to say hello and hold out my hand, palm up, for him to come and put his hand on top. Then *I* shook *our* hands. We sat down at the table on his veranda, overlooking the sea, on Ezra Pound Place; the hillside street is named for the writer who at one time lived in a villa about a half-mile away, within view of where we sat. As Alberto's mother, Patrizia Cadei got out his electronic typewriter and placed it in front of him, propped up on its case so that it tilted toward him, Alberto put his thumb in his mouth and began sucking it. His mother told him to take his thumb from his mouth and then reached over and flicked at his hands, as if to make sure it happened quickly. With the typewriter in front of him, Alberto began to type, slowly but at a regular pace. His mother translated into English as he typed in Italian.

"I am happy to reason things out with you," he wrote. He shook his head as in a tremor, squinted his eye, and typed with his right index finger, slowly. "Do we examine only the script mistakes or do we examine the actions I have described?" I smiled as his mother translated these words from the Italian. I suppose I was smiling because it was exciting to see him produce the words. As disabled as Alberto appears in body, the content of the text he was producing was perfectly conversational. He is thin and his movements are halting in everything from typing to walking, yet in our conversation that afternoon, I could not help but feel that Alberto was in charge of the direction it was taking.

He had written a dozen pages that he had sent to me earlier in the year. I had then commented on them, asking for clarifications and additional examples to illustrate some of his points. We emailed back and forth. He had made a number of changes, but now I was interested in getting him to elaborate further. The process reminded me of my work with university students, for here I was pleading with Alberto to provide more details to explain himself. He writes at a high level of abstraction, often leaving out or neglecting examples to illustrate his meaning. "Give me specifics," I begged. "I need to be able to visualize what you are telling me." Alberto is not one of my students, but that day he might as well have been, for I wanted to say to him: "specifics, specifics, specifics. For me, you cannot be too specific." A standard I often use to convey the level of detail needed is to imagine the reader as a film director who has to have enough concrete description in the script to be able to create scenes that the scriptwriter intended. I wanted Alberto to let readers see what autism means to him.

By Alberto's own description, and according to my observations, physical movements, particularly sequenced actions such as getting a glass of water, eating food, or taking out his typewriter, are difficult for him. It is not that Alberto has any palsy. He does not. It is just that he moves slowly and appears awkward. When grasping a spoon, Alberto uses his fingers to press it against his palm. He does not handle it with his index finger and thumb. If there is meat on the table, a dinner partner must cut it for him. He has not been able to do complex things such as cooking a meal, although he could stir a spoon in a pot. Nearly any action that requires sequencing leaves him stymied. When he walks, Alberto does so slowly—"I take mechanical steps [short steps] if I walk alone, but if taken by the hand or the arm, I walk regularly." On his own, he makes no quick moves. He resembles somewhat a person walking in the dark, feeling out the terrain as he goes. He sometimes flicks his fingers next to his left eye, and he often breathes shallowly. He does this when he feels anxious. It is, in his words, "hyperventilation."

Alberto is a person whom most autism experts and perhaps the public as well would describe as among the most disabled of all people labeled autistic. Anyone can see his extreme difficulty with movement. Anyone can observe that he does not speak. And anyone who has spent even a bit of time with him can see that without a typewriter in front of him he has quite limited ways to communicate other than to pull his mother or another person to something he might want or with a simple gesture: "at the tender age of 24 I have learnt to nod and say no with my head. I have difficulties to remember how to do it when requested and I make a big effort to do it." But what do halting, awkward, dissembled movement and difficulties in making gestures connote? Many people might look at Alberto and presume that somehow there is a correlation between physical awkwardness and impaired intellect. But they would be wrong. If one person could embody the contradictions that seem ordinary with autism, Alberto might be that person.

Alberto says that his difficulties are not with thinking and knowing but with doing or acting. Looking at his typed sentences, it is hard not to recognize that his many physical difficulties, with speech, movement, and any other actions cannot be taken as evidence of his intellectual abilities. His struggle seems to be in performance. When I asked Alberto to give me examples of things that are hard to do and things that he finds easier, he responded, in Italian, "Elementare Watson." He typed and his mother translated into English, with him explaining that literally "everything is hard." With but a few exceptions, he cannot do anything that involves more than one action, one step. Yes, he *has* learned to brush his teeth, but only because of repeated practice and with much prompting, step by step, "Open the toothpaste. Put the paste on the brush. Pick up the brush."

As he contemplates finishing secondary school and advancing to higher education, it is still the physical aspects of daily life that can be most daunting. In virtually every aspect of living, he must rely on others. He is frustrated, for example, with the fact that anytime his mother leaves the house to do an errand, he must accompany her. Recently, Alberto's mother Patrizia had to go shopping and so she insisted that he join her. It was a Friday afternoon and there was no one else to stay with him—Alberto's stepfather was at work and his regular care worker was off for the afternoon. "There was nothing I could do about it," Patrizia told me, "no one to stay with him." She sympathized with his frustration but told him, "Either you learn to defend yourself at home or you come with me." Naturally, he was angry. On the subsequent Sunday, he pulled her to the typewriter and typed out: "Let's talk. When you go out, you must leave one window open and leave the tape recorder." "What's the use of the tape recorder?" his mother asked. "You record your voice shouting for help," answered Alberto. "Teach me how to use the recorded voice," he typed. With more than a hint of skepticism, Patrizia at once asked and argued with Alberto, "In a panic you can do this? Why do you want to do this? It's too complicated." "He just lacks the practical," Patrizia told me. She felt that he sometimes comes up with ideas that, given his movement difficulties, are fanciful. With some additional discussion, however, they settled on the idea of Alberto learning to use a one-button panic alarm on the phone. While she regarded his own idea as too complicated, she admired his having grappled with the problem. Now, Alberto does stay at home alone for several hours at a time.

While Alberto's struggles with performance are more severe than those of most of the other contributors to this book, all the contributors do have significant movement problems that leave them on many occasions feeling and looking not only tongue-tied but also body-tied. This raises important questions: How should people who meet Alberto interpret him? Are his physical actions never indicative of his thinking abilities? If they *do* sometimes reflect his intentions, how can the observer know when they do and when they do not? And these practical questions lead to larger more theoretical ones. For example, if action does not necessarily reflect thought, what does this say about how scholars have constructed the meaning of mental retardation and of intelligence? What constitutes competence? Is physically independent action a component of intellectual ability? And, what constitutes fairness or justice for people who seek to participate in society in ways that differ from the so-called normal?

The Contributors

To date, firsthand accounts of autism have been produced nearly exclusively by people thought to be "high-functioning," including Williams (1989, 1994), Grandin (Grandin and Scariano 1986), and Barron (Barron and Barron 1992). The term *high-functioning* is not a technical term; it has been used in both professional and lay discussions to refer to individuals who evidence the ability to converse in oral dialogue, using speech. It is a highly problematic term, for it implies that those people who can carry on spoken conversations are intelligent and those who cannot, are not. Would anyone label Stephen Hawking, for instance, "low-functioning"? Classifying anyone as "low-functioning" is a potentially damning assumption, for it could easily forestall efforts to aid a person's participation in academic subjects in school or in community life.

Alberto and the other contributors to this book have been thought of by some as located at the opposite end of the autism spectrum.[1] At one point or another in their developmental years, all were given pessimistic prognoses. Even though an individual teacher, consultant, or diagnostician might have been optimistic about both their abilities and their potential, all but two were denied access to mainstream education for most of the developmental years. One of the contributing authors at age nine passed a state mathematics exam and could read at grade level, yet he was still not accepted in mainstream classes. Alberto, who did have legal access to regular classes, was thought by most educators to be unable to benefit from academic instruction. Educators typically believed the contributors to this book unlikely to develop literacy, unlikely to learn much more than rudimentary self-help skills, and unlikely to determine their own futures, even though some had already shown such abilities. In their early years, all of the authors were caught in the position where a few educators, diagnosticians, and consultants saw their competence, and yet such individual assessments were overwhelmed by the inertia of education systems that preferred to cast them as unworthy of full access to academic instruction. During their developmental years, all but one were unable to speak conversationally in complex sentences at the typical speed of conversation that others might use, although several could eventually do this if allowed to combine their speaking with typing. One can now speak in conversational sentences without also typing, as long as he can speak slowly—literally, one distinct syllable at a time—and if those listening to him are used to his pronunciation (it is sometimes necessary for the listener to ask him to repeat or spell out hard-to-understand words).

In their own ways, like Alberto, each of the authors included in this book is already recognized as having "broken through" to a measure of acceptance and respect in mainstream culture. Tito Rajarshi Mukhopadhyay was born in India and learned to speak and write after much intense support from his mother, a speech therapist, and others. By the age of eleven he had written a book, *Beyond the Silence* (Mukhopadhyay 2000), that was published by the National Autistic Society in England and was the subject of a BBC documentary (Terrill 2000), and he appeared on the U.S. television program *60 Minutes II* in 2003 (Mabrey 2003). He was home-schooled in India because no typical school would have him. Sue Rubin grew up in southern California and is now a college student; until age thirteen, however, she was diagnosed as both autistic and severely retarded and was thought incapable of academic work. She has been featured in several Public Broadcasting documentary segments in California and has published two opinion editorials in the *Los Angeles Times*. Richard Attfield lives in England, where he writes and has occasionally lectured on autism. He was accepted as a student at college; at the age of fifteen, he won his first writing award in the "Young Writers Competition" (1993) from among thirty thousand entries.[2] Prior to his late teen years, aside from being included in a playschool program, he attended only special schools, with the implication that he could not benefit from participation with students deemed nondisabled. During his segregated schooling he was given some "basic academic work, e.g. telling time, simple maths, reading and writing, science—repeating what I had learnt at home." Then, at age fifteen, he was given a "life skills" curriculum. At this point he demanded academics. Throughout his school years, his mother supported his communication. Jamie Burke lives in Syracuse, New York, where he attends high school. He was included in regular academic schooling from the age of three. In 2002 he wrote and narrated a documentary about how he learned to speak after first learning to communicate by typing (Kasa-Hendrickson et al. 2002) and was the subject of a research article on the same topic (Broderick and Kasa-Hendrickson 2001). Larry Bissonnette lives in the eastern United States and is an artist. He communicates through typing and through his paintings. His work was featured in a CNN news account and has been exhibited at art shows and in galleries in New York City, in Europe, and in the state of Vermont, where he resides (Sellen 2000). Lucy Blackman lives in Queensland, Australia, where she is a graduate student and writer. In 1999 she wrote an autobiographical book, *Lucy's Story: Autism and Other Adventures.*

In their chapters, the contributors discuss how autism affects their speech and most aspects of how they interact with other people and what they can do physically. I will not try to summarize here what each can do or what some have difficulty with, for they are complex individuals and evidence differing abilities in varied contexts, as will be revealed in their chapters. To this day, only one of the contributors can carry on a back-and-forth conversation without first typing his side of the dialogue; a few can say the words they type, before and as they type them, but for all of them communication is relatively slow compared to the rapid flow of speech they hear and respond to from others. Attfield, for example, *can and does* say sentences, and has been able to do so from the age of two, and yet his typing is more complex. In typing he carries on full, rich conversations. The sentences he has spoken aloud include, for example: "I am so annoyed; I will ask mum; of course I do like it; can I get some lunch please; I do not care; I would like some grapes please; it was all my fault; I wanted to speak; the telephone rang; maybe it was the doorbell." These are sentences that he said over a few weeks. "But as you say," he told me, "this is not holding a conversation." He had spoken such sentences "in response to being spoken to."

Despite the obvious accomplishments of the contributing authors, I do not want to imply that they are unusual among people classified as autistic, anomalies within an otherwise ordered taxonomy of disability. If they are unique in some ways, such uniqueness is probably typical. If there are similarities among them, these may give insight into alternative ways of interpreting autism. As will become obvious, for example, Alberto's characterization of the body as not easily complying with intention is repeated in multiple ways in several other narratives. Other authors introduce such topics as how to start speaking conversationally, how to differentiate speech that is meaningful from speech that is "automatic" and unintended, anxiety, obsessive routines, imagination, sensory awareness, self-abuse, and movement difficulties. In the concluding chapter, I discuss directly how these accounts might inform educational practice. First, however, it is useful to recall the origins of the concept of autism.

The Origins of Autism as a Disability Category, and the Idea of Competence

Leo Kanner, a doctor at Johns Hopkins University, first described and named autism. In an article titled "Autistic Disturbances of Affective Contact" (Kanner 1943/1985), he constructed the idea of autism from his clinical notes and parent reports on eleven individuals whom he saw at Johns Hopkins Medical Center between 1938 and 1943. Kanner concluded that his patients shared particular qualities that constituted a "unique 'syndrome,' not heretofore reported," and that they were not "feebleminded" or "schizophrenic" (Kanner 1943/1985, p. 41).[3] For the eleven children, he both described and hypothesized particular qualities. Among these were "a marked limitation of spontaneous activity";

"stereotyped movements with [the] . . . fingers, crossing them about in the air"; spinning objects; lack of initiative; requiring prompts; showing "no interest in our conversations"; not "good with cooperative play"; afraid of mechanical things, for example, a "vacuum cleaner . . . elevators . . . spinning tops"; and a desire to keep things in a fixed order (pp. 13–19). The principal "'pathognomonic,' fundamental disorder," he argued, "is the children's *inability to relate themselves* in the ordinary way to people and situations from the beginning of life" (p. 41; author's italics). Kanner called this *"inborn autistic disturbances of affective contact"* (p. 50; author's italics). The classification of autism was born.

Though an ocean separated them, Asperger's account of autism from his clinic in Vienna, Austria, resembled Kanner's in many respects. For example Asperger, observed motor difficulties of his subjects, not unlike Kanner's observation that some of his patients were "clumsy in gait and gross motor performances" (Kanner 1943/1985, p. 47). Asperger described a client named Fritz V. as having delayed "motor milestones" (1944/1991, p. 39). He characterized Fritz's participation in physical education as clumsy, "never physically relaxed," and lacking in rhythm. Asperger concluded that Fritz "had no mastery over his body" (p. 44). He found that another child, Harro, had poor handwriting, "as to be expected from his general clumsiness" (p. 55) Asperger surmised that Harro could activate only those muscles to which he directed "a conscious effort of will" (p. 57). Then, Asperger wrote, owing to movement problems, another child's (Ernst's) expressions were limited and "rigid," though there was no spasticity. Asperger determined that in general the children he called autistic had "a paucity of facial and gestural expression" (p. 69). "Even when he was being led in physical actions, Ernst's movements were," by Asperger's reckoning, "ugly and angular . . . never . . . natural . . . and spontaneous" (p. 57). And Ernst "behaved impossibly badly" in physical education, for he seemed completely unable to follow instructions to the group—today he might be thought of as dyspraxic. Asperger concluded that Ernst was both clumsy and undisciplined (p. 61). Similarly, a client named Helmut "could not possibly catch a ball" and when attempting to catch or throw looked "extremely comical" (p. 66).[4] Asperger determined that acquiring a repertoire of automatic motor skills was especially difficult for his subjects. It seems that he was nearing exasperation when he wondered aloud whether Ernst was either very smart ("particularly able") or "mentally retarded" (p. 63).[5]

Asperger identified many aspects of autism, including a tendency of some to use peripheral vision; presence of obsessive-compulsive tendencies, for example, to have objects in particular order; problems with spoken communication; and seeming inattention. Like Kanner, Asperger believed that his clients shared a principal characteristic, disturbed social interaction: "The autist is only himself," Asperger declared, "and is not an active member of a greater organism which he is influenced by and which he influences constantly" (p. 38). "The essential abnormality in autism," he argued, was a "disturbance of the lively relationship with the whole environment" (p. 74). In speaking of an absence of "lively relationship," Asperger seems to have been referring to what was outwardly visible and not necessarily to what the person might be thinking or feeling, for many of his comments about individuals suggest that he recognized his subjects' strong feelings and clearly responsive intellectual engagement with the environment. He could not help but see their uneven academic performance, but unevenness did not equate with incapacity to reason in complex ways.

The disturbance in social interaction was not, in either Kanner's or Asperger's mind, necessarily the product of impaired intellect or what is colloquially thought of in the United States as mental retardation or in Australia as intellectual disability. They saw autism in more specific terms. For one thing, there were nearly constant contradictions in the actions of the individuals they observed. Kanner argued that even though most of his clients at one time or another had been declared "feebleminded," he found them "all unquestionably endowed with good cognitive potentialities" (Kanner 1943/1985, p. 41). Even if they were not all necessarily able to demonstrate their cognitive abilities, he felt there was promise for all. He cited instances where students displayed remarkable vocabulary, "phenomenal rote memory for poems and names," and precise recollection of complex patterns as evidence of intelligence (p. 41). He described his patients as looking serious-minded.

The contradictions Kanner observed in his clients fascinated him. For example, Donald T, the first in his descriptions of the eleven, had many of the behaviors now seen as typical for people with the autism label.

Donald would walk around with a grin on his face, whispering, humming, shaking his head from side to side, and spinning "anything he could seize upon" (p. 13). At the age of six he still needed assistance with eating and dressing. When his father was trying to teach him the words *yes* and *no,* he told his son that he should say yes if he wanted to be put up on his shoulders. From that day on, Donald seemed to use "yes" as a request to be put up on his father's shoulders. It was as if he did not understand the conventional meaning of "yes." Yet, when he was asked to subtract four from ten, Donald responded, "I'll draw a hexagon" (p. 17). It was hard for Kanner to reason how it was that Donald seemingly could not master the uses of "yes" and "no" but *could* answer a math problem metaphorically. It was an odd juxtaposition of seeming at once obtuse and brilliantly inventive.

Another of Kanner's students (case nine out of a total of eleven), Charles N., could discriminate between eighteen symphonies at the age of eighteen months and would jump up and down at Beethoven (p. 33). Yet Charles's only form of conversation seemed to be echoes of words and phrases he had heard others say. He did not use language to carry on conversations, but he could name things such as "oblong block," "diamond," and "octagon" (p. 33). Ironically, even as he answered he would say, "What is this?"

Such contradictions and unevenness of performance caused Kanner to conclude that intelligence testing (e.g., the Binet test) would simply not work for assessing the competence of children classified as autistic. His patients were inaccessible to the "Binet or similar testing" (p. 47), and that, Kanner argued, was different from being unable to think in complex ways. Asperger provides even more detail on this point. One of his students, Fritz, responded to an assessment on differences in a way that revealed little. For "tree and bush" he simply said, "There is a difference" (Asperger 1944/1991, p. 45). For "fly and butterfly" he answered that they had different names. Yet when asked to subtract five from three, he responded, "2 under zero" (p. 45). A student might be able to solve complex mathematical problems at one moment but then completely fail at basic math skills in the school classroom. Asperger refers to such unevenness, where the performance is best when seeming to be spontaneous rather than done on request in a prescribed manner, as one of the "peculiar signs of 'autistic intelligence'" (p. 62). It seemed to Asperger that nearly nothing could be done on demand, hence the difficulty of testing in general. But if a problem, question, or comment was of particular interest, the student typically responded rapidly. Sometimes a question or topic could be understood but not expressed: Asperger cites a student who said, "'I can't do this orally, only headily.' He wanted to say that he had understood . . . but could not express it verbally" (p. 71). Further, he argued, the person he defined as autistic seemed exceptionally sensitive to teachers' personalities. They can be "guided and taught only by those who give them true understanding and genuine affection" (p. 48). He argued that the teacher's attitude and orientation would come across to the child "unconsciously" (p. 48). Asperger felt that people classified as autistic had excellent insight into the intentions of others: "they know who means well with them and who does not, even when he feigns differently" (p. 73).

During the 1970s, Rosalind Oppenheim, the parent of a boy diagnosed with autism, drew a similar conclusion. In the course of helping her son, she became a consultant to teachers and parents. Eventually she set up a school to teach children diagnosed with autism and wrote a book titled *Effective Teaching Methods for Autistic Children and Youth* (1974). Oppenheim observed that the same student could be competent in one setting where pushed to perform and thoroughly incompetent in another when expected to fail. She describes a student who one year is observed making statistical calculations with ease and another year seems incapable of the simplest addition calculation. She attributed the difference to the educational environment and to teacher expectations rather than to some changes internal to the child. She recommended that teachers be sure that curriculum placed in front of a student is not too simple. She explains that failure to respond in expected ways to the curriculum is often not evidence of inability to understand but rather may indicate lack of engagement. Harder, more complex, and more challenging work may trigger a response.

Oppenheim's point—she argues that people who look incompetent much of the time, even most of the time, may nevertheless be highly capable—is a hard one to prove, for it would have to be done individual by individual, situation by situation. It is a particularly hard sell when applied to individuals who do not speak and who have other qualities long associated with intellectual disability. Echoed speech, spoken seemingly out of context; tantrums; awkward movement; difficulty with sequenced tasks such as making a bed, setting a table, or dressing; and obsessive-compulsive behavior can make a person *seem* disconnected or "slow." Yet, if Alberto Frugone's accomplishments are any indication of what might be possible for others, the presumption of competence may actually be a precondition for working with individuals who have autism and who do not speak or who have highly disordered, echoed[6] speech.

Post-Kanner and -Asperger: Finding a Framework for Autism

It would be wrong to imply that the field of autism currently adheres to this presumption of competence. Rather, the world of autism expertise encountered by the contributors to this book seems divided between contradictory understandings, one far more pessimistic than the other. On the one hand, some experts characterize autism as a condition wholly internal to the person, as a collection of traits (see Duchan's 1998 discussion of how behaviors are often attributed to internal traits in experts' narratives of autism). On the other hand, autism may be seen as a set of qualities among many where the experience of the person can be understood only as being located and negotiated in complex social-cultural contexts. In the former, autism-inside-the-person viewpoint, there is a tendency to see the person as more or less static—not merely comprising particular neurophysiological characteristics but defined by them. In the latter instance, autism is more fluid; the person is seen as having particular qualities and as interacting with the environment, and thus as forever changing in complex ways.

In part, Kanner's original description of autism in 1943 evidences the autism-inside-the-person view. He speaks of children having "come into the world with innate inability to form the usual, biologically provided affective contact with people, just as other children come into the world with innate physical or intellectual handicaps" (Kanner 1943/1985, p. 50). Similarly, Asperger (1944/1991) argues that the very nature of the person diagnosed autistic is that of the isolated, self-directing, even oblivious person: "Autistic children are egocentric in the extreme. They follow only their own wishes, interests and spontaneous impulses, without considering restrictions or prescriptions imposed from outside" (p.

81). And yet also in their essays, Kanner and Asperger showed how their subjects did sometimes establish clear contact with a teacher or with a parent or other person, did respond to others, and did show keen awareness of others, albeit in unconventional ways or with unconventional timing. Thus, in addition to biology, context also mattered.[7] Kanner and Asperger were able to hypothesize internal pathology acting in conjunction with the environments, including social experience, which individuals encounter.

Essentially, in recent years the field of autism has come to agree that there are neurological differences between the brains of people with the autism classification and nondisabled persons. These concern brainstem and cerebellar abnormalities (Hashimoto et al. 1995; Courschesne 1995; Courschene et al. 1994; Bauman and Kemper 1986; and Bauman, Filipek, and Kemper 1997); the limbic system (Bauman and Kemper 1990); and the hippocampal complex and amygdala (Bauman and Kemper 1995). Courchesne summarized findings from brain-imaging research when he wrote that "brain-behavior evidence is consistent with the more general hypothesis that autism involves widely disturbed aberrant functional organization in cerebellar, cerebral and limbic regions, and these defects appear to underlie multiple cognitive behavioral deficits" (2002). Researchers disagree about which of these findings are accurate representations of autism and which may be the result of poor research controls, the point of onset (e.g., during pregnancy or in development), the degree to which autism may be explained in terms of genetic factors, and what other factors may prove influential to the onset of autism. Yet it would be hard to find experts in autism today who disagree with the finding that autism has a neurological basis.

The traverse from neurology to behavior is a tricky and remarkably elusive one, yet the tendency to treat it as direct, obvious, and specific can occur without hesitation. Trevarthan, Aitken, Papoudi, and Robarts (1998) exemplify this when they suggest that "the primary cause of autism is related to the 'instructions' for brain development that control the way a child's mind grows and learns from experience" (p. 4). Further, they argue, "most have marked deficits in attention and intelligence" (p. 2) and "the core of their motivation for relating to other persons is always characteristically 'absent' or inaccessible" (p. 3). To be sure, some researchers are more careful in their characterizations. For example, Bauman, Filipek, and Kemper (1997) write:

> There is mounting evidence for the importance of the cerebellum in the modulation of emotion, behavior, learning, and langu ge, and it is likely that the neuroanatomic abnormalities observed in the cerebellum in autism may contribute to some of the atypical behaviors and disordered information processing characteristic of the syndrome. However, the precise functional significance of these findings . . . remains to be elucidated. (p. 382)

Bauman and her colleagues are clearly not ready to enter into the metaphorical world represented in Trevarthan and colleagues' term *instructions for brain development* (Trevarthan et al. 199ζ, p. 4). Where Bauman and her colleagues refer to a possible relationship between neurological findings and performance, Trevarthan and colleagues claim specific cause and effect.

Unfortunately, metaphor is ubiquitous in the field of autism. For example, the manner in which many autism experts relate autism to intelligence illustrates how representations of autism are cultural constructions. In this instance, the particular representation implies a natural, physiological origin without having to prove it. Clinical literature often tends to characterize at least half, and often the majority, of people labeled autistic as *being* mentally retarded. Wing, for example, writes that, taking children similar to those Kanner wrote about in 1943, "about one-third have severe to moderate learning difficulties ['learning difficulties' is the British equivalent of what in the United States is referred to as 'mental retardation'], one-third have mild difficulties and one-third are in the low-average or better range" (Wing 2001, p. 46). Rapin (1997) says that for the 75 percent of persons classified autistic whom she believes to be mentally retarded, "their cognitive level is significantly associated with the severity of their autistic symptoms" (p. 99). Similarly, Jacobson, Mulick, and Schwartz (1995) link "general delays or deficits in language function" to "general delays or deficits in intellectual development" (p. 757). The presence of "linguistic and cognitive deficits of such persons" (i.e., individuals diagnosed as autistic) is, according to Volkmar and Cohen, more common than not (1985, p. 47). "There is little doubt," Carpentieri and Morgan write, "that most children with autism suffer from substantial cognitive impairment. Indeed, about 75% . . . " (1996, p. 611). Their use of the term *suffer* implies that autism is a kind of wound. Further, Carpentieri and Morgan argue, compared with individuals who test at the same level of cognitive ability/disability, people classified as autistic are more impaired in verbal reasoning abilities and substantially more impaired in everyday socialization and communication skills (p. 611).

In these accounts (e.g., Rapin 1997; Jacobson, Mulick, and Schwartz 1995; Volkmar and Cohen 1985; and Carpentieri and Morgan 1996) a metaphor has emerged. Problems in speech and performance are presumed to be based in impaired minds, *as if* the person were held back (i.e., retarded) in thinking. These accounts abandon the reference to metaphor in favor of a deficit-oriented reality. Rapin (1997) refers to "cognitive level[s]"; Jacobson, Mulick, and Schwartz (1995) to "delays or deficits in intellectual development"; Volkmar and Cohen (1985) to "cognitive deficits"; and Carpentieri and Morgan (1996) to "substantial cognitive impairment"—all terms that imply certainty, thus reifying the metaphor.

Several other prevalent arguments in the autism-inside-the-person tradition are the ideas of *mindblindness, central coherence,* and *executive function.* Again, metaphor operates as reality. First, consider mindblindness, also referred to as theory-of-mind (ToM). To convey the basic idea of mindblindness, Baron-Cohen describes a study conducted by Perner, Frith, Leslie, and Leekam, in which a researcher shows a child a Smarties candy container and asks, "'What do you think is in here?' The child naturally replies 'Smarties.' The child is then shown that the tube actually contains pencils" (Baron-Cohen 1996, p. 71). The experimenter subsequently asks the child two belief questions: what the child first thought was in the container, before being shown that pencils were in it, and what another child might think is in the Smarties container if the other child had not seen the pencils. Perner and colleagues reported that nondisabled child participants respond "Smarties" in both instances and a majority their subjects classified as autistic answer "pencils." From this, Perner and colleagues conclude that children with the autism label "answered by considering their own knowledge of what was in the box rather than by referring to their own previous false belief or to someone else's current false belief" (p. 71). The researchers then concluded that "in autism there is a genuine inability to understand other people's different beliefs" (p. 71).

The argument among "mindblindness" theorists is that nonautistic persons are born with a "mechanism for manipulating representations of mental states" and therefore, with age, develop the ability to recognize "pretense and belief" (Frith 1991, p. 19). People who have been diagnosed as autistic are, by contrast, thought to lack this *mechanism* of theory-of-mind. Frith hypothesizes that "this particular component of the mind is faulty" (p. 19) and that *lacking* this "mechanism," people are limited in their ability to develop "social imagination and communicative skills" (p. 19). She argues that with autism this impairment may also come with "aggravating factors, such as additional handicaps" that further exacerbate problems of participation in the social world (pp. 20–21).

Popular accounts suggest that the "mechanism" of mindblindness mandates a way of being. Park (2001), for example, describes her daughter as not having a "'Theory-of-Mind' to allow" her to see "something from another point of view" (p. 148). Thus, she explains, her daughter will scrape "ice off the windshield on the passenger's side, her side, leaving the driver's side obscured. She thinks I can see what she sees; if she knows something, she thinks the person she's talking to knows it too" (p. 148).

As with the autism–mental retardation construction, the metaphorical nature of the mindblindness representation goes unacknowledged. Frith and other researchers have not actually located a physical mechanism. Thus reference to a mechanism, a "component of the mind" (p. 19), or to what another person "thinks" (Park 2001, p. 148) can only be metaphorical. That it is *easy* to consider other possibilities should give readers pause about the explanatory power of mindblindness theory. In the ice-scraping example, Park's daughter, Jessy, might indeed be thinking of herself, imagining herself looking out the car window. So she prepares for that by scraping off her side, never giving attention to her mother's side of the windshield. Yet this does not prove that Jessy *cannot* imagine her mother also needing to peer through a clear windshield, only that she *has not* imagined it or attended to it. Park hints at this latter possibility at the very end of her book *Exiting Nirvana,* when she describes Jessy's remarks at a memorial gathering to mark the death of one of her companions. Jessy recalls the thoughtfulness of this person who helped her have her first one-person art show and who took her to sketch the Flatiron Building in New York City. Jessy spoke in a "quiet sadness" (p. 207).

People classified as autistic or self-identifying as autistic have been particularly critical of theory-of-mind as a construct, finding it vague, misleading, and inaccurate. One of the first times I became aware of this was in an interaction I had with Donna Williams. She was scheduled to give a keynote address at a conference to which I had invited her in Syracuse, New York. A month or so before the event, she called me to say that because of a family crisis, she might not be able to come and give the talk. I was deeply disappointed and told her as much, for I knew that many of the more than four hundred people planning to attend the conference were likely coming precisely because she was on the program, and only secondarily for other sessions. She suggested that we could arrange a satellite feed from England where she was living at the time. I acknowledged this would be possible but that it would be a poor substitution to her actually being present. I told her I understood her predicament but hoped she might still find a way to attend the conference. The next day she called back and explained that she had resolved the family crisis and would be able to speak after all. Then she said, "See, I have empathy." I laughed. She had made an insider's joke; for this was as if to say a person with autism *could* understand that others may have feelings different than their own, and *can* imagine those other feelings, despite what official definitions of autism may claim.

The challenge to mindblindness theory has also come from other people labeled autistic. In a presentation before Autism Europe's Congress 2000, Blackburn, Gottschewski, McElroy, and Niki (2000), members of Autism Network International, who define themselves as autistic, presented a series of criticisms. Speaking from their own experiences, they argued that theory-of-mind research demanded that participants have verbal abilities, attention and attention-shifting skills, and information-processing as well as other capabilities that mimic the nonautistic person's. Citing time as another type of difference, one of the presenters explained that she "may not pick-up on certain aspects of an interaction until I am obsessing over it hours or days later. So in practical situations, I have impaired social cognition, with problematic results, while I may seem to have good insights into people at other times." Another said, "I don't think well on my feet." He explained that he could not think about his own perspective and the other person's "at the same time, especially if I am talking or actively listening to the other person talk." Another person said she often attends to how a person is speaking as much as to the content, noting that some people "tend to be slower [in frequency] beat-like" while others "tend to be flashier" to the point of making "my teeth itch." With this focus, she is "not sure what kind of information about them" she is "attempting to process," their "behavior" or "them."

Given such complexities, theory-of-mind comes off as a crude concept, incapable of capturing the multiple ways different people experience the world. One of the presenters puts it sympathetically, in a *Country of the Blind* (Wells 1911/1997) manner: "ToM works between NTs [i.e., neurotypicals], and it works between ACs [people with autism and their 'cousins,' i.e., people with related disabilities] but it fails when ACs and NTs interact together" (Blackburn et al. 2000). Thus, from a phenomenological perspective, the explanation is not that people labeled autistic are defective or lacking a key "mechanism" but that they may experience the world differently than do so-called neurotypicals.[8]

A second explanation of autism is that people so classified cannot easily connect details to wholes; they are seen as not have the capacity to draw relationships between specifics and more global understandings. Frith (1989) argues that while autism is characterized by what Wing and Gould (1979) call a triad of impairments—social interaction, communication, and imagination—there may be a still more fundamental explanation for the nature of this disability. Frith posits that the "triad," all related to central processing (1989, p. 97), may reflect a disinterest in or failure to recognize the value of generalizing, stemming from what she calls "a weakness in a drive for central coherence" (p. 107). The problem, she argues, is not that people classified as autistic get caught up in an endless focus on details, the proverbial trees rather than the forest, and not that "they are too good at discrimination" (p. 106), but that perhaps they demonstrate an "inability to see the 'need' for generalizations across differences" (p. 107). Frith suggests that where a person labeled autistic may maintain interest in one thing for a long period of time, "a normal child would attend to it briefly, finding it interesting only as part of a greater pattern" (p. 109). Frith speaks of an "impaired brain" of the person labeled autistic, characterized by a "disengagement" between central coherence (i.e., generalizing) and "peripheral devices" (p. 117). Naturally, communication relies heavily on a person's ability to relate a complex array of particulars to generalizations. Once stuck on one or a few details, a person would lose the plot of nearly any conversation. Then, for even more complex matters, such as considering others' perspectives—what Frith refers to as "mentalizing" and what Baron-Cohen has called theory-of-mind—the person labeled autistic would be at even further disadvantage, since thinking about what others might be thinking requires taking lots of specifics and interpreting them to make a larger whole. In a three-part examination designed to test the theory of "central coherence" with "high-functioning adults with autism or Asperger syndrome," Jolliffe and Baron-Cohen (1999) reached a more modest conclusion than that people with the autism designation are unable to process spoken and written language for meaning. Rather, they suggest the possibility that "individuals with an autism spectrum disorder have to make a greater than normal effort to process for meaning, with the result that they tend not to fully process for meaning unless requested to do so or unless they make a conscious decision to do so" (p. 166).

The recent availability of imaging technology would seem to present an opportunity to test the relevance of the central coherence theory as well as other theories of autism, but if one wanted to examine central coherence, upon what exactly would the researcher focus? Belmonte and Yurgelun-Todd note that research in autism has produced numerous accounts of difficulties with "updating the scope and focus of attention" and "operational rigidity [that] may stem from an inability to reorient attention rapidly" (Belmonte and Yurgelun-Todd 2003, p. 651), with individuals demonstrating difficulties in "dividing attention between auditory and visual channels" (p. 652). Working with six individuals whom they describe as "non-retarded" adults with diagnoses on the "autism spectrum" (p. 653), Belmonte and Yurgelun-Todd conducted an experiment in which their subjects were to maintain visual fixation on a target while attending covertly to "one of two stimulus locations and ignoring the other" (p. 654); participants did this task while having their eye movement monitored and while undergoing neuroimaging (MRI).

When the person detected the target stimulus (a colored square), he or she was then expected to shift attention to the alternate location and await the next target stimulus. Upon shifting attention, the person also had to move "the index finger of the dominant hand in the direction of this shift" (p. 654). The researchers found that the subjects with the autism diagnosis revealed different patterns of brain activation than the control group, leading the researchers to propose a

> pattern of information flow . . . characterized by three elements: hyper-arousal, that is, primary sensory processing that is abnormally intense . . . [a]nd abnormally generalised across anatomical regions and functional systems . . . and (2) impaired early selection of relevant stimuli . . . leading to (3) overloading of higher-order processes. (Belmonte and Yurgelun-Todd 2003, p. 660)

If overaroused by stimuli and in effect overloaded to the point of not being able to effectuate higher-order thinking, so the argument goes, the young, developing mind might "likely evolve a cognitive style that emphasizes low-level features" and "eschew reliance on global patterns" (p. 660; see also Belmonte et al. 2004). At the same time, Belmonte and Yurgelun-Todd consider that this could be top-down effects of "higher-order deficits" (p. 661), or that other factors could be involved, for example, anxiety in the experimental situation. Moreover, they note in the introduction to their study that research on attention that does not involve rapid attention shifting shows people on the autism spectrum performing at "normal or near-normal levels" (p. 652).

Bara, Bucciarelli, and Colle (2001) suggest that the notion of "central coherence" is excessively broad. What has been described as weak central coherence could reflect other, more specific difficulties related to, for example, perception, attention, and context. In their own research, they found that the ability to generalize and intuit intent of others, for instance, could be affected dramatically by context, thus suggesting that what may appear as difficulty with central coherence in one situation disappears in another. Bara, Bucciarelli, and Colle hypothesize that a single, rather narrow impairment, such as attention difficulties, could affect a range of other cognitive functions, thus causing a person to appear incompetent in higher-order thinking, when the problem is really more one of performance (2001 p. 219) under particular conditions. In making this argument, Bara and colleagues reject the presumption of overall deficits found within the individual to a more complex view that individual qualities are always operating in social context, where social context may dramatically influence performance. Perhaps most important to their analysis, particular conditions, such as when the subjects in their study did a theory-of-mind assessment on computers, may assist individuals in bypassing a particular problem such as attention shifting. Their subjects might well have found themselves defeated by the theory-of-mind tasks had they been asked to perform them verbally rather than with the medium of the computer.

This is not to suggest that the computer is somehow the antidote waiting to rescue people with the autism diagnosis. Rather, as Sue Rubin, one of the contributors to this book, explained in an earlier article, the struggle with attention can involve complex interactions of various factors. She described herself as having "obsessive compulsive behavior" where she gets "stuck with certain thoughts and actions" (Rubin et al. 2001, p. 421). With echolalia, she explains, "I say a word or sound and am unable to switch it off or change to a different sound" (p. 421). Yet, when attending a class where she is "cognitively engaged," her echolalia disappears (p. 421). In short, an organized teacher or other factors, including a computer, may aid attention and thus performance.

A third explanatory metaphor for autism is the idea of executive function. The term *executive function* refers to the ability to plan sequenced actions, where a person begins with first steps and then follows through with a series of actions, modulating performance over time, leading to an end result that approximates intention (Damasio and Maurer 1978; Welsh and Pennington 1988). On one level, the term would seem to be primarily descriptive, including such functions as "planning, flexibility of thought and action, set-shifting, inhibition, and holding a mental representation 'on-line' or in working memory" (Griffith et al. 1999). In short, it describes actions to carry out a purpose. But does it explain autism?

As with any of the broad concepts (e.g., mindblindness and central coherence), treating executive function as a global explanation (i.e., cause) of autism may mistake difference and difficulty with incapacity.

Griffith, Pennington, Wehner, and Rogers (1999) conclude that there is a "serious challenge to the executive dysfunction hypothesis of autism" in the fact that preschoolers in their studies demonstrated abilities in many of the areas considered fundamental to executive function. These included memory, maintaining information over a period of time during which a task takes place, using and manipulating information, shifting focus across different sets of information, and inhibition of responses (p. 830). If lack of executive function could be a cause of autism, then young children would not demonstrate such abilities. In a more recent study, with slightly older children, Joseph and Tager-Flusberg (2004) find that executive function skills correlate with communicative functioning, but note that a correlation does not demonstrate causation. Further, they do not find a relationship between executive function skills and "reciprocal social functioning" (p. 151). Thus they find "limited relationships between . . . executive functions . . . and symptom severity in autism" (p. 152).

On a more fundamental level, researchers are asking themselves (Miyake et al. 2000) whether the skills identified as comprising the construct called executive function are closely interrelated or whether they are actually quite distinct. Or, in studying one skill, such as memory, does another skill, such as inhibition or attention, intrude? Miyake and colleagues found that "set-shifting," "monitoring," and "inhibition"— their research was with college students with no identified disabilities— may be skills that correlate with each other but that are also "clearly separable" (p. 49).

The issues raised by Miyake and colleagues, as well as by Griffith and colleagues (1999), suggest the problem of seeking any overarching explanation of autism. First, there is the fact that executive function is a metaphorical construct and not an identifiable mechanism. Second, the concept proposes a global deficit within people classified as autistic. But is the person who struggles with a particular task (note that not everyone with the autism label would have difficulty with the following example), for instance compiling a set of disks on a pole in the order previously observed in a model, really unable to think about actions and steps required to carry out actions, and really missing a cognitive mechanism? Is the person actually unable to see and interpret different sets of information and their possible relation to an action? Or, rather, does one or several things get in the way of successful performance? Similarly, is this a problem consistent across every setting, or do differences or difficulties in performance intensify under particular conditions? For example, delayed attention shifting could affect performance, as could anxiety, including environmentally induced anxiety; difficulties with timing; problems of sequencing; poor proprioceptive awareness; or any other specific elements that can be essential to overall success.

Each overarching construct on causality, including theory-of-mind, central coherence, and executive function, implies that autism can be understood as essentially internal to the person. In this sense, such explanations resemble the *nature* side of debates about intelligence (for an excellent discussion of this, see Hayman 1998). The "nature" argument holds that people are born smart or not, thus exonerating socially created inequities such as poverty and poor educational opportunity from culpability for stunting a person's development. Similarly, when a theory treats autism primarily or exclusively as an internal state or trait, it may, albeit possibly unintentionally, imply biological determinism. Save for the unlikely prospect that science could cure a person of the presumed internal flaw, such a theory is fundamentally a pessimistic stance. The theory defines the person as more or less bound in and made static by trait, with any chance of "improvement" (i.e., becoming more "normal") being modest or unlikely. Wing appears to represent this viewpoint when she writes, "Children who do not exhibit any signs of good cognitive ability are very unlikely indeed to develop skills through any method of teaching" (Wing 2000, p. 2). If a person *does* improve dramatically, the autism-as-internal-trait framework holds that while education may have been important, the person him- or herself is unusual (see, for example, the description of Tito Rajarshi Mukhopadhyay as "remarkable," in Wing 2000, p. 2). Within the framework of "big theory" explanations of autism, an individual who demonstrates dramatic change is likely to be regarded as a statistical outlier, or as Wing says, "remarkable." Thus prevailing notions about autism remain intact, undisturbed by particular contradictory evidence.

On the "nurture" side of the debate, the person classified as autistic, *like any person,* remains elastic. Autism is not all-defining. The experiences of Alberto Frugone or of the presenters in Glasgow, mentioned above, demonstrate the proposition that performance of anyone is situational. Des Lauriers (1978), in an early case study that preceded recent autobiographical accounts, makes this point when he describes his investigations of Clarence, one of Kanner's original eleven clients. Des Lauriers finds that Clarence understands that his social interactions often are different in degree from normate[9] expectations but are nonetheless situationally defined. Clarence worries about losing his job to new technology and about whether he will be able to satisfy his wife sexually—Des Lauriers points out that these are the kinds of things that a person without autism might also worry about, for instance, "the mild rumblings of panic" that surround the transition from being single to getting married (p. 227). Des Lauriers concludes that while autism may describe differences in Clarence's subjectivity, Clarence owes his accomplishments to early exposure to social interaction and education. He understands and explains himself and his possibilities in terms of opportunity.

Autobiographers and the Myth of the Autistic Person Alone

The field of autism, by which I mean professional experts, researchers, parents, teachers, and others who contribute to an autism literature, inhabits a different location vis-à-vis people classified as autistic than do the people themselves. The outsider perspective can never definitively know what the other person experiences or understands. The outsider is always in the position of having to ask, "What am I seeing here? What does this mean?" The tendency in the field to frame a response to such questions has been deficit-oriented. Within this deficit model, the outsider develops hypotheses or theories (e.g., the theory-of-mind, cognitive deficit) from a normate perspective and applies them to and tests them on people defined as disabled, in effect saying: What does the person labeled autistic lack that the "normal" person possesses? An alternative stance would be to identify individual subjective understandings or assumptions by eliciting perspectives of people classified as autistic, and to interpret multiple meanings of autism with an eye to placing the perspectives of labeled people in the foreground. The latter might be termed a critical phenomenology model, for it presumes that ideas about autism derive from many sources, always reflect power relationships between the defined and those who do the defining, and shift over time and in relation to social and cultural contexts. The contributing authors to this book follow in a recent tradition, most notably Grandin (Grandin and Scariano 1986; Grandin 1995), Williams (1989; 1994), and Barron (Barron and Barron 1992). Clearly, Grandin's 1986 book, *Emergence: Labeled Autistic,* signaled a period of transformation where people diagnosed as autistic began to define the experience of autism from the inside out. Instead of giving evidence of being broken and fundamentally out of touch (i.e., alone and perhaps uninterested) with the world around them, Grandin revealed a life in progress, very much in negotiation with social contexts.

Predictably, however, professional scholars tended to view Grandin through a deficit lens. Happé, in writing about Grandin—a Ph.D. researcher, consultant, and designer of animal feedlots, as well as a prolific writer about autism—refers to the latter's writing as "remarkable and an achievement of which almost anyone would be proud" (Happé 1991, p. 213). She finds particular passages where Grandin tells about her friendships, her imaginative games, strategies she used to win games by matching wits with other children, and "feigning sympathy and lying about who had done" something as a way of avoiding punishment as unusual for a person diagnosed as autistic. Happé cites these examples as evidence of an ability to "manipulate another person's beliefs and emotions" (p. 209) and therefore as indicating that Grandin is atypical of people classified as autistic. In other words, Grandin's accounts do not correspond to particular "known" deficits of autism.

Happé finds some of these descriptions so remarkable as to be suspect. Grandin's having a coauthor for her first book, *Emergence* (Grandin and Scariano 1986), casts "doubt," Happé argues, "on exactly those passages which are most interesting and challenging to our ideas about autism" (p. 208). Happé seems to be holding onto a Cartesian notion of the individual as separate from the rest of the world. From this perspective, autism can be understood in terms of individuals' qualities (including presumed deficits), more or less independent of outside influence—in effect, as within the autonomous individual. To have a "reliable" analysis of Grandin's autism, Happé writes, it would be necessary to examine "the autistic writer alone" (p. 209).

Happé describes Grandin's "unghosted" work as "hard to follow in places" (p. 209), as if to say that her initial book with Scariano is basically "ghosted." Seeming to pull Grandin back into the theory-of-mind construct of autism, Happé points to "changes of topic that do not run smoothly for the reader" (p. 210). She sees the deficits of autism in what she considers Grandin's abrupt shifts "from talking about her squeeze machine to talking about how to handle cattle" (p. 210). Happé seizes on this to say it is "as if she [Grandin] fails to appreciate that her reader does not share the important background information that she possesses" (p. 210), suggesting that Grandin is unable to distinguish between what knowledge is shared and what knowledge is personally known (p. 215). Here she makes an obvious, if implicit, reference to the theory-of-mind construct. She faults Grandin for introducing the existence of her squeeze machine (a device Grandin designed to help her with sensory awareness) many pages before she actually describes it, creating a bit of a mystery for readers (p. 210).

As useful as these examples might be for buttressing the deficit-oriented, theory-of-mind explanation of autism, they do as much to undermine it. After all, it is common that writers, myself included, and especially new writers, must go through multiple edits to sort out such things as order of events and descriptions, transitions, development of ideas, proper amounts of background information, and other adjustments to meet readers' expectations. So why would it be different for a person labeled autistic? Anyone who has heard one of Grandin's lectures on autism knows that she has developed into a most entertaining, highly imaginative presenter. As with other writers, it would be remarkable if her writing did *not* change over time, reflecting her experiences with the craft and with working collaboratively with others. Thus it is not surprising that Oliver Sacks refers to her book *Thinking in Pictures* (Grandin 1995), written ten years after *Emergence* (Grandin and Scariano 1986), as "a new much more deeply pondered and integrated narrative essay" (Sacks 1995, p. 12).

Now, consider Grandin's writing from a critical phenomenology stance. In her first autobiographical account (Grandin and Scariano 1986), she describes how her mother would read with her each day after school, and how through a process of trial and error she came to understand herself. She explains as issues of performance such things as her reactions to touch, the contradictions between the words she wanted to say and the automatic (i.e., as opposed to intentional) words that came out of her mouth, and her difficulty with achieving rhythm when clapping. It is simply impossible to read her narrative without recognizing that the author has lived what she describes. By sharing detailed accounts of her coming-of-age experiences, she confirms her understanding that they would be of interest to readers who do not have autism and who may interpret the world differently.

Far from confirming the deficit model, where the person labeled autistic is presumed isolated and uninterested, recent autobiographical accounts reveal people in search of connections with the world. Granted, Barron (Barron and Barron 1992) acknowledges being consumed by compulsions, such as repetitively throwing crayons down the heat register in his home to see if the pattern of each one's disappearance would replicate itself. He describes his fascination with throwing kitchen utensils into a tree, each time to see how high they would go, to see where they might hit the tree, to hear them make a rustling sound with the leaves and branches, and to see them fall, again and again. He loved patterns, and so he explored them. Yet, as with Grandin, Barron's narrative describes a struggle to achieve connectedness. He gives an accounting of his many strategies to acquire skills that would allow him to be seen as a participant with nondisabled people. Even if other people were unaware of his strong desire to change, to learn, and to interact— in other words, to socialize and to be socialized with—he kept hard at work. He explains that he felt proud of himself that he knew the names of all fifty American states. At every opportunity, he would ask his parents' friends if they had ever visited particular states, for example, Montana, West Virginia, or Kentucky. By asking about particular states by name, he could show that he knew them. He says he liked to talk about the states because it gave him a structure for conversation and allowed him to feel he was in control of the conversation. In retrospect, he realizes that he "conducted conversations that were fragmented and disjointed, that led nowhere," but he forgives himself for needing this step in the climb to communication (p. 107). "What mattered" at the time, he writes, "was that doing it made me feel a little closer to being a normal human being. I got recognition, and I felt powerful for at least a while when I steered the talk where I wanted it to go" (p. 107). As annoying as these conversations might have been to those he buttonholed, they gave him an alternative to being left out of "normal" conversations. "Everyone else talked effortlessly," he explains, "conversations flowing as smoothly as a creek, and I felt very inferior, shut out, less important" (p. 104). His listing-the-states narrative meant Sean Barron could converse. Such speech, albeit a kind of script, was indeed speech, and he was getting better at it. So autism had not made him uninterested in the world or in other people's perspectives. Also, the fact that he had a strong agenda did not mean that he was incapable of recognizing that others viewed the world differently. If anything, awareness of others' different points of view gnawed at him. In retrospect he believes that the topic of travel to far-off places, even if he had limited knowledge of what the states were actually like, allowed him into a fantasy that helped dampen "the pain" of his "present situation" (p. 106).

Barron sees autism as part of who he is, but who he is cannot be understood simply as autism. Extreme anxiety, for example, is one element that he attributes to his autism. But whatever its neurological basis, how Barron experiences anxiety shifts as he negotiates real-life situations. He describes taking a speech class in high school and literally gouging his arms as he clenched himself in fear, attempting to speak before the class; slowly, after his teacher drew his attention to his clenching hands, and with practice, he became more relaxed and better able to speak. Toward the end of his growing up, Barron's family moved to a different community, and so he and his sister found themselves in a new high school. Barron read this as an opportunity to achieve a new persona, or at least a new reputation. He became more successful in conversing with other students. It was as if the new context gave him license to try out newly acquired skills, without feeling bound by how others might define him from previous encounters. It worked.

He applied himself to developing a sense of humor in much the same, deliberate way that he had tried public speaking. He decided that he needed a sense of humor, something he had observed in other people. In fact, he "resented the fact that everyone else seemed to have one" (p. 180). He might have been comforted to know that not everyone does have a sense of humor, but in any case, he wanted one. He knew that he would need to pick up on nuances, and to do so more quickly than he had in the past. So he set about watching *Gilligan's Island* (Schwartz 1964) reruns repetitively until he was able to "recite a whole scene word for word." It was helpful, he says, that the program itself was "repetitive . . . easy to follow, predictable, and a comedy" (Barron and Barron 1992, 180). He believed that if he could capture the nuance of *Gilligan's Island*'s humor, he could repeat the lines and make other people laugh. What he found, though, was that people laughed at his unusual way of repeating the lines, not at the lines themselves. What he was coming to see was that his idea of what was funny often differed from what others took as funny. Also, he often could not stop his own patterns of actions. For the moment, he felt caught in compulsions.

That Grandin and Barron have interests and seek new skills, that they can chart their histories of change, and that these are always connected to social interactions render the notion of the "autistic person alone" unrealistic, even mythical. From a critical phenomenology perspective, their accounts reveal them as growing, changing, and achieving new subjectivities through engagement with the world.

The first definitions of autism did define autism in deficit terms, as a state of "aloneness"—Asperger wrote that "the autist is only himself [cf. The Greek word *autòs*]" (1944/1991, p. 38). Yet, as noted earlier, Asperger himself provided evidence to contradict the aloneness stereotype. The person classified autistic can no more be thought of as alone than can any person. This is apparent in Barron's writing, as it is in Grandin's. The idea of the writer as always existing in context could not have been more clearly illustrated than in how Barron came to write his part of the book *There's a Boy in Here* (Barron and Barron 1992). I first met Sean and his mother, Judy, in 1993 at a Syracuse University conference on disability. When I said how much I enjoyed their writing, Judy told me of her first reactions to Sean's writing. She was initially disappointed with Sean's prose. In her estimation, it was too general, showing little passion, to the point of being boring. To get Sean to write more specifically, and thus in a more interesting and instructive way, she gave him Tobias Wolff's memoir, *This Boy's Life* (1989), as an example of fine writing. "Write like this," she said. Apparently, that is all it took. After reading Wolff's book, Sean began to write detailed, compelling, dramatic accounts.

Seeing Past the Big Disconnect, Reading the Body

As has been the case for many people who have spent years trying to understand autism, a hint of pessimism surrounded my own early work, for I wondered how much people classified as autistic understood of the world. It was not that I wanted to declare them mentally retarded or cut off from the world; rather, I simply did not have a way to conceptualize what the other person understood or felt. In face-to-face encounters, like many educators, I suppose I vacillated between two stances—on the one hand, talking rather normally to the person as if he or she understood me perfectly, and on the other, wondering to myself if the person really did understand or, instead, was in his or her own world. The point at which I shifted clearly to the more optimistic of these two standpoints occurred when I met several people labeled autistic who, like Alberto Frugone, could not speak effectively but could reveal their intelligence in other ways. One of these people was Lucy Blackman. I want to describe my meeting her and learning from her writing in order to set the stage for a question that pervades this book: How should the nonlabeled person interpret the speech and actions of the person labeled autistic, when both may seem unusual, even unfathomable?

One Saturday morning at a communication center in Australia, in conjunction with a research project (Biklen 1990), I had a conversation with Blackman, then a high school student. Later, she would go on to graduate from Deakin University in Australia, write her autobiography (Blackman 1999), and give lectures at autism conferences in the United States and at Syracuse University. Attwood, a leading scholar on autism and Asperger syndrome (see, for example Attwood 1998) has written about Blackman, "Over the . . . years [between 1990 and 1999] she has taught me more about autism than any academic text" (Attwood 1999, p. vii). He found her classically autistic in appearance, as "she appeared to live in her own world, made few intelligible sounds and at times her behaviour was quite bizarre," yet he came to see her as "a person of remarkable intelligence and fortitude" (Attwood 1999, p. vii).

I feel similarly instructed by Blackman. My first meeting with her was one of several events that provided a foundation for my coming to a *presuming competence* stance toward the person labeled autistic. Blackman had spent most of her school years in segregated centers for students with mental retardation and had only recently been admitted to a typical secondary school when we met in Melbourne, Australia. During a visit to her high school, I observed that she seemed unable to speak in words aloud, frequently paced in the hallway of the school, and did not always stand and listen to me when I spoke to her. Also, I was told that she had previously displayed other unusual behavior, for example, climbing a tree and peeing on the ground in public. In short, she behaved in ways that struck me as unconventional. And yet, on the Saturday morning that I recall as a turning point in my orientation toward autism, she drew me into a debate that was not easy to forget.

Blackman typed her side of the conversation:

Lucy: "You put emphasis on integration. What really does integration have to offer to some terribly retarded people?" She had heard me speaking on the local radio and also at a gathering of teachers about school inclusion.

Me: "It offers the chance to be seen as an ordinary person. Of course that depends on other people being able to see them in this way," I responded.

Lucy: "You must be so idealistic," she said. To this I responded that I thought of myself as optimistic more than idealistic. She then continued, saying that it is "too mean to judge people by ability." I wondered if she was referring to her own judgment where she had referred above to "some terribly retarded people." Then she added, "Most people need proof [of the student's competence]. How can the disabled meet such a gauntlet?" It was highly unlikely that people with disabilities would ever find acceptance in the world as long as there was "no profit in disability," she argued.

Within this brief interchange, Blackman revealed complex thinking that might seem unimaginable if we had seen only that she paced in the school hallway, seemed unable to speak, and walked away from social interactions.

There were several lessons here. Her physical actions do not necessarily reveal her thinking abilities. Occasionally they do, for example, when she looks up from her typing and waits for a companion to read her text. But often, from a normate/outsider perspective, her actions can mislead. For instance, her walking away from a conversation may reflect excitement or a desire to manage excitement, not indifference to the conversation.

In our debate over inclusion and attitudes about disability, she showed a keen sense of social justice; she is quite aware of discrimination practiced on the basis of disability, and obviously she knows that other people's ideas about disability are not always similar to her own. She has framed her own ideas about disability in terms of political economy, recognizing that if inclusion of people with disabilities could be made profitable, it might also become popular. Hers is no ordinary take on disability.

Another message from this interchange with Blackman struck me as particularly important. She impressed on me that her disability or difference needs to be acknowledged and accommodated. Her life will not necessarily improve if those around her adopt the attitude that "everyone is the same." While she insists on being treated as a competent person, treating her disability as invisible would leave her vulnerable. She is the first to point out that in some ways she *is* different from most other people. In practical terms, she requires an assistant by her side, someone who exudes calmness and who on occasion will remind her to shift her attention to a next task or to a person wishing to interact with her. She depends on several well-trained assistants to support her using augmentative and alternative communication systems. Also, she told me that she appreciates being treated as smart; she pointed out which teachers or classmates appreciated her intellect—students in her literature class, for example, opted to join her section so that they could benefit from her comments. On a still more practical level, her means of communicating dictates that she have time to type out the words she wants to say; if she is going to be heard, people around her must be willing to wait as she types. Also, her attendance at school is dependent on school officials recognizing that she needs ways of dealing with her anxiety, including pacing in the hallway. These factors, and possibly others as well, all appear to be a *sine qua non* for her participation in school. Without them, she has no chance of demonstrating her complex ideas.

I label my learning from Blackman as "getting beyond the big disconnect," because she confirmed for me the fact that it is impossible for the outsider to know what she is thinking by simply observing her actions. If all I have are my observations, then the best I can do is to hypothesize.

This is what has for so long made understanding the autism of people who do not speak virtually unfathomable. Blackman illustrates this in her book, *Lucy's Story: Autism and Other Adventures* (1999), when she explains how, as a young child, she heard other people's words: "someone would release some spoken sounds in my direction, but unless I already knew what they were trying to say, I floundered because only part of the speaker's intended information package got through" (p. 36). Interestingly, her mother *did* grasp that Lucy could understand things if given in another form. Her mother's notes from this period include the comment that "communication with Lucy is most effective when reinforced with signals which are almost over-dramatic" (p. 37).

Blackman has always had problems with spoken expression. She could not speak to say what she wanted, so she developed other strategies. Unfortunately, the logic of these strategies is often lost on the normate observer. In *Lucy's Story,* Blackman describes how she would sit "on a potty on . . . [the] kitchen floor" to indicate that she wanted something to eat (1999, pp. 36–37). Of course, the people around her were not likely to decipher the meaning of her sitting on the potty. It turns out that during her childhood one of her caregivers had taken to bribing her with food when giving her toilet training; years later, Lucy could not perch herself next to the kitchen table and "whine with the other kids that I wanted a second (or fourth) cookie." Sitting on the potty had become her "equivalent strategy" (pp. 36–37). Her example is reminiscent of Kanner's account of Donald, who would say yes to mean that he wanted to be hoisted onto his father's shoulders. Prior to her having a reliable means of communication, to interpret the possible meanings of Blackman's actions was often to play a guessing game.

"Real speech," she explains, was her "downfall." She might be able to reproduce the tone of someone's voice in a parrot-like fashion, but making sounds for communication was limited to saying "single vowel sounds" (p. 41). Today, Blackman says that, if very relaxed, she may greet a person, saying, "Hello, so and so [i.e., the person's name]," but typically even greetings that for most people are automatic are, for her, impossible, unless someone with her tells her to say hello or goodbye. If reminded or thus prompted, she can give off a "'bye bye' as woodenly as twenty years ago [i.e., when she was a young child]" (p. 42) and perhaps wave, but even through this she is likely to glance away, or worse walk away, "my eyes often flashing back to the person who has reminded me of what to say, and on whom I am relying for timing and reinforcement" (p. 42). This seems to illustrate what Goode (1994) meant in his book *World without Words* when he concluded that certain "communication can be *necessarily* dyadic (or triadic) and *only* dyadic" (p. 199).

More often than not, if left to her own devices, Blackman's direct interaction with someone in public triggers ritualistic responses that leave the observer confused, for the dyadic or triadic quality is missing or incomplete. For example, she describes a situation where, at the age of eighteen, an older woman stood next to her at a crosswalk. "I assume she was concerned at my odd movements. She asked me if I were all right. Confused by the fact that she expected me to respond, I started running in a little circle" (1999, p. 41). A half hour later, Blackman was still making her circles and the "would-be benefactor was standing aghast" (p. 41). Her movements were social overtures, attempts to engage, but they were so outside the normate notion of how to connect socially that it would have been hard for any passersby to realize her intentions. Only people especially close to her would have any chance at all of accurately guessing her meaning. The seeming mismatch (from a normate perspective) between her actions and intent was frustrating to Blackman but not easily improved upon, and certainly not an indicator of her thinking: "The strange thing was that I could see the ridiculous and comic scenario in my mind's eye, but I could not alter the behaviour" (p. 41). Doing what someone else expects, *when* expected, seems to be among the hardest tasks for her to achieve.

Ever since meeting Blackman, I have been impressed with how often other people diagnosed as autistic have similarly described the disconnect between their ideas and their actions. Rubin (Rubin et al. 2001), another of the contributors to this volume, has described her performance as on-again, off-again: "When someone asks me to do something, sometimes I can and other times I can't. I understand the request but I can't follow it. I absolutely will eventually be able to do it, but no one waits long enough" (p. 423). Imagine the difficulty that her need for extended time of response could have on how people assess her. In other instances, Rubin comes out with automatic actions that either impede her doing what she wants to be doing or simply precede more intentional actions. As she says, "I certainly understand why I was assumed to be retarded. All my very awkward movements and all my nonsense sounds made me appear retarded" (p. 419). Like Blackman, she asks that people not judge her based on her every action (or inaction). Her body's attempts at intentional action are simply too unpredictable.

More Evidence against a Static Conception of the Person Classified Autistic

In 1996, several years after meeting Blackman, I received a tape recording from Richard Attfield, another of the contributors to this book. This package would further shift my perspective on autism. It would strengthen my conviction in the presuming competence stance toward people labeled autistic and would deepen my sense of the complexities involved in interpreting others. Especially, I was to learn more about autism and speech and what the process of personal change looks like.

Along with the tape, Attfield enclosed a typed page. In a letter to Richard some weeks later, I reported my reaction to the tape:

> I listened to your tape just last week and was thrilled by it. At first I put it into my tape machine in my car and heard your gentle, ever so intentional voice. It was hard for me to understand all the words at first, but some popped out full formed, easy for me to understand. It would have been far easier if I had been in the same room with you, watching you mouth them. But then I pulled my car over next to a stand of trees along the road and picked up your "Assessment of Me by Me" and read along with your reading. Then of course all of your words became crystal clear. How glorious it was. I wanted to shout for your success, to tell the world.

This was one of the first times I realized that communicating by typing might create a path for some individuals to begin speaking as well. Once I understood that the tape and typed text were one and the same, I listened to the tape several times. With the text in front of me, each recorded word became clear. As for content, it was rich with Attfield's anger at having been treated as if he were retarded and at being segregated into special education, and with rightful indignation at being held back from access to academic instruction. He was determined to overcome his fright to speak up for himself:

I want to go to college to gain an education. I do NOT want to go to a Day Centre [a segregated, disabled-only setting]. I am not retarded. . . .[10]

All my life I have been considered stupid. I understand that autistic people are intelligent and if you people admitted that you cannot understand us then perhaps we could try in a way to understand each other as fellow human beings. I get so frustrated in this useless body. If you just expressed some understanding and treated me as an intelligent person I could try to talk to you instead of feeling frightened to express an opinion. I know that I am intelligent . . . will you ever take what I say seriously?

At the point of hearing this tape, I had not yet met Richard Attfield. In my letter to him, I asked if he would let me videotape him as he read aloud. In a return letter, Richard informed me that he would be too nervous to be videotaped, but perhaps he would be capable at some point in the future. Several months passed before he wrote me again. To my delight, he now agreed to meet. Within two weeks of hearing from him, I was en route to England, video camera in tow.

Richard was among the first people with the autism label who I had heard could read aloud what they wrote or typed, even though extemporaneous conversation was still very difficult. When he read aloud, he could say things of great complexity. An irony of this situation was that he had been able to read text aloud from the time he was five years old. What was new, at least in my experience, was that he could type his side of a conversation or essay and then read his own words aloud. Yet with speech alone, without any text to read, he seemed limited to a few phrases or, as he explained later, "sentences peppered here and there." It was not for several years that I would learn that others could do the same thing Richard was demonstrating, that is, reading text as they wrote or typed it (see, e.g., Broderick and Kasa-Hendrickson 2001).

At the disabled-only schools that he had attended, much of the curriculum was nonacademic, such as cooking, telling time, physical exercise, gardening, shopping, visits to the library, ice-skating, horse riding, swimming, and what Richard refers to now as "real basic reading." He persisted in asking for more academic subjects. Some were at length adopted, but "not a full academic programme."

I knew very little about Richard other than that he had been classified as having both cerebral palsy and autism, that he was now attending college, and that he aspired to become a writer. When I arrived at his house, Richard greeted me warmly by saying, "Hallo." Then, on the first day of my visit, Richard demonstrated to me that he could read aloud. He held several typed pages in front of him, looked intently at the lines and began to read, ever so slowly and quietly. I did not know at the time—and he had not mentioned it to anyone, including his parents (he did not want to give them further cause for concern)—that he had noticed a deterioration in the sight in his right eye.[11] I angled my video camera toward him.

He told me that the camera made him nervous, but I did not initially realize just how much of an intrusion it was. It was only later, during the actual writing of the book, that Richard told me he was concerned about how he would come across on the tape: "I was feeling miserable because I knew I would not be able to read as fluently, as I am able to do to myself." He explained that he had taken half an hour to read aloud what he could read to himself in two minutes. "It was extremely annoying," he told me.

I did my best to blend into Richard's living room by sitting in a corner chair for hours, alternately talking to him and reading some of his car magazines—he had a rather large collection of magazines about Jaguars, motorbikes, Fords, the British Mini, and also 4 x 4 vehicles. At midday each day, we would take a ride with his father and mother in their auto, to see nearby villages and the coast. On these outings, Richard sat in the backseat with his mother, typing away in rich conversations. These times in the car seemed far more relaxed than our mornings together in his living room, probably because we were then out of the presence of the video camera. In the car, Richard seemed more talkative (through typing). As much as I wanted to be able to record Richard's reading aloud on video, it had become obvious that the camera made him uncomfortable.

On the morning of the last day of my visit, I told Richard that we should give up trying to videotape his reading aloud; "It's not that important," I said. "After all, I have seen you reading aloud and I have it on audio"—I had the original audiotape he had sent to me and now I had observed his reading aloud firsthand. "It's not so crucial that I capture it on videotape." But Richard said he would like to try again. At this point, he picked up a cassette-tape player, put a tape in, and pressed the fast-forward button. When the tape came to the end, he set it to go in fast reverse, and so on. I do not know that Richard ever told me the meaning of this action, though I interpreted it as him creating a sound barrier, a kind of homemade white noise between himself and the environment, the sort of whirring noise that libraries often use to dampen the sound of individuals' voices. As the tape ran in fast-forward and rewind, Richard read aloud for the camera. The hum of the tape recorder was not so loud as to overwhelm the audio-recording part of the video. I concluded that Richard had created an accommodation that allowed me to capture on video his ability to read aloud.

I don't mind admitting that, once again, I felt exhilarated at Richard's ability. It felt like a success for us both. My thought was that he could become an inspiration to others who wanted to learn to speak aloud. To my surprise, Richard later told me that he felt he "had failed because it was not good enough." He explained that "because of being denied access to structured speech therapy sessions," he was "ill-equipped to deal with an expressive communication difficulty; inside was a person screaming to get out. I could not live up to my own conception of myself so therefore I felt that I had failed."

I could not help but reflect on the fact that this situation spoke to the question of what it means to assess competence. The particulars were different, but in terms of the larger lesson, my visit with Richard was partly a replay of what I had learned from observing and getting to know Lucy Blackman. The only way I could come to understand Richard was by talking to him, and for him to instruct me on what he was experiencing. It was a kind of catch-22 where, if I ever expected to get to know Richard, I first had to accept that he thinks and feels in complex ways. In actuality, this was not a leap of faith on my part, for there were many clear signs that I observed after spending even a little time with him, whether his smile, or his few spoken words, or his nervousness when I brought out my video camera and proposed to capture him speaking, or his gentle eyes and interested look in my direction, or all these things. Subconsciously, I know I expected that Richard and I would get to know each other and that I would learn from him. I never stated that expectation explicitly to myself, but I also never assumed anything less. As it turned out, I earned a friend as well. Richard and I have now known each other for nearly ten years. We correspond regularly and, on occasion, Richard calls from England on the phone, reading aloud his side of the conversation as he types it.

After our mutual success with the videotaping session that morning in 1997, we set off with his parents for an afternoon visit to Cambridge, where we wandered through narrow streets, watched university students paddle along the river in punts, and browsed in bookstores. The trip was Richard's idea. He had wanted to show me Cambridge, for which I will always be grateful. I had not previously been to Cambridge but had read about it and knew the work of some of its faculty.

We also stopped at a cemetery filled with American soldiers who had died in World War II. Later, the opening scene from the film *Saving Private Ryan* (Spielberg 1998) would remind me of our outing, for the film depicts a family strolling through just such a cemetery. Richard wrote about our stop, "I felt like my life, my suffering was insignificant in contrast to the sacrifices those servicemen had made."

Over the years, I keep being struck by how dramatically Richard has changed, at least in my eyes, becoming ever more outspoken, confident, and humorous. When we first met in the mid-1990s, Richard gave me examples of his early writing. In 1992, his prose included some unusual sequencing. For example, he wrote, "When I was asked stupid questions reply I always would words decide safe were to answer. I did try to trust people then friends with them I would be." By 1996, Richard's writing had become more fluent. In a letter to the director of Student Services at his college, he wrote the following:

> I am grateful for your help in organising a course for me to study "A" levels. I am looking forward to studying English Literature and The History of Art. I am also looking . . . to attaining a better understanding of the old English in Shakespeare's plays. I have read the first scene of King Lear [a play the class was to study] and thought it was good.

By 2001, three and a half years after Richard had read aloud in front of my video camera, I was back in England for a second visit. As it turned out, during this visit I made a mistake that led to Richard explaining something I had not yet recognized. I happened into a newsstand one morning, just a few minutes before departing by car to his house for another day of conversations. At the newsstand, I noticed a rack of magazines about automobiles. Remembering Richard's interest in the British Mini and four-wheel-drive cars, I purchased two of the car magazines. When I arrived at his house that morning, I presented Richard with the magazines. He then said, "I loved my magazines but one must move on." Referring to my gift, Richard explained, "It's like coming off cigarettes for a year and then someone giving you a packet."

My first interpretation of this interchange was of Richard owning up to an obsession with car magazines. I later learned, however, that this was an imposed understanding. Richard told me, "I had realised how expensive the magazines were. I calculated how much money I was spending on magazines and decided that I could spend the money on trendy t-shirts and jeans or hair gel instead." He further explained his reaction to my bringing him the car magazines:

> When you gave me the magazine, I tore the front page off; my mother nearly died in horror. I tore the page of the magazine because I did not want to read it. I had decided that it was time to move on. [Previously] I would bury myself in a magazine as a front for the fact that I could not participate in a conversation. I remembered a time when I did not buy magazines to read, so I was quite proud of myself on your first visit to my house that I read them. I read the car magazines because I was interested in them. I had visions of buying myself a car at some point in the future. . . . [But then] I had decided I spent too much money on magazines. It [the gift of two magazines] was like coming off cigarettes for a year and then someone giving me one, but I no longer wanted to read them. I no longer felt the need to hide behind them because I had a means by which I could express myself. Do people hide behind newspapers on train journeys or when eating by themselves so they do not have to acknowledge other people?

I suspect my initial interpretation of Richard and his magazines is evidence of how I had imposed an aspect of the prevailing, official definition of autism on Richard, making an interest into a "fascination" and collecting into an "obsession."

During the same visit, I asked Richard whether he still watched videos, as I had observed him doing on my first visit when I had parked myself in his living room for the better part of a week. But this, too, was something that had changed. He still has a large video collection, but he explained that he was now two years older and his interests had changed. At his request, his mother had taken his prior collection of tapes to a charity shop and he had purchased new ones. At one time, the earlier tapes had been interesting, but then he said, "I had put one on and was bored stiff with it." Now, he said, it is "hard to understand what their attraction had been." "Wasting . . . life doing repetitive things," he explained, might well have been a reaction to being physically isolated in disabled-only schools, and not having access to intellectual work.

Today, we often e-mail back and forth, mentioning different films we have seen, comparing our reactions to them. About the film *Notting Hill,* for example, Richard told me that he especially likes the ending where Hugh Grant looks at Julia Roberts: "their eyes meet and for that instant they make a connection." And about *Finding Forrester* he told me, "I loved the bit where Forrester questioned the Professor over the meaning of a word, because it was something I did myself and therefore I felt that I had made a connection." He also enjoyed seeing *Shakespeare in Love,* "because I was studying Shakespeare at College and it brought the Elizabethan age alive for me."

During my second visit to his home I realized how many questions he asked me, and on so many topics. Ostensibly, I was interviewing him, but more often he was questioning me. He is more outwardly inquiring than any person with the autism label that I know, and more inquiring than most other people as well, autistic or not. Indeed, he is a gifted conversationalist. Alberto Frugone asks me questions as well—recall, for example, that he asked me whether I had come to speak with him about his grammar or about his life. And Lucy Blackman had questioned me the very first time we met, arguing with me about my thoughts on inclusion. But Richard literally peppers me with questions, although always in the most open-minded, truly inquiring way. One day when we were talking about his writing a chapter for this book, he joked, "I would settle for the Nobel prize for literature." Then he asked, "What are you writing about?" As quickly as I answered, he asked, "What are other people writing about?" and "Who are the other people who are contributing?" Then he asked me what I thought of his writing; then "How many books do you think will sell?" he asked. "Do you think a book by me [alone] would sell?" Perhaps to needle me in my role as an editor, he asked me if I would permit him to edit my writing. I said I'd be afraid to, but in the end I have asked for his comments. He asked if I knew other people who battled anxiety. When I said I did and described one person, Richard commented, "The anxiety. To hell with it. It rules your life if you let it." Richard asked why I had not immediately seen him at the Heathrow Airport in the arrival lounge when I came through the doors from Customs: "Was it because you were unable to recognize me or because you did not look my way?" He wanted to know if I thought he had changed in the three years between my visits. "What about my language?" he asked. "In terms of vocabulary?" I asked. "Yes, topic and conversation, structure of sentences then [compared to now]." He told me that he felt that some individuals he has met speak in a steady stream rather than so much back and forth—I have heard this sometimes explained as a protective response to difficulties in processing incoming speech. Richard wanted to know how I thought his communication compared to others labeled autistic. No one else had asked me such a question, so it gave me pause. I told him that his questioning of me was distinctive, that he was more inquiring than others.

Reflecting now on the many conversations we have had, ranging from Richard's probing questions to his reflections on events we shared, I keep returning to thoughts about what all this means for prevailing ideas about autism. In his book *Mindblindness* (1996), Baron-Cohen cites Pinker's work on language where Pinker says that a common vocabulary in any language community enables people to converse in and recognize concepts "mind to mind virtually instantaneously" (p. 84). But not so for people diagnosed autistic, Baron-Cohen argues:

> Consider a person who has an intact language faculty but who cannot mindread [editor's note: i.e., appreciate that others have points of view independent of their own] . . . autism arguably being such a case. . . . Such a person would be able to reply in perfectly well formed sentences when asked a question like "Where do you live?" but would be unable to engage in social dialogue—normal communication. (p. 131)

As will become apparent in his contribution to this book, long before he could express himself in sentence-level, back-and-forth dialogue,

Richard Attfield had a keen sense that many people did not interpret him as he did himself. He was a part of the language community well before many people recognized it.

A Social Constructionist Way
of Thinking about Autism

I argue that autism is best understood as a social and cultural construction, that the particular aspects of autism's construction are complex and multilayered, and that people classified autistic as well as those around them, including the autism field, have choices to make concerning which constructions to privilege. Autism is not a given condition or set of realities—at least, it is not "given" or "real" *on its own*. Rather, autism is and will be, in part, what any of us make it.

By way of explaining and justifying these assertions, I present five related principles that frame this book. The first concerns the importance of *interpreting the mind and body from an insider perspective*. Ever since the middle of the nineteenth century, disability has been increasingly framed as medical abnormality, in need of being studied, cataloged into new or available taxonomies, and explained. In the context of utilitarian politics, where individual economic worth depends on the person's perceived productivity, any condition that might be thought to violate prevailing norms is subject for analysis, with difference being treated as pathology, to be reformed, isolated, or blotted out. Autism, like other disabilities, was initially described as a deviation from an ideal norm of behavior or performance and is increasingly studied as an example of deviation in neural structure. In this collection of essays, I do not take the position that autism is pathogenic and certainly not that autism demands a cure—these are not my judgments to make. But neither do I want to suggest that the body is irrelevant to understandings of autism.

Autism as an identity, like gender and race, has been linked to particular externally imposed interpretations of the body. The contributing authors have a history of being interpreted, often pejoratively, based on what they looked like and how well they perform in particular situations, according to particular normate standards. This is not unlike cultural treatment of race:

> Racial identities, like those along the dimensions of gender and sexuality, are defined in a peculiarly corporeal way: one's identity as an African American is rooted in one's embodiment as a black body. (Appiah and Gates 1995, p. 4)

Yet, *unlike* the case with race or gender, the person labeled autistic has been known to complain about an unruly body that will not always comply with intention. Nevertheless, I do not enter this discussion through the framework of pathology. Rather, I am interested in how people labeled autistic perceive others' representations of their bodies and performance and, perhaps even more important, how they themselves experience and interpret their bodies.

In using the term *body*, I mean to refer to the mind/body and how the person participates in the world. This is not basically different from the idea that all learners have preferential learning styles. Williams, speaking from her own experience with disability, has written that "some people need to use physical involvement with" a topic and thus engage learning through "kinesthetic sense and not just the visual and auditory because they can't hold much in conscious awareness without it all floating off, fragmented (for me [Williams adds] it's like confetti in there a lot of the time)" (in Biklen 2002, p. 19). In essence, Williams is saying that for some people to understand a cup is a cup, they need to hold it, not just see it or hear about it.

Richard Attfield also seemed to implicate the body, at least eyesight, when he described how he saw the written word, yet his difficulty, unlike what Williams describes, was not with meaning but with how he actually saw words. He could not "read easily," he explained, for while he "had no trouble identifying anything"—for example, a cup—"words tumbled, jumbled, jumped away, danced about when I read." As can be observed in many autobiographical narratives (e.g., Grandin 1995; Williams 1989; 1994; Barron and Barron 1992), people with the autism label often discuss their ways of seeing or feeling, sense of body parts and their locations (i.e., proprioception), motor planning, and other aspects of mind/body performance.

Autobiographical narratives afford a window on the specific nature of these experiences. To the extent that they are different from other people's experiences, such accounts suggest how these differences can be negotiated in social and cultural contexts and how others can make performance easier. Williams's advice in this regard, to offer multiple modes of learning, implies another main principle about understanding the experiences of people classified as autistic: context matters. Simply stated, the second principle for framing this book is: *in order to begin to understand the person labeled autistic, as to understand any person, it is necessary to examine social context.* What is the world that the person inhabits? And how does the person negotiate different environments?

I am often asked, "What percentage of people with autism can be expected to achieve the communication abilities that Alberto Frugone or Richard Attfield or Lucy Blackman has achieved?" Clearly, such a question grows out of the pathology perspective. It imagines people and their neurology inhabit a continuum of ability, ranging from extreme pathology to less pathology, verging on normalcy. I answer by talking about privilege or opportunity. It has always seemed to me that representations of autism and educational practices are only partly related to individuals' neurological makeup; and really the same point must be made about anyone and any educational regime. For example, the likelihood that a particular student will be included in a regular class or sent off to a special school will have more to do with local educational policy toward students with autism than with any neurological assessments—for a more elaborate discussion of this point in relation to all disabilities, see my article "The Myth of Clinical Judgment" (Biklen 1988). Similarly, the educational performance of any nondisabled student is invariably related to family wealth, geographic location, and other social factors. So, in response to the question about how many people with autism might develop excellent, alternative communication abilities, I suggest that the percentage is likely to be a reflection of context. How many have parents—in the main this has been mothers—who can contribute huge amounts of time and energy to their education? How many have access to academic school curricula? How many enjoy access to communication training and hundreds of hours of practice? It is likely not insignificant that Attfield, Frugone, and Blackman all had mothers who devoted themselves to providing intense instruction and who interceded with schools to see that they received academic content even when social policy and prevailing professional and social doctrine and attitudes discouraged it.[12]

The intimacy that parents and family friends have with children seems to play a role in their ability to see how they interact with contexts and in turn encourages them to support contexts in which the children thrive. In an earlier study, a colleague and I (Kliewer and Biklen 2001) described how a respite worker, Carol Schroeder, supports a sixteen-year-old labeled autistic:

> "Steven knows everything there is to know about butterflies," Carol explained in an interview in which Steven also participated. He interjected, "Monarch butterflies. Would you like to see?" Steven had with him his ever-present notebook filled with tattered pages of his own detailed drawings of various types of butterflies and cocoons. "Pupa or chrysalis," he corrected. "Steven's read everything there is in the library on butterflies," Carol noted. Indeed he had with him, as always, several different public library books, all related to butterflies and insects. He laid three of the books, opened, on the floor, then centered himself among them, glancing at each of the exposed pages. He then flipped to the next page of each book and repeated the process. Carol shrugged, "That's how he reads. I tried to get him to do it one book at a time, but it wasn't worth the battle—didn't I, Steven?" Immersed in his reading, he appeared to not hear the question." (pp. 4–5)

Sadly, neither Carol nor Steven's mother, Nikki, was successful in getting educational officials to recognize Steven's interests or his reading ability. They were told, "Steven's not a reader yet," and he can "decode, but doesn't process" (p. 5).

Apparently, Steven's school does not recall Asperger's and Kanner's warning that context is crucial to performance. Both Asperger and Kanner observed that their students often would show understanding of a complex math problem or other intellectual work when their response was unexpected; it was as if they did better when approached indirectly. This seems quite like Steven's way of reading; Carol Schroeder might try to teach him to read a book at time, but he insists on scanning three at a time. Could it be that he finds that approach useful? Instead of framing different performance as failed performance, Asperger and Kanner understood that contexts needed to be examined and often adjusted to the person's interests and idiosyncratic ways of interacting.

More recently, Williams has proposed a style of teaching that puts the teacher in an oblique relation to the student, thus protecting against heightening the person's anxiety. Like Nikki and Carole's style of interacting with Steven, Williams's approach provides a nonconfrontational way of fostering engagement. It might include "open ended statements, multiple choice or questions left on the page rather than directed at the person, with the social 'floodlights' turned down as we allow them their own uninvaded space to answer using an indirectly confrontational media such as typing or pointing [which are via objects] then we increase the chances of getting an intelligible, less self protective response" (in Biklen 2002, p. 16). Williams's suggestions are reminiscent of Kanner's observation of the student Donald, who answered math problems metaphorically but seemed unable to answer yes/no questions. Presumably, autobiographical accounts may illuminate how and why some contexts allow for more successful performance than others.

Third, *the person labeled autistic always participates in defining him- or herself, even if by default.* The contributing authors to this book may be unusual in that, irrespective of autism, each is highly reflective and articulate about how he or she got to this point. Frugone, for example, recalls how he instructed his mother on how he might become more independent at home. Similarly, Attfield recounts his campaign to challenge school officials. When the special school officials recommended placement in a sheltered, segregated activity center, he asked for and applied to college. Having decided on his own that he must enter regular schooling, he made a tape-recorded plea outlining his goals, wrote letters of application for college education, and eventually won access to one.

Burke, another of the contributors to this book, a boy who first began to speak in complex sentences at the age of thirteen, explains that he did so only after deciding he must, and then only with a raft of strategies, including hours of practicing pronunciations by repeating words his mother said and by attempting to speak aloud lists of words that his mother posted on his refrigerator at home (Broderick and Kasa-Hendrickson 2001). In each of these instances, the person steps outside the position of being the observed or the judged (i.e., assessed and categorized) and describes how he or she took a hand in self-definition.

The idea of learning-by-doing may be a *sine qua non* for some learners. When asked what might constitute the ideal learning situation,

Williams cited, "one which relies on exploring concepts through movement and through the senses for one's own benefit and not as a matter of eagerly awaited proof" (in Biklen 2002, p. 20). Clearly, this approach will not be required for everyone with the classification of autism, but for some it may be essential. The narrative accounts in succeeding chapters include much about how the contributing authors have defined their own learning.

A fourth principle is that *autism may not be easily understood through majority assumptions* (i.e., it requires a critical phenomenologist's openness to multiple subjective understandings). It is common for educators to assume that actions bespeak intention or interest. But what if the so-called normal person observing the person classified as autistic misinterprets an action as having an intention that it does not? Blackman illustrates this problem in the incident mentioned above. How was the elderly woman at the road crossing to interpret Blackman walking in circles? And how was Blackman's mother to make sense of her sitting on the child potty in the kitchen? In the former instance, Blackman was flustered, and in the latter, she was requesting a cookie; but who would have known? The reasons why people labeled autistic may have difficulty with many kinds of conventional performance—with activities that are multistep ones (e.g., crossing a street at the right moment), with speech (e.g., asking for a cookie), and with social interaction—are multifaceted and hard to decipher. They require careful observation, a willingness not to judge quickly and negatively, and, ultimately, an interest in listening to people as they attempt to interpret themselves.

Attfield mentions general difficulties with movement as well as intense anxiety and sensitivity to particular sounds, although he notes that these changed over time and even from moment to moment, depending on context. To begin to understand them, he argues, it is necessary to interpret them in the contexts in which they occur. About sounds, he told me that as a young child certain noises were jarring:

> The first time I was perceived as having sensitivity to noise in the environment was when I was a year of age. I reacted to the noise of an electrical kettle boiling in the kitchen at a friend's house, by lying on the floor and screaming in terror, putting my hands over my ears. Another time I recall in school at the age of 15/16, I experienced the same sensitivity to the noise of

a kettle boiling; the kettle was standing on a metal tray at the time. I did not lie on the floor and scream in terror but I felt like going A.W.O.L. I complained bitterly about the noise but was told I had to accustom myself to it. Extractor fans or cold air fans, irritated the life out of me, rather like a dentist's drill. For a time, around the age of eleven, I had one or two panic attacks if I heard the sound of a hair dryer—again in school if I was overly anxious—especially if I was not allowed to move away from the noise source which was often the case; at home where I felt safe, the noise did not unduly bother me.

It is noteworthy that Richard is careful not to internalize his reactions to his environment, for example, his reaction to sounds, as things that can be understood simply as specific to his own biology. He points out what is obvious for anyone but not always granted the person who has been classified with disability labels, namely, that all performance is a reflection of the person in context.

The autobiographical accounts in this book should give clues to parents, educators, and others on how to see a person's distinctive forms of performance, how to distinguish intentional from unintentional or automatic actions, and how to support the person doing and saying what he or she wants. But as Attfield's account attests, this always requires consideration of context and becomes more reliable only if the affected person can explain the issues of performance him- or herself.

At the same time, building understandings from autobiographical narratives may prove challenging precisely because it requires a shift in perspective from the so-called normal body to other bodies, and from enforcing narrowly defined, dominant ideas of normal to embracing difference as normative. In general, the distinction of disability is fundamentally connected to the notion that there *is* a normal body. The person with the nondisabled body runs in a particular way, eats with utensils in a particular way, crosses the street, builds objects, dances, and speaks in sentences. The person classified as autistic, who might not do some of these things or who might do them in clearly different ways from the so-called norm, is in the position of being seen as awkward or inadequate, or even as an "individual failure." (For a discussion of the concept of failure in relation to disability, see Ferguson 1994.) Thomson puts it this way about disability in general:

So powerful is the cultural imperative to structure experience with absolute categories that figures who seemingly defy classification—such as mulattos, freaks, transvestites, bisexuals, and other hybrids—elicit anxiety, hostility, or pity and are always rigorously policed. The rigidity of social order testifies to the destabilizing threat of ambiguity. (1997, p. 34)

The policing of people classified as autistic may include, for example, desires to "cure" autism, forced segregation of people labeled autistic in special schooling and housing, and insistence that the person perform within completely normate standards, rather than in ways that reflect how autism is experienced. The idea of being policed runs through the autobiographical accounts. Fortunately, the contributing authors also explain how they often resist regulation.

The fifth and last principle is the *importance of presuming competence*. Kanner and Asperger went to some pains to explain that the performance they observed in their subjects was uneven and that formalized assessments, say, through intelligence tests, were unlikely to give a fair representation of ability. As Grandin confirms, even nontest situations can be unpredictable. Grandin quotes her mother's observation made in a letter to a child psychiatrist: "[Temple] wants someone near her in whom she has confidence. Her improvement is tied in, I'm sure, with appreciation and love. Until she is secure in her surroundings, knows the boundaries and feels accepted and actively appreciated, her behavior is erratic" (Grandin and Scariano 1986, p. 48). Grandin's mother's description seems prescient, for in working on this book, I found that the contributors could converse fluently with me, but only if their mothers or other trusted, familiar persons in whom they felt confident were nearby. Also, trivial or demeaning content from me would surely never have elicited meaningful dialogue. Related to this issue, Attfield, in his chapter, writes about the frustrations he felt when educators and diagnosticians treated him as incompetent during his early years. It drove him to despair when teachers gave him the same elementary curriculum—for example, money counting and time telling—year after year.

The "presuming competence" theme arises in all the autobiographical accounts that follow, albeit in distinct forms. In its simplest articulation, presuming competence means that the outsider regards the person labeled autistic as a thinking, feeling person. This is precisely the stance that every educator must take—failing to adopt this posture, the teacher would forever doubt whether to try to educate at all, and would likely be quick to give up the effort. Aside from the optimism it implies, another benefit of the presuming competence framework over a deficit orientation—where particular levels of incompetence (e.g., belief that the person is incapable of learning to read or lacks the ability to appreciate other people's perspectives) are presumed—is that when a student does not reveal the competence a teacher expects, the teacher is required to turn inward and ask, "What other approach can I try?" The narratives that follow are filled with instances where the authors discovered ways of revealing their inner selves, nearly always in the context of someone else (a parent, teacher, or friend) expecting as much.

Notes

1. Terms such as *high-functioning* and *low-functioning* are inherently problematic. For instance, Williams and Grandin may today be classified by some as *high-functioning*, yet both report that early in their development they had trouble speaking the words they wanted to say. Even upon publication of her first book (Williams 1989), Williams would have reporters prepare their questions, to which she would type responses; she would then read from her text and also expand on her prepared texts. Terms such as *high-functioning* and *low-functioning* fail to capture the complexities of how these individuals, or for that matter anyone, communicate.

2. Ted Hughes, British poet laureate, chaired the judges for the competition. Sir Simon Hornby, chairman of the W. H. Smith Group, wrote the introduction for the book-length collection of the winning selections, *My Hand Is Elastic*.

3. References are to the 1985 reprinted version of Kanner's article.

4. While I have observed many people with autism who could not catch a ball, I have also observed some who *can* catch a ball if it is thrown directly at them, as long as they can do so automatically. But if the ball is thrown in the air—for example, a high fly ball—and they have to run toward it to catch it, this they would find impossible. Doing something automatically (i.e., without having to contemplate steps of action) seems to work for some, while intentional actions (i.e., contemplating steps of action) are more problematic.

5. More recently, Asperger's name has been used to refer to those children with autistic characteristics who "tend to speak fluently by the time they are five, even if their language development was slow to begin with, and even if their language is noticeably odd in its use for communication . . . they remain socially inept in their . . . interactions" (Frith 1991, pp. 3–4).

6. The terms *echoed* and *echolalia* are often used in the field of autism to refer to language a person repeats, having heard others say it. This may refer to repetition of a phrase just heard or a phrase or sentence said some time earlier, even several years earlier.

7. To a qualitative researcher, part of the appeal of Kanner's and Asperger's accounts of autism is that they adopted an inductive approach to understanding their clients. Of course, this was to an extent forced on them, for they did not have an available framework that seemed to work for describing the people they were seeing. They recognized that if prevailing disability categories did not fit, and they wanted to arrive at a useful, new diagnosis, the only tools they had to do that were careful observation, suspended judgment, and analysis and interpretation.

8. This conclusion seems to be supported by a study published in *Brain and Language* in which researchers modified the test conditions for theory-of-mind testing by asking people with autism to type out their responses rather than speak them. In an article titled "Communicative Abilities in Autism: Evidence for Attentional Deficits," Bara, Bucciarelli, and Colle (2001) recruited "twenty mute male children diagnosed with autism [DSM-IV] . . . ages . . . 7–18 years [mean age: 11 years]" who were all able to type to communicate (p. 226). Before conducting the actual investigation with "mindblindness tests," the experimenters had each of the participants with autism and controls (nondisabled persons) take part in "cognitive tests" involving sequential ordering of pictures and memory and attention tasks "where the participant is invited to consider a sequence of pictures in order to complete it with one of a series of cards" (p. 227). In these pretesting activities, the participants with autism did more poorly than the nondisabled controls. Yet when given the actual theory-of-mind, Sally Anne–type problems, the persons with autism actually slightly outperformed the nondisabled participants. Citing other research in which people with autism benefited from "computer instruction and interactive games" (e.g., Heimann et al. 1995), Bara and colleagues argue that their own participants' successes with the theory-of-mind tasks may have resulted from the use of the computer typing and written formats "to focus children's attention on the task" (p. 233):

> It is certainly true that, under normal conditions, communicative performance in autistics is blatantly disrupted; but once attentional and emotional support is offered, performance is restored. Our results contradict the hypothesis of a lack of communicative competence in autistics. (p. 234)

Thus Bara and his colleagues offer a less-nuanced explanation than that of the people with autism who presented in Glasgow, but it is along the same line of reasoning.

9. Thomson (1997) introduces the term *normate* in her book, *Extraordinary Bodies: Figuring Physical Disability in American Culture and Literature*, to refer to the socially constructed notion of the "normal person." I have adopted the term here and elsewhere in this book to draw attention to the idea that "normal" is purely a constructed idea, subjectively created and applied, and forever shifting in meaning.

10. During the editing of this book, Richard told me that he questioned including the sentence "I am not retarded." He did not want to cast aspersions on individuals who remained at day centers. The point is that such centers have typically come to be modern-day dayrooms, not unlike institutional wards, where people are given crafts or other "activities," where they are segregated from the rest of the world, and where employment tends to be makework, if it is work at all. In my view, by saying "I am not retarded," Richard was not making judgments about others who were sent to such centers, but I appreciated his sensitivity.

11. He was later diagnosed as having keratoconus.

12. I do not want to imply that children who do not seem to flourish are somehow the victims of poor or inadequate mothering. After all, fathers can also play important roles in child rearing, as can schools and others social settings. I mean only to draw attention to the very gendered nature of current societal practices with regard to disability. Others have written about the gendered quality of this work and the fact that accomplishing it depends on a measure of middle-class privilege, as well as willingness to resist dominant professional discourses of disability that are so often pessimistic (Harris 2003; Morris 1991; Traustadottir 1991a; 1991b); the role of parents, and particularly of mothers, comes up in many of the autobiographies of people with so-called high-functioning autism, and so it is not surprising that it arises in the context of those who had been defined as "low-functioning." At the same time, there are examples in the literature of individuals who have found other people and opportunities for support (see e.g., Williams 1989 and 1994).

References

Appiah, K. A., and Gates, H. L. Jr. (1995). *Identities.* Chicago: University of Chicago Press.

Asperger, H. (1944/1991). 'Autistic psychopathy' in childhood. In U. Frith (ed. and trans.), *Autism and Asperger syndrome* (pp. 37–92). Cambridge: Cambridge University Press. Originally Asperger, Hans. 1944. 'Die Autistischen Psychopathen.' In *Kindesalter, Archiv. Fur Psychiatrie und Nervenkrankheiten, 117,* pp. 76–136.

Attwood, T. (1998). *Asperger's syndrome: A guide for parents and professionals.* London: Jessica Kingsley Publishers.

—— (1999). Foreword. In Lucy Blackman, *Lucy's story: Autism and other adventures* (p. vii). Redcliffe, Queensland, Australia: Book in Hand.

Bara, B. G., Bucciarelli, M., and Colle, L. (2001). Communicative abilities in autism: Evidence for attentional deficits. *Brain and language, 77,* pp. 216–240.

Baron-Cohen, S. (1996). *Mindblindness: An essay on autism and theory of mind.* Cambridge, MA: MIT Press.

Barron, J., and Barron, S. (1992). *There's a boy in here.* New York: Simon and Schuster.

Bauman, M., and Kemper, T. L. (1986). Developmental cerebellar abnormalities: A consistent finding in early infantile autism. *Neurology, 36* (suppl. 1), p. 190.

—— (1990). Limbic and cerebellar abnormalities are also present in an autistic child of normal intelligence. *Neurology, 40* (suppl. 1), p. 359.

—— (1995). Neuroanatomical observations of the brain in autism. In J. Panksepp (ed.), *Advances in biological psychiatry* (pp. 119–145) New York: JAI Press.

Bauman, M., Filipek, P. A., and Kemper, T. L. (1997). Early infantile autism. *International review of neurobiology, 41,* pp. 367–386.

Belmonte, M. K., Cook, E. H. Jr., Anderson, B. M., Rubenstein, J. L. R., Greenough, W. T., Beckel-Mitchener, A., Courchesne, E., Boulanger, L. B., Powell, S. B., Levitt, P. R., Perry, E. K., Jiang, Y. H., DeLorey, T. M., and Tierney, E. (2004). Autism as a disorder of neural information processing: Directions for research and targets for therapy. *Molecular psychiatry, 1,* pp. 1–18.

Belmonte, M. K., and Yurgelun-Todd, D. A. (2003). Functional anatomy of impaired selective attention and compensatory processing in autism. *Cognitive brain research, 17,* pp. 651–664.

Biklen, D. (1988). The myth of clinical judgment. *Journal of social issues, 44,* pp. 127–140.

—— (1990). Communication unbound: Autism and praxis. *Harvard educational review, 60,* pp. 291–314.

—— (2002). Experiencing autism: An interview with Donna Williams. *TASH connections, 28,* June, pp. 15–21.

Blackburn, J., Gottschewski, K., McElroy, K., and Niki, L. (2000). A discussion about theory of mind: From an autistic perspective. *Proceedings of Autism Europe's 6th international congress,* Glasgow, Scotland.

Blackman, L. (1999). *Lucy's story: Autism and other adventures.* Redcliffe, Queensland, Australia: Book in Hand.

Broderick, A., and Kasa-Hendrickson, C. (2001). "Say just one word at first": The emergence of reliable speech in a student labeled with autism. *Journal of the Association for Persons with Severe Handicaps, 26,* pp. 13–24.

Carpentieri, S., and Morgan, S. B. (1996). Adaptive and intellectual functioning in autistic and nonautistic retarded children. *Journal of autism and developmental disorders, 26,* pp. 611–620.

Courchesne, E. (1995). New evidence of cerebellar and brainstem hypoplasia in autistic infants, children and adolescents: The MR imaging study by Hashimoto and colleagues. *Journal of autism and developmental disorders, 25,* pp. 19–22.

—— (2002). Deciphering the puzzle: Unusual patterns of brain development in autism. Paper presented at the World Autism Congress, November, Melbourne, Australia.

Courchesne, E., Lincoln, A. J., Townsend, J. P., James, H. E., Akshoomoff, N. A.,

Saitoh, O., and Yeung-Courchesne, R. (1994). A new finding: Impairment in shifting attention in autistic and cerebellar patients. In S. H. Broman and J. Grafman (eds.), *Atypical cognitive deficits in developmental disorders: Implications for brain function* (pp. 101–137). Hillsdale, NJ: Erlbaum.

Damasio, A. R., and Maurer, R. G. (1978). A neurological model for childhood autism. *Archives of neurology, 35,* pp. 777–786.

Des Lauriers, A. M. (1978). The cognitive-affective dilemma in early infantile autism: The case of Clarence. *Journal of autism and childhood schizophrenia, 8,* pp. 219–232.

Duchan, J. F. (1998). Describing the unusual behavior of children with autism. *Journal of communication disorders, 31,* pp. 93–112.

Ferguson, P. (1994). *Abandoned to their fate.* Philadelphia: Temple University Press.

Frith, U. (1989). *Autism: Explaining the enigma.* Cambridge, MA: Blackwell Publishers.

Frith, U. (1991). Asperger and his syndrome. In Uta Frith (ed.), *Autism and Asperger syndrome* (pp. 1–36). Cambridge: Cambridge University Press.

Goode, D. A. (1994). *World without words.* Philadelphia: Temple University Press.

Grandin, T. (1995). *Thinking in pictures, and other reports from my life with autism.* New York: Doubleday.

Grandin, T., and Scariano, M. (1986). *Emergence: Labeled autistic.* Novato, CA: Arena.

Griffith, E. M., Pennington, B. F., Wehner, E. A., and Rogers, S. J. (1999). Executive functions in young children with autism. *Child development, 70,* pp. 817–832.

Happé, F. G. E. (1991). The autobiographical writings of three Asperger syndrome adults: Problems of interpretation and implications for theory. In Uta Frith (ed.), *Autism and Asperger syndrome* (pp. 207–242). Cambridge: Cambridge University Press.

Harris, P. (2003). "Mom will do it." The organization and implementation of friendship work for children with disabilities. Unpublished doctoral diss., Syracuse University, Syracuse, New York.

Hashimoto, T., Tayama, M., Murakawa, K., Yoshimoto, T., Miyazaki, M., and Harada, M. (1995). Development of the brainstem and cerebellum in autistic patients. *Journal of autism and developmental disorders, 25,* pp. 1–18.

Hayman, R. L. (1998). *Smart culture.* New York: New York University Press.

Heimann, M., Nelson, K. E., Tjus, T., and Gillberg, C. (1995). Increasing reading and communication skills in children with autism through an interactive multimedia computer program. *Journal of autism and developmental disorders, 25,* pp. 459–480.

Jacobson, J. W., Mulick, J. A., and Schwartz, A. A. (1995). A history of facilitated communication: Science, pseudoscience, and antiscience. *American psychologist,* pp. 750–765.

Jolliffe, T., and Baron-Cohen, S. (1999). A test of central coherence theory: Linguistic processing in high-functioning adults with autism or Asperger syndrome: Is local coherence impaired? *Cognition, 71*, pp. 149–185.

Joseph, R. M., and Tager-Flusberg, H. (2004). The relationship of theory of mind and executive functions to symptom type and severity in children with autism. *Development and psychopathology, 16*, pp. 137–155.

Kanner, L. (1943/1985). Autistic disturbances of affective contact. In A. M. Donnellan (ed.), *Classic readings in autism* (pp. 11–50). New York: Teachers College Press.

Kasa-Hendrickson, C., Broderick, A., Biklen, D. (producers), and Gambell, J. (director) (2002). *Inside the edge*. Video documentary. Available from Syracuse University, 370 Huntington Hall, Syracuse, New York.

Kliewer, C., and Biklen, D. (2001). "School's not really a place for reading": A research synthesis of the literate lives of students with severe disabilities. *JASH, 26*, pp. 1–12.

Mabrey, V. (producer/director) (2003). *Breaking the silence*. Documentary. *60 Minutes II* (United States).

Miyake, A., Friedman, N. P., Emerson, M. J., Witzki, A. H., Howerter, A., and Wager, T. D. (2000). The unity and diversity of executive function and their contributions to complex "frontal lobe" tasks: A latent variable analysis. *Cognitive psychology, 41*, pp. 49–100.

Morris, J. (1991). *Pride against prejudice*. Philadelphia: New Society Publishers.

Mukhopadhyay, T. R. (2000). *Beyond the silence: My life, the world and autism*. London: National Autistic Society.

Oppenheim, R. (1974). *Effective teaching methods for autistic children*. Springfield, IL: Thomas.

Park, C. C. (2001). *Exiting nirvana: A daughter's life with autism*. Boston: Little, Brown and Company.

Rapin, I. (1997). Current concepts: Autism. *New England journal of medicine, 337*, pp. 97–104.

Rubin, S., Biklen, D., Kasa-Hendrickson, C., Kluth, P., Cardinal, D. N., and Broderick, A. (2001). Independence, participation, and the meaning of intellectual ability. *Disability and society, 16*, pp. 425–429.

Sacks, O. (1995). Foreword. In T. Grandin, *Thinking in pictures, and other reports from my life with autism* (pp. 11–16). New York: Doubleday.

Schwartz, S. (1964). *Gilligan's island*. Television series (United States).

Sellen, B., with Johanson, C. J. (2000). *Outsider, self taught, and folk art annotated bibliography*. Jefferson, NC: McFarland.

Spielberg, S. (producer/director) (1998). *Saving private Ryan*. Motion picture. Dreamworks (United States).

Terrill, C. (producer/director) (2000). *Inside story: Tito's story*. Documentary. London: BBC.

Thomson, R. G. (1997). *Extraordinary bodies: Figuring physical disability in American culture and literature.* New York: Columbia University Press.

Traustadottir, R. (1991a). The meaning of care in the lives of mothers of children with disabilities. In S. J. Taylor, R. Bogdan, and J. A. Racino (eds.), *Life in the community: Case studies of organizations supporting people with disabilities* (pp. 185–194). Baltimore: Paul H. Brookes.

————— (1991b). Mothers who care: Gender, disability, and family life. *Journal of family issues, 12,* pp. 211–228.

Trevarthen, C., Aitken, K., Papoudi, D., and Robarts, J. (1998). *Children with autism.* 2nd ed. London: Jessica Kingsley Publishers.

Volkmar, F. R., and Cohen, D. J. (1985). The experience of infantile autism: A first-person account by Tony W. *Journal of autism and developmental disabilities, 15,* pp. 47–54.

Wells, H. G. (1911/1997). *Country of the blind and other science fiction stories.* Edited by M. Gardner. New York: Dover.

Welsh, M. C., and Pennington, B. F. (1988). Assessing frontal lobe functioning in children: Views from developmental psychology. *Developmental neuropsychology, 4,* pp. 199–230.

Williams, D. (1989). *Nobody nowhere.* Garden City: Doubleday.

————— (1994). *Somebody somewhere.* New York: Times Books.

Wing, L. (2000). Foreword. In T. R. Mukhopadhyay, *Beyond the silence: My life, the world and autism* (pp. 1–3). London: National Autistic Society.

————— (2001). *The autistic spectrum.* Berkeley, CA: Ulysses Press.

Wing, L., and Gould, J. (1979) Severe impairments of social interaction and associated abnormalities in children: Epidemiology and classification. *Journal of autism and childhood schizophrenia, 9,* pp. 11–29.

Wolff, T. (1989). *This boy's life: A memoir.* Boston: Atlantic Monthly Books.

2

■　■　■　■　■　■　■　■　■

I. An Introduction to Sue Rubin

I first met Sue Rubin in the mid-1990s when, as a teenager, she was just emerging into communication. She is short in stature and thus appears younger than her years. At that time, her mother held her arm as she pointed to letters on a letter board. Several years later she developed the ability independently to point to letters on a letter board or on a computer or hand-held communication device. When I met her in the mid-1990s, she had just moved from segregated special education into inclusive academic classes.

Up until that point, she had been defined as autistic *and* retarded.[1] Rubin was tested throughout her early schooling. At the age of seven, psychologists declared her to have a "mental age" of two years, eleven months on the Stanford-Binet; two years, ten months on the Merrill Palmer Scale of Mental Tests; and one year, one month on the socialization domain of the Vineland Adaptive Behavior Scale. By the time she was nine years and eleven months old, little had changed. Psychologists rated her at "2 years 11 months on the Merrill Palmer Scale of Mental Tests, 2 years 6 months on the Peabody Picture Vocabulary Test-Revised (PPVT-R), and between 1 and 3 years on the motor skills, social and communication, personal living skills, community living skills portions of the Inventory for Client and Agency Planning (ICAP), and an overall assessment of 2 years 1 month in adaptive behavior" (Rubin et al. 2001, p. 428). Psychologists described her behavior: "self injurious behaviors, scratching arms, forehead"; "yelling/screaming . . . becomes part of a cycle towards biting/pinching when angry, up to 10 times per day"; "[a]ggressive behavior pinching, scratching others, biting adults . . . behaviors function to communicate that she is angry or upset and allow for stress reduction. Susie may become angry if routine is altered or people in the routine are changed. May tantrum without identified reason"; "[s]elf isolation . . . [she] will not interact with others unless prompted to do so even when children are within close proximity . . . self stimulatory activities usually occur during self isolation" (p. 428). She was retested at the age of twelve years, ten months, just before she began to learn how to communicate by typing. The psychological report stated that she was operating at the level of "2 years 6 months on the Arthur Adaptation of the Leiter International Performance Scale, 1 year 4 months on the Developmental Test of Visual Motor Integration, 2 years 3 months on the Normative Adaptive Behavior Checklist, and 2 years 1 month on the broad independence rating of the Inventory for Client and Agency Planning" (p. 428).

Once she had a way to communicate, Sue Rubin took a full load of academic classes in high school, published two opinion editorials in the *Los Angeles Times,* and was featured in documentary segments developed by a local public broadcasting station. She has since become a leading disability rights advocate and keynote speaker at many disability conferences.

Her emergence as an excellent writer occurred simultaneously with her gaining skill in the mechanics of communicating through typing. In the late 1990s, Margaret Himley, a professor in the Writing Program at Syracuse University, invited Sue to participate in a writers' workshop at a disability conference. Sue agreed, but when the time came for her actually to enter into conversation in the workshop session, she was too anxious; instead, she stood outside the door of the meeting room and listened to the conversation. Six months later, I invited Sue to present at a disability conference in Los Angeles. This time she was able to make her presentation. She gave a prepared address—she had typed it into her computer beforehand and so was able simply to hit the "Enter" key to have the lines appear up on a screen in front of the audience. Upon completion of the presentation, she answered questions from the audience, typing independently.

Sue has since gone on to win a fellowship at Whittier College, where she is earning a baccalaureate degree, and to live in her own home, with personal attendants whom she hires. When she first purchased her house, I visited her there to observe the transition she was making to life as a college student.

For the chapter contribution that follows, I asked Sue Rubin to respond to quotations from the original Kanner article on autism (Kanner 1943/1985). Sue wrote a draft that I reviewed and commented on. I had only a few questions where I asked for elaboration or clarification. She returned the completed draft a few days later. It appears here.

■   ■   ■   ■   ■   ■   ■   ■   ■

II. A Conversation with Leo Kanner

Sue Rubin

Editor's note: In this chapter, Sue Rubin comments on quotations from Dr. Leo Kanner's classic article from 1943 in which he first defined and described autism (Kanner, L. [1943], Autistic disturbances of affective contact, *Nervous Child, 2,* 217–250; page numbers cited below are from Kanner 1943/1985).

In Kanner's (1985) description of Donald, he concludes:

There is a marked limitation of spontaneous activity. He wandered about smiling, making stereotyped movements with his fingers, crossing them about in the air. He shook his head from side to side, whispering or humming the same three-note tune. He spun with great pleasure anything he could seize upon to spin. He kept throwing things on the floor, seeming to delight in the sounds they made. He arranged beads, sticks or blocks in different series of colors. Whenever he finished one of these performances, he squealed and jumped up and down. Beyond this he showed no initiative, requiring constant instruction (from his mother) in any form of activity other than the limited ones in which he was absorbed. (p. 13)

Although behavioral characteristics of people with autism are so vast, I find many similarities and many discrepancies between Donald's behaviors and my own. Autism is a world so difficult to explain to someone who is not autistic, someone who can easily turn off the peculiar movements and actions that take over our bodies. Donald's wandering smiling is something that I simply cannot do. His ability to show emotion, whether appropriate or not, in my opinion works to his advantage. My abilities limit me to smiling only when prompted. In a social setting, an example of being prompted might be, someone placing their hand on my back to get my attention, followed by a directive to make a response. This action of a greeting does not come naturally. I require a level of focus and prompting in order to react in a socially acceptable fashion. In a society that has not yet accepted us as being normal, what a great advantage it would be to always appear like everything is rosy. That, all-is-well look is something I see most often: people, normal people, falling to social context, walking around with a permanent smile shielding what they really feel. Yet, *we* are termed abnormal or peculiar. My compulsions are different than Donald's. He finds pleasure in spinning items. I find pleasure in holding and collecting things, which gives me comfort and, strangely enough, support. As someone would carry around a lucky coin or rabbit's foot, I tend to walk about with a plastic item such as a spoon or plastic button in hand. Yet similarly both Donald and I find great pleasure in the way things fall. For him it might be the sound, for me the action. I see it almost in slow motion. The different angles, the way it moved, perhaps the changing colors. Water, in which I also find great comfort and joy, is something that falls with an unexplainable grace. For that split second the water falls, I can almost see into another world. Many times [this is] my second salvation. Unlike Donald, I was never very good at organizing and arranging. I do not have the patience to strand beads or put objects in some sort of order. It is however possible that with constant instruction, prompting and reinforcement the daunting tasks may be completed. As I have matured, I have become more aware of the outside world and my place in it socially. I may not show great excitement to see you, but I know of people's presence and, depending on what you have for me, my delight to see you varies. As far as initiation of interaction, if the person has autism, don't count on it. If I feel very strongly about something and can turn off my world, I will initiate communication. My way of being anti-autism is to stay as close to reality as I can. I mean by this, I try not to spend too much time alone, but to be with friends and to not get caught up in my own head.

Observations by Donald's mother show his increasing independence both physically and intellectually:

> He continues to eat and to wash and dress himself only at my insistence and with my help. He is becoming resourceful, builds things with blocks, dramatizes stories, attempts to wash the car, waters the flowers with the hose, plays store with grocery supply, tries to cut out pictures with scissors. Numbers still have great attraction for him. While his play is definitely improving, he has never asked questions about people and shown no interest in our conversations. (Kanner 1985, p.15)

With enough reinforcement, I too have become increasingly more independent. I use the term *reinforcement* in the sense that I require some type of prompting. If for example it is bath time. I need verbal reinforcements to start and follow through with the process. The prompting begins with a verbal cue to remove my clothing. With the water running and my favorite CD playing, I then know the steps to follow. I do however have some motor limitations that restrict my ability to competently complete simple tasks like brushing my teeth. A little help in that department makes for more pleasant dental visits. However, over the years I have become more self-sufficient in daily living activities, with constant prompting from staff and of course my mother. Hand over hand is a technique used to help me fulfill many tasks that I otherwise may not be able to do by myself. Tasks that include uses of sharp objects or kitchen appliances, is where I seek most help. I enjoy being part of meal preparations or tending to the lawn. Yet my participation also requires some assistance. As a young child I remember being much like Donald. Not wanting to be involved in gatherings and becoming somewhat upset when disturbed by people I really didn't want to see. My mother is very active and I have always been surrounded by people and rarely left to play alone. Yet it was not until I became an active communicator that I wanted to be around people. And as I have matured, people's lives now impact me. Everyone I meet has shown me what it is to be "socially normal." As daunting a task as it may sound, at the age of 23, I now want to surround myself with people that I can relate to. I enjoy listening to problems and gossip and the most rewarding of all is how all the people in my life relate to each other. I am the silent fly on the wall that listens and watches everything. I may not initiate conversation, but I am fascinated by the conversations going on around me. Many of the times I am included in these exchanges and always have an ear open on those that I am not.

Donald's mother continues to speak of his success:

He talks very much more and asks a good many questions. Not often does he voluntarily tell me of happenings at school, but if I ask leading questions, he answers them correctly. He really enters into the games with other children. One day he enlisted the family in one game he had just learned, telling each of us just exactly what to do. He feeds himself better and is better able to do things for himself. (Kanner 1985, p. 16)

As stated before I rarely find the strength in my autistic capabilities to initiate a conversation. There may be times where something pertinent eats away at me until I either find a moment where my body and mind coincide and I am able to go get a device to converse with. Sadly though, most times I am not able to do this unless one of my friends initiates or prompts me to get a device for communication purposes. Very much like Donald however, if I am prompted with leading questions I am more than happy to answer in great detail. Sometimes, though, these details will become repetitive because I have become stuck on minor details, which are of little or no relevance to the situation. I am very aware of when I get stuck on a moment. It takes someone who knows me very well to be able to stop those moments. It varies though as to what I am going through. Sometimes a verbal prompt is enough, yet other times I feel the desire to start my statement over, and need to be able to have that opportunity to restart my thinking process. I rarely initiate anything in my life unless it concerns my basic needs, I will tell someone when I need to go to the bathroom or if I am hungry, but I rarely tell a friend that I would like to have a conversation about a certain topic. I am very fortunate that my friends and family are people who know me very intimately. Many times I feel as if oral communication is over rated. Much of how I express myself is through my eyes. Those close to me are easily able to tell if I am sick, tired, or happy, by just looking at my face. My expressions are not always appropriate yet my eyes are the windows to my soul.

Kanner's accounts of the eleven individuals he followed spanned several years. In the case of Donald, two years later than the previous entry, his mother wrote: "His interests change often, but always he is absorbed in some kind of silly, unrelated subject. His literal-mindedness is still very marked; he wants to spell words as they sound and to pronounce letters consistently" (Kanner 1985, p. 17). Many times I change my interests just as Donald does, but to me they have a certain tie that weaves them together. Many people do not understand my fascination with certain objects, but they are somewhat my salvation, such as my love for water and plastic objects, which people dismiss as having no use. These are my addictions, just as a smoker needs a cigarette; I need my items to give me physical comfort. I admit that they are not always appropriate, such as when I go to college and end up following someone down the hall only because I am perplexed with the button on the back of their pants. I find myself not wanting to do these embarrassing things yet my body and mind are both perplexed with needing to see and touch that little button whether or not it is an invasion of someone's privacy to come up to them and start fondling their buttocks. I have a tendency to ignore what others may feel as being too invasive. I don't believe anyone who I've ever gone up to touch their buttons has ever really enjoyed that experience but to me it doesn't matter. Autism is not a polite disorder, nor does it care what others perceive as being wrong or right.

I am a very sarcastic person and very much enjoy my own wit. Sometimes people think that I am being crass, yet they find my intellect quite stimulating. I prefer non-fiction to fiction; this is due to my literal-mindedness. I chose my major, History, based on the knowledge that it is easier for me to digest facts than to absorb material which is fictionalized. I am still working on understanding when others are being facetious. I am quite lucky that the people who surround me know when to elaborate on a joke or comment to let me in on the situation. Sometimes this can be a very confusing ordeal, as I tend to frustrate myself for not understanding others' sarcastic notions, though I expect them to understand mine.

Kanner (1985) reports on Donald's father's confusion:

> His father, trying to teach him to say "yes" and "no," once asked him, "Do you want me to put you on my shoulder?" Don expressed his agreement by repeating the question literally, echolalia-like. His father said, "If you want me to, say 'Yes'; if you don't want me to, say 'No.'" Don said "yes" when asked. But thereafter "yes" came to mean that he desired to be put up on his father's shoulder. (p. 14)

Typically I find myself having the same problem as the one Donald and his father share. I am able to say "yes" or "no" to questions if in fact they are not leading (i.e., do you need to go to the bathroom?). If someone asks me "Do you want to go to the bathroom? Yes or no?" I will typically answer with a yes because it is the first word in the sentence that my autistic brain got stuck on. So what might appear not to be a leading question does functionally become a leading question if it triggers an automatic response. This by no means is a literal answer. My "Yes" answer does not mean that I do not understand the question. The problem that I believe Donald experienced is one that I often find myself getting stuck on.

Here is a different but similar example of the same thing. There are key intersections in my town which I know are on the way to my mother's house and if I am taking that certain route even though I know I am not going there I will verbally with the help of echolalia get stuck on that notion. This does not mean I don't understand where I am going, instead it is a trigger of familiarity, which I am very consumed by. Another example of this is seeing my regular staff person on Friday mornings. I know that she is the one who brings me to my parents on Friday afternoons to spend the night there. I rely on this every Friday because I have become familiarized with our routine of packing my overnight bag after my morning routine. It does not matter to autism if my parents are out of town, I still know that on Fridays I am to pack my bag and get to my mother's by mid afternoon. People with autism like routines, and if those routines are broken it does not mean that we don't understand what is happening it just means that it is harder for us than most to stop our brains from spinning off into their regular patterns. It is a process that is hard to understand and also hard to fully explain, but it can be terrifying to an autistic person not to be given repeated warnings when in fact their routine will change.

What Kanner (1985) thought unusual I find quite reasonable. "Many of his replies were metaphorical or otherwise peculiar. When asked to subtract 4 from 10, he answered: I'll draw a hexagon" (p. 17). Often what happens is that someone with autism hears key phrases and concepts and associates them with something that makes sense to them, but to the outside world has no commonality. To Donald a key word or phrase in that sentence most likely made a comparison to that object or concept of a hexagon. I believe that Donald's interpretation of what he was asked to do was very relevant, it may not have been the typical answer someone wanted, but literally if one subtracts 4 from 10 the answer is 6. A hexagon also has 6 angles and 6 sides, which is most likely what Donald pictured in his mind with this mathematical equation. To me his answer makes sense. It is a very literal interpretation of the number 6.

Kanner (1985) wrote, "He was still extremely autistic. His relation to people had developed only insofar as he addressed them when he needed or wanted to know something. He never looked at the person while talking and did not use communicative gestures. Even this type of contact ceased the moment he was told or given what he had asked for" (p. 17). I have found in my experience that it is very hard for an autistic person to initiate relations with others. This does not mean that we do not desire communication. Instead *our* social rules are not socially acceptable. I have explained many times that my inability to look at someone when speaking to him or her does not mean I am avoiding the person as many presume. Sometimes, eye contact literally is painful for me to achieve. This has become easier for me to achieve however with those in my life with whom I am extremely comfortable. There are certain days, though, where eye contact is not something I am able to achieve, regardless of who the person is. Autism is not a social way of life. Many times, solitude is one's best friend. Other times it can be my own worst enemy, spinning me into an autistic mind-frame, which is very much like an echolalic pattern which will not stop. One of my greatest goals is to become more social. This is slowly but surely being achieved with my core group, which surrounds me. They keep me social by bringing me out into new environments, an undertaking which I would never have imagined possible before I met them. They are my friends, which means for the first time in my life I am able to meet others through them. I go to parties with them and their friends, which I now can consider mine. I have never been happier. My friends respect me and love me for all that I am, silly autistic tendencies and all. Many times I must put up with a lot of their "normalities" as well, so I suppose we are even. My friends know when I need time alone and when they need to get me out of my autistic mind and interact with the world around us. Interaction varies day-to-day just as it does in any person's life. There are days where everyone needs solitude and other days where all you need is a friend to accompany you. The last thing I want to clarify is that no matter how much social interaction one has, one will never be free of autism. The tendencies to be and act in certain ways may subside but they will always be autistic.

Also about Donald, his mother writes:

He really enjoys the movies now but not with any idea of a connected story. He remembers them in the order in which he sees them. Another of his recent hobbies is with old issues of Time magazine. He found a copy of the first issue of March 3, 1923, and has attempted to make a list of the dates of publication of each issue since that time. So far he has gotten to April, 1934. He has figured the number of issues in a volume and similar nonsense. (Kanner 1985, p. 17)

I read much in the same way as is described in this excerpt. I see words on a page in pieces and then my mind connects them the way it should to make sense as a whole. Ever since I can remember learning new pieces of information, this is the way my brain has processed them. I can read and make sense of something extraordinarily quickly as opposed to how other people do. I tend to not like to watch movies either, unless there are subtitles at the bottom of the screen for me to follow along with. It makes the experience much easier for me to understand and digest as a whole.

Frederick's mother describes her 6 year old:

> The child has always been self-sufficient. I could leave him alone and he'd entertain himself very happily, walking around, singing. I have never known him to cry in demanding attention. He was never interested in hide and seek, but he'd roll a ball back and forth, watch his father, shave, hold the razor box and put the razor back in, put the lid on the soap box. He never was very good with cooperative play. He doesn't care to play with the ordinary things that other children play with, anything with wheels on. He is afraid of mechanical things; he runs from them. He used to be afraid of my egg-beater, is perfectly petrified of my vacuum cleaner. Elevators are simply a terrifying experience to him. He is afraid of spinning tops. (Kanner 1985, p. 17)

Being left alone is sometimes my only sanctuary. Although not extremely productive, I like to spend parts of my day listening to music and playing in the sink. As trivial an activity as that may sound, I stand in front of the sink and play with the water. Nothing else is on my mind but what is in front of me. School, home life and family escape my mind for that brief moment, oh yes, and they keep it brief. "They" is in reference to my family and friends. I enjoy my time alone, yet being as busy as I am with school and conferences, my day is quite full. I use the time in front of the sink as an outlet during crowded times. It is a relaxation tool that I can too tear myself away from.

Like Frederick I find much comfort in phrases with a singsong type tone. Although my words are less clearly pronounced than I suspect his are. I succumb to my echolalic tendencies and repeat phrases that correlate to different tunes from Christmas carols to the Mickey Mouse Club theme. My echolalia and my infatuation with spoons are two aspects of my autism that I have yet to successfully control. Autism is a constant struggle. It takes every ounce of energy I have to sit somewhat quietly during a two-hour lecture. I force myself to stay as focused as possible on what is being discussed in class. The professors play a huge role in staying quiet and focused. Male professors with dominating voices and little breaks in their lecture is where I find the greatest comfort. However, jumbled and easily intimidated professors with little continuity to their lectures is where I find it most difficult to stay focused. Finally, when class is over, I feel almost that my mouth is going to explode with everything I would have said, had I been allowed to say it.

Like Fredrick, I too am consumed by certain objects. My need for plastic spoons or anything plastic for that matter has come to define how many people look at me. As if my short stature is not enough, carrying around plastic spoons or toys makes me look child-like. It is difficult to describe how it feels to have someone look down at you and say, "How cute she is with her little toys." The amusing part of the scenario is to see their faces when my friends tell them I am 23 years old and I am a sophomore at Whittier College.

Fear plays an intense role in my life. As Frederick is fearful of many mechanical items, I too am afraid of certain senses. The sound of cars driving quickly by sets off something in my head that makes me very uncomfortable. Similarly, I recall when I was a child being very disturbed by the sound of the vacuum cleaner as well as lawn mowers. It is the unexpectedness of sound that catches me off guard. A feeling that I cannot put into words forces me to react. Many times my reaction is to inflict pain on myself, whether it is to bang my head against the wall or to pinch myself. In a strange way it brings me back to reality.

Fredrick's mother continues describing his behavior:

> To a certain extent, he likes to stick to the same thing. On one of the bookshelves we had three pieces in a certain arrangement. Whenever this was changed, he always rearranged it in the old pattern. He won't try new things, apparently. After watching for a long time, he does it all of a sudden. He wants to be sure he does it right. (Kanner 1985, p. 18)

This describes classic autism. As a child, change was a bit difficult, but I have learned to accept and sometimes embrace change. There are certain items I like to have in special places. When it comes to my spoons or plastics I will not tolerate much change, yet at school or social events, some variance is needed.

Frederick is described as having unusual speech and an exceptional memory for songs at an early age:

> He had said at least two words ("Daddy" and "Dora," the mother's first name) before he was 2 years old. From then on, between 2 and 3 years, he would say words that seemed to come as a surprise to himself. He'd say them once and never repeat them. One of the first words he said was "overalls." At about 2 ½ years, he began to sing. He sang about twenty or thirty songs, including a little French lullaby. (Kanner 1985, p. 18)

This is a bit harder to identify with. My speech is very limited and most of the time echolalic in nature. For instance, the names of my friends and family, I often repeat. [I might say] "See Rita," my mother, not necessarily because I want to see her, yet it is a familiar tape running through my head. "Do da dee newt na nay," is always a favorite echolalic phrase. It has a sing-song rhythm to it and has been termed my signature phrase. My recollection of my childhood speech patterns is difficult for me to comment on [for it is hard for me to remember]. As I said before, I find much comfort in songs and music.

Frederick's parents recall how they tried to influence his speech:

> In his fourth year, I tried to make him ask for things before he'd get them. He was stronger-willed than I was and held out longer. And he would not get it but he never gave in about it. How he can count up into the hundreds and can read numbers, but he is not interested in numbers as they apply to objects. He has great difficulty in learning the proper use of personal pronouns. When receiving a gift he would say of himself: "you say Thank you." (Kanner 1985, p. 18)

In listening to myself talk I observe the lack of recognition of myself. Instead of saying, "I want to go home," I'll say, "Go home." This is only in verbal communication. Through typing, I am able to express all of my thoughts grammatically and contextually correctly, as I am sure is clearly evident.

Further descriptions of Frederick follow:

His facial expression was tense, somewhat apprehensive, and gave the impression of intelligence. He wandered aimlessly about for a few moments, showing no sign of awareness of the three adults present. He then sat down on the couch, ejaculating unintelligible sounds, and then abruptly lay down, wearing throughout a dreamy-like smile. When he responded to questions or commands at all, he did so by repeating them echolalia fashion. The most striking feature in his behavior was the difference in his reactions to objects and to people. Objects absorbed him easily and he showed good attention and perseverance in playing with them. He seemed to regard people as unwelcome intruders to whom he paid as little attention as they would permit. (Kanner 1985, p. 19)

In this respect Frederick and I are most alike. A room full of people does not intrigue me as much as a toy or object on the other side of the room. What goes on in my head can be described as a scene out of a movie. Picture me walking into a room, the crowd of people parts and the object I desire most on the other side of the room has every ounce of my attention. There is a glow around it that draws me in and nothing else matters but having it in my hands. The people are just background noise and obstacles in my way. That is the life I lead. I have learned over the years that more is expected of me. I can't run around a room aimlessly, but need to network, make acquaintances, and socialize to the best of my ability in order to prove to people that I am a highly intelligent, thinking and feeling human being.

Richard's autistic behavior is described:

[H]e climbed on a chair, and from the chair to the desk in order to reach the switch of the wall lamp. He did not communicate his wishes but went in to a rage until his mother guessed and procured what he wanted. He had no contact with people, whom he definitely regarded as an interference when they talked to him or otherwise tried to gain his attention. (Kanner 1985, p. 22)

I also sometimes have trouble being able to communicate my needs to those around me. It has been a struggle I have dealt with my entire life. I am ashamed to say this, however I too have thrown many a tantrum to get my needs met. This entire process can be emotionally draining on everyone involved. I am now seeing that when I need something I must communicate it, in other words by using a verbal prompt such as the two basic words of "need help." These types of verbal prompts are my way of getting a reaction out of my friends and family. My staff are very accustomed to helping me in rough situations and are adequately trained to understand not only my verbal, but also my prompted needs, for example pointing to an object or pulling on their arm. I rarely feel the need to throw a tantrum to get one of my needs met. Living on my own with the help of others has given me far greater independence than my parents or I ever expected. My staff push me to be able to do things with the least amount of support necessary. They are constantly teaching me that I must rely on myself first and then ask for the aid if I am not able to accomplish something on my own. I have experienced problems with staff on whom I become co-dependent. I find that I am happier being tested to see what my strengths and weaknesses actually are. I am not afraid at all to ask for help from my staff and friends because they are truly there for the purpose of aiding me in my times of need. I feel much more independent than I could have ever imagined, and that feeling alone is intensely gratifying.

Paul differs in that,

> when with other children, he ignored them and went after their toys. His enunciation was clear and he had a good vocabulary. His sentence construction was satisfactory, with one significant exception. He never used the pronoun of the first person, nor did he refer to himself as Paul. All statements pertaining to himself were made in the second person, as literal repetitions of things that had been said to him before. He would express his desire for candy by saying, "You want candy." He would pull his hand away from a hot radiator and say, "You get hurt." Occasionally there were parrot-like repetitions of things said to him. Formal testing could not be carried out, but he certainly could not be regarded as feebleminded in the ordinary sense. He could count and name colors. He learned quickly to identify his favorite Victrola records from a large stack and knew how to mount and play them. (Kanner 1985, p. 24)

It is extremely difficult to explain to someone that I have normal intelligence though I look as if I am disabled. Many do not understand that my intellectual functioning is far greater than is perceived by looking at me. I have a difficult time communicating with the outside world because other than echolalia and verbal prompting I am very limited in my oral speech. I am a junior in college and have a GPA of 3.67. I am not aided in test taking or writing of essays, my college work is my own, contradictory to what many perceive when they view me and my staff in my classes. I do have an aide that takes my notes in classes and that is there for emotional support. Other than that, I am the one responsible for the grades that will appear on my semester grades. Things are not always what they seem. I sometimes feel as if I am the eighth wonder of the world as people stare and marvel at my irregular behaviors which lead to poor assumptions that I am simply mentally disabled with little or no intellectual functioning. My appearance is very deceptive, and day after day I am working, as an advocate for all autistic individuals, to let the world know that we are intelligent and witty, should not be judged for our quirky behaviors because they are only a minute reflection of our true capabilities.

In Barbara's case,

> she showed no interest in test performances. The concept of test, of sharing an experience or situation, seemed foreign to her. She protruded her tongue and played with her hand as one would with a toy. Attracted by a pen on the desk stand, she said: "Pen like yours at home." Then seeing a pencil, she inquired: "May I take this home?" When told that she might, she made no move to take it. The pencil was given to her, but she shoved it away, saying, "It's not my pencil." She did the same thing repeatedly in regard to other objects. (Kanner 1985, p. 25)

It has taken me years to become somewhat comfortable in testing situations. I use the word tentatively because I realize that no one is perfectly comfortable in testing situations. Like Barbara, I often find myself paying much more attention to anything other than the testing at hand. Although I sometimes portray an uninterested, unengaging brat, that is not to say that I do not value the importance of testing. When it comes down to it, I work as hard as I can to complete the tasks accurately and intelligently.

Virginia's experiences with testing are similar to mine:

With the non-language items of the Binet and Merrill-Palmer tests, she achieved an IQ of 94. "Without a doubt," commented the psychologist, "her intelligence is superior to this. She is quiet, solemn, composed. Not once have I seen her smile. She retires within herself, segregating herself from others. She seems to be in a world of her own, oblivious to all but the center of interest in the presiding situation. There was no manifestation of friendliness or interest in person. On the other hand, she finds pleasure in dealing with things about which she shows imagination and initiative." (Kanner 1985, p. 27)

With non-language items on a test, I have a significantly more difficult time. Although I know in my head what shapes might correlate, I find it difficult to make my hand point to the right answer. The action I will my hand to take is not always what really occurs. And unfortunately I score much less well on those sections of standardized testing than on the verbal sections. Again, when I use the word verbal, I am referring to my use of typing devices that aid me in completing my thoughts. In many testing situations I realize that all of the attention is on me. Unlike Virginia, I do not retreat to segregating myself from the people in the room, but relish all of the attention. I have been given very positive attention in my life and I am appreciative of all those who see past my child-like looks and odd behavior to see the person that I truly am.

Virginia illustrates classic autistic behaviors:

When a group was formed around the piano, one child playing and the others singing, Virginia sat among the children seemingly not even noticing what went on, and gave the impression of being self-absorbed. She did not seem to notice when the children stopped singing. She had an intelligent physiognomy, though her eyes had a blank expression. (Kanner 1985, p. 27)

This clarification must be made. Although it may seem that we are uninterested in our surroundings, that is not entirely true. In my case, I might be fixated on an object in my hand, but I am very much aware of what is going on outside my world. I listen very closely to conversations going on around me and despite looking in another direction, I see the actions of the people in the room. I may not look at you when you talk, but I am always listening and I always understand.

Unfortunately, I do not possess the creativity of Herbert.

> Within certain limits, he displayed astounding purposefulness in the pursuit
> of self-selected goals. Among a group of blocks, he instantly recognized
> those that were glued to a board and those that were detachable. He could
> build a tower of blocks as skillfully and as high as any child of his age or even
> older. He could not be diverted from his self-chosen occupations. He was
> annoyed by any interference, shoving intruders away (without ever looking
> at them), or screaming when the shoving had no effect. (Kanner 1985, p.
> 29)

I may be eloquent in my writing, and adorable in my behaviors, but creative I am not. I do not have the astounding ability to recognize glued and unglued blocks. I cannot make towers or entire cities with blocks, for that matter. But there are many things I do excel at. I read faster than most people, and have a large capacity for learning. I in no way want to discount Herbert's activities; they are just not skills I possess. I have always desired a more creative ability. Wanting to draw pictures or paint is an attribute I want to explore. Frustrations run high when I cannot get the pencil or brush to move in the fashion I crave and that hindrance has made it difficult to delve into my creative side.

Again Herbert is much more meticulous than I: "Both times he entered the office without paying the slightest attention to the people present. He went after the Seguin form board and instantly busied himself putting the figures into their proper spaces and taking them out again adroitly and quickly" (Kanner 1985, p. 29). This seems like a redundant activity. I have certain places I like to keep things. But I never recall, moving things then replacing them, over and over again. Of any of the people with autism that I have discussed in this narrative, my behaviors are far different than those of Herbert. These types of redundant activities are the ones that bore me the most.

In Kanner's (1985) description of Alfred, a 3 ½ year old boy's behavior is portrayed:

> He frets when the bread is put in the oven to be made into toast, and is afraid
> it will get burned and be hurt. He is upset when the sun sets. He is upset be-
> cause the moon does not always appear in the sky at night. He prefers to play

alone; he will get down from a piece of apparatus as soon as another child approaches. He likes to work out some project with large boxes (make a trolley, for instance) and does not want anyone to get on it or interfere. (pp. 30–31)

Fear plays an enormous role in our lives. With one worry of one action comes other feelings of nervousness. I never feared so much the results of contact with electrical appliances as I did the appliances themselves. In fact, unlike Alfred, I like my bread toasted and enjoy the somewhat burnt and crusted ends. The sun and moon, although intriguing, rise and set, illustrating to me only the time of day. They evoke little emotion in me. Again the references to being alone and others' interferences have been consistent throughout my reflection and consistent over much that I know to be autism.

As part of Alfred's communication, it is said that "he was often confused about the meaning of words. When shown a picture and asked, 'What is this picture about?' he replied, 'People are moving about'" (Kanner 1985, p. 33). This seems like a normal response to me. His response of, people moving about, tells me that the people in this picture are obviously on the go. On the other hand, if he is repeating the word *about* in his answer merely because it was asked in the question and in fact people are not moving about in the picture, I could see the cause for concern. And yet here is another similarity to my own behaviors. When speaking verbally, which in my case cannot and should not be taken as fact, I tend to repeat what is being said to me. For example, if someone were to say, "What is the book about," instead of regurgitating an appropriate answer, I would respond, "About, alright." Although not touching on what the correct response is, I appease you to the best of my verbal abilities so you might understand that I have digested what you have asked. Yet I cannot find the words to accurately express my thoughts verbally.

Alfred seems to be much more aware than I was at such a young age:

He once stopped and asked, very much perplexed, why there was "The Johns Hopkins Hospital" printed on the history sheets: "Why do they have to say it?" This, to him, was a real problem of major importance, calling for a great deal of thought and discussion. Since the histories were taken at the hospital, why should it be necessary to have the name on every sheet, though the person writing on it knew where he was writing? The examiner, someone he remembered very well from his visit six years previously, was to him nothing more nor less than a person who was expected to answer his obsessive questions about darkness and light. (Kanner 1985, 33)

Testing, therapies, questions and answers can get all too boring. Alfred is thoughtful, bright and obviously not afraid of questions about anything and everything. People do not realize what it is like to be poked and prodded, looked at as strange, or medically unexplainable. It was difficult for me, and I am sure for all of these children, to sit day after day in front of clinicians who have no idea how to help you. How to change or help modify your behaviors, or better yet how to give you the strength to turn them off? Although many of these children are still young enough not to realize what is going on, or how they are different, someday it will become all too apparent, their oddities.

In the case of Charles he was depicted, "as a baby, the boy was inactive, 'slow and phlegmatic.' He would lie in the crib, just staring. He would act almost as if hypnotized. He seemed to concentrate on doing one thing at a time" (Kanner 1985, p. 33). It is hard for me to describe my behaviors as a small child, but consistency shows that this is a very real attribute of autism. Withdrawn behavior and self-entertainment is a staple in what is autism throughout a person's life.

Charles's mother took her cues from Charles as to what he might benefit from: "His enjoyment and appreciation of music encouraged me to play records. When he was 1 ½ years old, he could discriminate between eighteen symphonies. He recognized the composer as soon as the first movement started. He would say 'Beethoven'" (Kanner 1985, p. 33).

Such a remarkable talent. It may be cliché, but I never forget a tune. The enjoyment and recognition of music is a skill that I would bless on all. Such a collection of sound brings exhilaration to my body that is almost unexplainable. Music therapy is one of the best ways to induce relaxation and serenity. I favor many different types of music. Tom Petty is by far my songwriter of choice. I listen to his CD on a daily basis and it is used as a prompt to begin the bathing process. I also enjoy Jazz and many other instrumental compilations.

Charles went through phases in his selection of activities:

> At about the same age, he began to spin toys and lids of bottles and jars by the hour. He had a lot of manual dexterity in ability to spin cylinders. He would watch it and get severely excited and jump up and down in ecstasy. Now he is interested in reflecting light from mirrors and catching reflections. When he is interested in a thing, you cannot change it. He would pay no attention to me and show no recognition of me if I enter the room. (Kanner 1985, p. 33)

Once again this touches upon our infatuations with our belongings. As I have explained, this behavior is much like my fascination with plastic and water. Something that although many people have tried effortlessly to alter still remains strong as ever. Charles's mother saw him as disconnected from the world or bound to his own:

> The most impressive thing is his detachment and his inaccessibility. He walks as if he is in a shadow, lives in a world of his own where he cannot be reached. No sense of relationship to persons. His entire conversation is a replica of whatever has been said to him. (Kanner 1985, p. 34)

An autistic person's degree of detachment varies. As a small child it is difficult to control and they have yet to come to the realization that being a social person means, being a person. You are, autistic or not, defined as a person based on social abilities. As I have matured I have learned that in order to be recognized as a thinking, feeling adult, I must learn to be social. Setting aside my desire to be alone or my craving to give in to my spoons is something I have had to struggle with and will continue to struggle with for many years. As discussed previously I tend to detach myself from social situations at times where autism is in control of my capability to relate to those around me. This does not mean that I don't enjoy socializing with my peers but at times autism will not allow me the desire to socially interact.

Charles's mother continues her description:

> When the book was taken away from him, he struggled with the hand that held it, without looking at the person who had taken the book. When he was

pricked with a pin, he said, "What's this?" And answered his own question: "It is a needle." (Kanner 1985, p. 35)

Charles has completely detached himself from the outside world, without looking at anyone, acknowledging their presence or even resorting to answering his own questions. My feeling is that he will soon realize that his need for people is much greater than his need to be left alone. Kanner reports that Charles "never used language as a means of communicating with people. He remembered names such as 'octagon,' 'diamond,' 'oblong block,' but nevertheless kept asking, 'What is this?'" (Kanner 1985, p. 35). Charles has communicative abilities, but has yet to learn how to properly utilize them. As withdrawn as he may seem, at the same time he does seek out some form of communication. He asks questions of himself for which he already knows the answer. This should show his potential for effective communication. As I am sure they have, his parents should have encouraged such dialog regardless of how insignificant it might seem. We all have to start somewhere and it would be interesting to find out how far Charles has gotten.

The next person, John, is also described as seemingly wanting a particular order to his interactions and as having unusual patterns of speech:

> At the end of his fourth year, he was able to form a very limited kind of affective contact, and even that only with a very limited number of people. Once such a relationship had been established, it had to continue in exactly the same channels. He was capable of forming elaborate and grammatically correct sentences, but he used the pronoun of the second person when referring to himself. He used language not as a means of communication but mainly as a repetition of things he had heard, without alternation of the personal pronoun. (Kanner 1985, p. 36)

My communication with those around me has baffled many who have crossed my path. When I was younger I remember my relations with individuals being very ritualistic. If I saw someone for a week while they were on vacation, then the next week I expected them to still be part of my life. I did not understand that because someone leaves there is still a relationship between friends. Contact also has played a huge part in terms of echolalia. I still to this day have a hard time when someone I care about leaves me. I have had staff and friends I truly felt close to. After they moved on in their lives, I was not able to move on away from them. Their names very much formed a part of my echolalia. There are times where I will be reminded of old staff and their names take over my echolalia.

Charles is described as conforming to particular routines:

> There was very marked obsessiveness. Daily routine must be adhered to rigidly; any slightest change of the pattern called forth outbursts of panic. There was endless repetition of sentences. He had an excellent rote memory and could recite many prayers, nursery rhymes, and songs "in different languages." (Kanner 1985, p. 36)

I need routine in my life. It is something I can depend and rely on in this crazy life. I am not as strict about my routine as I have been in the past, and I believe this is beneficial for me to be able to deal with life's little surprises. My staff are the biggest reason routine is not as pivotal in my life anymore. I will admit things are done loosely based on a structure or routine, yet my staff have been able to teach me that things in life are not predictable and that is ok, as long as I am willing to be patient. College is another arena in my life, which my staff can only structure to some extent. There are many days in college where the schedule will change due to some celebration of a holiday, or times of classes will change for finals. My staff is very good about letting me know in advance when they see a change in my schedule coming up, they are very sensitive to my needs, whether this is done for their sanity or mine we still don't know.

Some of what Charles said, from an early age, was interpreted as being literalist:

> At 5 1/2 years, he had good mastery of the use of pronouns. . . . He saw a group photograph in the office and asked his father, "When are they coming out of the picture and coming in here?" He was very serious about this. His father said something about the pictures they have at home on the wall. This disturbed John somewhat. He corrected his father: "We have them near

the wall" ("on" apparently meaning to him "above" or "on top"). (Kanner 1985, p. 36)

I have never been one to correct grammatics, due to the fact most of my speech is echolalia, and my mother always concentrated on this. However, I do understand what it is like for John to have strict relations with certain objects and be very literal. This is something to this day I am working on as I continue to practice on relating to those around me. An example of my literal thinking is that when I see a Lexus I shout out Rita (my mother's name), this shows how my autism associates all Lexus cars with my mother, though I know this cannot be possible. My staff will tell me they see the same Lexus but that Rita cannot possibly be driving every Lexus I see. Charles speaking of the pictures in the office is another version of echolalia and autism's way of viewing things in a literal manner.

The description of Elaine speaks to the unpredictability of autism:

> When taken to the playgrounds, she was extremely upset and ran back to her room. She was very restless but when allowed to look at pictures, play alone with blocks, draw, or string beads, she could entertain herself contentedly for hours. Any noise, any interruption disturbed her. Once, when on the toilet seat, she heard a knocking in the pipes; for several days thereafter, even when put on a chamber pot in her own room, she did not move her bowels, anxiously listening for the noise. (Kanner 1985, p. 39)

This is one depiction of autism that I am very sensitive to. Autism plays on a person's five senses. It can vary from day to day and is not something one can control or see coming. As a child I remember being stimulated by a noise others would classify as a hum of an air conditioner and it would drive me crazy. There have been other times where my sight is stimulated in a car, watching traffic go by, and my only release of all this tension would be for me to bang my head violently on the glass. I am not saying this is appropriate behavior, but people with autism cannot control this "spinning" that goes on in their head. It is not something we are able to control or express concern about in most cases. Many times it has been a mystery to those around me as to what sent me off into a tantrum. Those very close to me can usually figure it out, but this does not mean they have any control over the situation, except for physically moving me out of that environment so that they can protect me from my own autistic demons.

Kanner reports about Elaine,

> She frequently ejaculated stereotyped phrases, such as, "Dinosaurs don't cry"; "Crayfish, sharks, fish, and rocks"; "Crayfish and forks live in children's tummies"; "Butterflies live in children's stomachs, and in their panties, too"; "Fish have sharp teeth and bit little children"; "There is war in the sky"; "Rocks and crags, I will kill" (grabbing her blanket and kicking it about the bed); "Gargoyles bit children and drink oil." (Kanner 1985, p. 39)

I believe this is one autistic person's echolalia. These are words or phrases that one becomes stuck on, and cannot get out of his or her head and instead repeats verbally to the world. I do this all the time and find myself as well as my staff being annoyed by the repetitive nature of echolalia. This does not mean I am in control of it. There is no one rule regarding my echolalia. At times it may mean I need to express a thought or idea, other times it can mean I need to be stimulated and do something, and yet other times it can just be my playful tactics to have someone sing along with me. I cannot speak for others, but with my echolalia I need a response of some kind otherwise I will spin out of control. Many times echolalia is stopped by a person's acknowledgement to what I have said, other times I need someone to tell me to stop or use the phrase "turn it off."

Kanner further notes that, "Here speech is rarely communicative. She has no relation to children, has never talked to them, to be friendly with them, or to play with them. She moves among them like a strange being, as one moves between the pieces of furniture of a room" (Kanner 1985, p. 40). Some perceive autistic people to be rude and antisocial, I view it as being true to one's self. Many people in society do not want to interact with those around them, but instead of ignoring them or being polite and saying they need to be alone they will sit and be passive and interact with those around them, the entire time wondering how to get out of the situation. I never have to deal with this. When I don't want to be around others I won't place myself in their existence, I will stay away.

Most of the time my friends are very understanding that I need time alone. Most people do, but just don't, for whatever reason, allow themselves the luxury.

A central theme of Kanner's about autism is as follows:

> The outstanding, "pathognomonic," fundamental disorder is the children's inability to relate themselves in the ordinary way to people and situations from the beginning of life. There is from the start an extreme autistic aloneness that, whenever possible, disregards, ignores, shuts out anything that comes to the child from the outside. Direct physical contact or such motion or noise as threatens to disrupt the aloneness is either treated "as if it weren't there" or, if this is no longer sufficient, resented painfully as distressing interference. (Kanner 1985, p. 41)

I believe I have tried to correct this notion at least through my views in this commentary, yet I do not want to be the poster child for autism. I do not want to carry that burden. I hope that reading my responses has given insight to some that may have not been something they had thought about before. As I have stated many times throughout my responses, every autistic person is heterogeneous [i.e., comprised of different qualities] and certain things will not apply to certain other people.

About speech, Kanner noted, "In none of eight 'speaking' children has language over a period of years served to convey meaning to others" (Kanner 1985, p. 42). My only message here is that not all communication is best served through speech. Art and music are great examples of languages that do not have to be spoken to be conveyed. I am asking those who have read this to look beyond the obvious. Peel more layers, look deeper than the obvious, stop being lazy and look at things and others from a new perspective. It may not be comfortable, but at least it will broaden one's horizons.

Kanner describes the behavior of people with autism as more or less constant. "There is a marked limitation in the variety of his spontaneous activities. The child's behavior is governed by an anxiously obsessive desire for the maintenance of sameness that nobody but the child himself may disrupt on rare occasions" (Kanner 1985, p. 44). There are definite instances where I find myself being more or less autistic than on other days. This is not something I am able to have any control over. This being said, my most realistic way of explaining these are as good and bad days to which everyone, regardless of disability, is entitled. I do have a longing desire for things to remain the same. In many conversations with my friends I have come to realize that we all like a small degree of variability in our lives. I would say that autistic persons do like routine and most often welcome it. However it takes time to adjust to the "real world," the one that is often unpredictable and sometimes unforgiving. I believe this has been one of my truest hardships with autism and living in the world around me. Thanks to the patience of all those who stand beside me, I am able to overcome all obstacles.

Another observation of Kanner's is that people with autism get along well with objects. "Objects that do not change their appearance and position, that retain their sameness and never threaten to interfere with the child's aloneness, are readily accepted by the autistic child. He has a good relation to objects" (Kanner 1985, p. 46). As I have stated before I believe that all people like and crave uniformity in their lives. Autistic people also want a certain aspect of predictability and sameness. I will admit that life is much simpler when I know exactly what is going to happen and the time and place it will happen. Living on my own though, has made me realize everyday is different, everyday has new challenges for me to overcome. Some days I look forward to them and others I cringe in fear. Assume I am like all others when I say we all, to a varying degree, want predictability.

One of the mysteries that Kanner tries to unravel is the comparative importance of people and objects in the lives of people with autism:

> The children's relation to people is altogether different. Every one of the children, upon entering the office, immediately went after blocks, toys, or other objects, without paying the least attention to the persons present. It would be wrong to say that they were not aware of the presence of persons. But the people, so long as they left the child alone, figured in about the same manner as did the desk, the bookshelf, or the filing cabinet. (Kanner 1985, p. 46)

I often look at inanimate objects before paying any attention to who is in the room with me. I have a desired craving for plastic objects and will search a room for those objects before I pay any attention to anyone around me. I am very aware there are others in a room with me, but my autistic tendencies focus on the irregular, the unpredictable. I don't know how or why, I just know that it is a characteristic that I will always have. I don't want others to take offense with this lack of rationale or be intimidated by the fact that inanimate objects take preference in autism. I just hope that not everything has to be clearly defined or understood for it to be accepted. I find it similar to people who, when they first notice someone new in the room, they look at their shoes. I don't necessarily understand this, but am quite intrigued all the same.

Thankfully, Kanner did not assume that people with autism were not intelligent:

> Even though most of these children were at one time or another looked upon as feebleminded, they are all unquestionably endowed with good cognitive potentialities. They all have strikingly intelligent physiognomies. Their faces at the same time give the impression of serious-mindedness and, in the presence of others, an anxious tenseness, probably because of the uneasy anticipation of possible interference. The astounding vocabulary of the speaking children, the excellent memory for events of several years before, the phenomenal rote memory for poems and names, and the precise recollection of complex patterns and sequences, bespeak good intelligence in the sense in which this word is commonly used. Binet or similar testing could not be carried out because of limited accessibility. But all the children did well with the Seguin form board. (Kanner 1985, p. 47)

Being looked upon as feebleminded is something I have been forced to endure my entire life. What an extremely difficult hole to have to climb out of, to fight for your own intelligence and capabilities. As I have said throughout, my conduct is much like the children explored, with some differences and many similarities. Although individuals with autism are exactly that, individuals, there are basic characteristics that make up autistic behavior and those mentioned are definitely the staple of who we are. It is funny how we are considered strange or different, even though our recollection of complex patterns, memory for precise detail, and overall capabilities many times exceed those of the people who are pointing or starring. That realization often times is my greatest joy. I have found that there are many tests in the scientific realms that are quality measurements of intelligence. Yet, those that are most highly noted are the ones most incapable of scratching the surface of our minds.

It is certainly one of the most controversial of Kanner's ideas that he believed parents might have some role in fostering a limited interest in people:

> In the whole group, there are very few really warmhearted fathers and mothers. For the most part, the parents, grandparents, and collaterals are persons strongly preoccupied with abstractions of a scientific, literary, or artistic nature, and limited in genuine interest in people. Even some of the happiest marriages are rather cold and formal affairs. The children's aloneness from the beginning of life makes it difficult to attribute the whole picture exclusively to the type of the early parental relations with our patients. We must, then, assume that these children have come into the world with innate inability to form the usual, biologically provided affective contact with people, just as other children come into the world with innate physical or intellectual handicaps. (Kanner 1985, p. 50)

Without a doubt, I have been the most blessed with parents who support and drive me to be successful at anything I do. They far surpassed warm-heartedness in everything they have given me, not material but emotional. My mother is my strength. She has devoted her life to my successes and to the education of people around the globe about autism. I only wish that someday I can be half the woman she is and pray that every daughter in the world is as blessed as I am. I have been surrounded by educated people and have learned something from every one I meet. One thing I have never felt is aloneness, although at times retreating to my own world, there has always been someone there to pull me out and drive me to be a rational, and logical person in our perplexing society. To my sincerest gratitude I have been motivated to be an intellectual, social individual with goals very much attainable.

Note

1. The term *mental retardation* is still used widely in the United States, while other jurisdictions have long since abandoned this term in favor of *intellectual disability*

(Australia) and *learning difficulties* or *learning disabilities* (United Kingdom). I use the term here because it is the term that was applied to Rubin by educational authorities. The term *mental retardation,* like *intellectual disability,* is, of course, socially constructed, and its meaning has shifted often over the years. Colleagues in the United Kingdom tell me that the terms *learning disabilities* and *learning difficulties* are still routinely debated and are constantly shifting in meaning.

References

Kanner, L. (1943/1985). Autistic disturbances of affective contact. In A. M. Donnellan (ed.), *Classic readings in autism* (pp. 11–50) New York: Teachers College Press.
Rubin, S., Biklen, D., Kasa-Hendrickson, C., Kluth, P., Cardinal, D. N., and Broderick, A. (2001). Independence, participation, and the meaning of intellectual ability. *Disability and society, 16,* pp. 425–429.

3

■　　■　　■　　■　　■　　■　　■　　■　　■

I. An Introduction to
Tito Rajarshi Mukhopadhyay

Tito Rajarshi Mukhopadhyay was thirteen years old when we completed the interviews that were the basis for this chapter. Tito grew up in India, mainly in the city of Bangalore, where his mother moved so that he might be near schools and medical services. As it turned out, he was not accepted into academic schools and so was mainly home-schooled. By the age of eleven he had written a book, *Beyond the Silence: My Life, the World and Autism* (Mukhopadhyay 2000) and was the subject of a BBC documentary titled *Inside Story: Tito's Story* (Terrill 2000). He has subsequently been written about in a *New York Times* article ("A Boy, a Mother" 2002) and was the subject of a CBS television *60 Minutes* story (Mabrey 2003). When he writes, he requires his mother to be sitting nearby; he told me that his mother sitting next to him "creates an environment." When he speaks in sentences, he does so in a quiet voice, word by word, syllable by syllable, and sometimes letter by letter—he reverts to spelling only when the listener does not understand the word he has pronounced—with his mother, Soma, near him, repeating the words he says. For the text in this chapter, he wrote all of it in longhand—since he was six years old "he has written by himself using a pencil" (Wing 2000)—and I then reorganized the questions and responses into topical areas. Tito approved the final version.

I first heard about Tito when Anne Donnellan, a professor at the University of Wisconsin, introduced me to the BBC documentary and to his book. As soon as I had read his book several times, I began an e-mail correspondence with him. Although he said he did not want to write a chapter for this book on his own, Tito told me that he would happily respond to questions and be interviewed. Within a few weeks of our beginning to correspond, I had gone through his book in considerable detail and had developed twelve pages of questions in which I asked him to elaborate on particular themes. As Tito began to submit responses to the questions, I readied for a trip to Bangalore so that we could continue the interview face to face. In addition to the chance to work with Tito, I wanted to get to know him in his own environment, to see what his daily life was like.

The morning after my arrival in Bangalore, I set out for Tito's apartment by taxi. The driver had to stop several times to ask passersby where his street was located. It is a dirt street diagonally opposite a theater. There were many shops on the adjoining street but none on the street where Tito lives. The taxi driver had to circumnavigate an ox that was standing in the middle of the road. The driver used the telephone at a nearby shop to call Tito's mother, and she came down to lead me to their apartment. Following Soma, I entered a two-story cement building. We climbed to the second level and walked across an open area before entering their apartment, which comprises a living room, a bedroom, a small kitchen, and a bathroom. A television and small mattress were in the living room—"With Tito there must be a place to lie down in each room," Soma said—as well as a couple of stools, a coffee table, a mat, and a half-size refrigerator that had milk, water, eggs, and other basics. The walls were light green, with some dirt and dust stains. There was a calendar on the wall and several paintings by Soma, including one of a horse, one of a cat, and another of flowers. There was also a plastic box mounted on the wall, in which were two baby dolls, about five inches tall. An overhead fan in each room churned, making a clacking sound. As we entered, Soma directed Tito and me to the left along a narrow hallway to a rectangular room that had a small desk, a portable computer, a bed that also doubled as a couch, and a plastic chair. It was the only chair in the house; Soma insisted that I sit on it as she and Tito sat on the bed/couch. At the end of the room was a metal utility bookshelf filled with books about philosophy, literature, science, and history.

Tito sat and pointed to letters on a paperboard; he rested his hands at times and pivoted his hand, slapping down his index finger on letters. He typed out, "I am honoured that you have come. What do you teach?"

It seemed that from the outset, Tito was going to make my interview an easy process; he was going to raise topics quite apart from any I might have prepared. I said, "Well one of the courses I teach is on research methods, specifically what is called qualitative research or participant observation and open-ended interviewing. Sometimes it's called ethnography. I teach about how to learn the other person's perspective."

Tito pointed to letters and said, "Is that like anthropology?"

"Yes," I replied. At this point Tito began to speak with his voice, syllable by syllable, and Soma announced the full words as she heard them. Later she explained that this gave Tito feedback as he was speaking, to confirm that she had understood his words, and so he could go on.

"Never saw such a small tape," Tito said, remarking on my mini–cassette recorder.

"Yes, isn't it. It's small so it is easy to carry around," I said.

"I suppose that's very pocketful. I will talk now. We can discuss," Tito said.

"We can discuss," I repeated.

Tito's mother was surprised that I could understand his speech: "Oh you understood. So you are used to bad speech."

I laughed and said, "Bad speech? This is your son's speech you are talking about!" Actually, I found it easy to understand Tito, as his pronunciation was clear.

Tito said, jokingly, "I suppose that it will be a nice voice taped." Tito then asked, "How do you rate my autism?"

To this I responded, "I'm sure people would say it's severe because severity has always been in terms of, you know, moving the arms, stereotypes, and difficulties with speech. But then people might see your speech and that would raise their assessments of you. The dominant view is still that three-fourths of people with autism are thought to be mentally retarded. It's not true, but that's the view. It's a great barrier to get past."

For the next week and a half, I went from my hotel to Tito's home each morning. We would talk for an hour or two before we set out for sightseeing around Bangalore, as we continued to converse. Tito told me, "I think that you should see the city and then tell me how you find it. I think it is everything in a city. In the market you will find India."

During each of the morning sessions, we would typically get through ten or twelve lines of discussion before Tito would lope out onto the open space between his apartment and the stairs to the ground level. His mother would say, "Tito, okay, but after fifteen minutes you come back and talk." Then she would call him back, insisting that he talk some more before we would go out sightseeing. Most days, it seemed that Tito simply wanted to pace about during these interludes. One day, we were talking along, and he said the word *eraser.* Then he got up from the couch and headed outside. Soma explained to me that an eraser of his had fallen behind part of the building and was lodged where he could not get at it; he was focused on it. Soma explained, "Sometimes little things become so big in his mind."

When Tito came back into the room, he sat and began to rock back and forth. "I cannot. I'm sorry but I cannot help it," Tito said. "I need it [the rocking] to feel my body." As it turns out, his relation to his own body is a key theme he takes up in his chapter.

At times, Tito focused on monitoring his appearance; at other times he jumped from one observation to another about the world around him. One day, we went to a large park in the town. As we sat on a bench, a deaf man came up to us, begging. Tito remarked, "I will go around like that"—he was apparently worrying about his own future. As he walked away, Tito said, "I think that it will rain today and tomorrow will get cooler. This tree is deciduous. You have conifers [i.e., in the United States]." Tito then asked me if we had oxen in the United States. "I love them. They are huge and tall. I wanted to see redwoods in California. Last time I could not. I will look for a mentor." Tito was jumping from one topic to another in a kind of stream of consciousness.

We touched on many topics. Tito explained that with practice, initially copying letters and words that his mother showed to him, he had learned to write with a pencil strapped to his hand. He told me that he learned to speak by having his mother pat him on the back, to help him initiate getting sounds to come out. Then he progressed to getting words out with her prompt; she used her hand in a waving motion, as if she were directing traffic.

As we talked, a man came by selling cookies. After the man passed, Tito remarked to his mother, "Isn't it good I did not ask for it?" Some girls were playing in the park, giggling. Tito said, "Young people are too happy."

Soma replied, "They are enjoying themselves."

I then asked, "What's the problem with young people?"

Tito answered, "I cannot have that memory."

Soma said that he meant remembering childhood, for his had been difficult. Tito found it hard to engage with other children in unstructured situations. Soma explained that Tito had a hard time managing "a very open situation. Because here we are engrossed in a very focused conversation he can handle it. But if it's too open . . . "—she shrugged, as if to say it's too challenging for Tito. Again, this is a theme he takes up in more detail in the chapter.

I told Tito that I had heard other people with autism make a similar comment, that structured situations were typically easier than open-ended ones. I added, "Others with autism tell me that they only like movies with a few characters."

"Make movies like that," Tito said. "Read my mind. Make movies with only one character."

"I tried taking him to a movie," Soma said, "but he watches for a short while and then leaves and comes back. So I usually go with my husband and my husband takes him out. I ask for a seat near the door so he can go in and come out."

One day we took a trip to a retreat several hours outside of Bangalore. As we set out, Tito was sniffing my shirt. Then he said, "I am sniffing and that is bad manners."

"Does the shirt smell okay?" I asked.

"Nice," Tito responded.

When we got to the retreat, Tito asked me, "How is that taxi charging?"

I told him that it was by the distance and that by U.S. standards it was very inexpensive.

As it turned out, the trip we made to this retreat caused Tito tremendous anxiety. He did not want to get into a car for several weeks after that. He easily stepped inside a bus or even an open-air, three-person scooter taxi, but not an automobile. He searched for a reason to explain his anxiety. It seemed as if he was trying to understand it so that he could overcome it.

"Car travel is no problem for me," Tito said initially. "I think the problem lay in the ritual of traveling that route by bus. I thought in the beginning that I was afraid of the bends and curves of the road and waited for them to get over. However, when the anxiety persisted, I began to search for the exact cause. Because every effect should have some logical cause. My cause was my ritual of traveling that route by bus. This may sound illogical to you. So you can blame the whole thing to my autism." Later, I asked Tito if he would write a poem on the topic and this is what he gave me:

> *When I enter the little room space*
> *of your pretty car*
> *wonder what happens to me*
> *I get a sort of fear*
> *And what or how should I explain*
> *About this fear of mine*
> *Call it a thing to worry about*
> *Maybe a test of time.*
> *And how should I describe*
> *What happens*
> *When your pretty car is near*
> *All I find my gets goosed*
> *And I call it fear.*
> *Do I feel too big for it*
> *Your humble pretty car*
> *How worthy am I to sit inside*
> *Your pretty lustrous car?*
> *Call me this or call me that*
> *I remain a misfit wit*
> *Don't you realise this a bit*
> *I am so autistic?*

A day or two later, I told Tito that I had had a harrowing trip to Mysore to see a palace. "I must say I was so frightened by the drive in the car. I wish I had gone by bus. I think I would not make a trip like that again. All the way back to Bangalore, I tried to look down and read a book. But each time I looked up, the oncoming traffic scared me." I found that the cab would be going along and large trucks would come from the other direction, directly in front of us, moving aside only at the last minute.

My description of the traffic seemed to evoke a different explanation for Tito's anxiety over car travel: "That same thing happened to me in the car. I could see the vehicles coming but I was not getting the distance. And the wind hitting my face was awful."

We covered many topics over the days we were together. Tito explained to me that he is exceedingly active, walking all about the city with his mother. Soma remarked that "with Tito everything is done fast. He comes in and writes a poem. It is done so quickly. He wants his poem and in no time he has completed three pages. Finished. So then he says, 'Now I have to search for a new thought.'"

A good part of his activity is in learning new skills. He told me that he struggles with himself. He said it is hard sometimes to remain calm and not to run off or become agitated. "I must continue to be calm," Tito told me. "I must continue to talk to do that." Being engaged in conversation is a way of staying calm.

As he describes in his chapter, that his mother is a bit of a battle-ax seems to be at the heart of Tito's successes with speech and writing. Soma told me that she wants to help Tito become more initiating in his actions. She wants him to be able to talk about what he wants to do and then to be able to do it. "That's my dream, that he's going to talk and then do things. Then, only then, his behavior will come under control. I have to start with small words: 'Let me pick this up.' Just small words. And then go on to 'I have to behave.' Or, 'I need to keep still.' It has to be an active verb and then after saying it, doing it."

As Soma described this strategy, I turned to Tito and asked him what he thought of her idea.

"I think she has started that," Tito said.

"Oh really? Already?" I said. "And what's the reaction from the willing subject?" I asked. "Or is it the unwilling subject?"

"I have to do it," Tito said. "I need to do it because she is rewarding me."

"Yes, I am rewarding him," Soma said.

"You are rewarding him?" I asked. "So is this behavior modification?"

"Yes," Soma said.

"And what are the rewards?" I asked.

"Anything," Soma explained, "whatever bit of biscuit or what we have."

"So Tito, what are your feelings about this strategy?" I asked.

"Not to comment on," Tito said.

I laughed and said, "That's it?"

"Yes," Tito said.

■ ■ ■ ■ ■ ■ ■ ■ ■

II. Questions and Answers

Tito Rajarshi Mukhopadhyay and Douglas Biklen

Imagination and Performance

Biklen: You once described going on a train, and seeing a middle-aged gentleman sitting nearby. It sounded as if he was a kind of reassuring, if imaginary, companion.

Mukhopadhyay: When I wrote about a middle-aged man [Mukhopadhyay 2000], I meant that there was this hypothetical character around me who seemed to be everywhere. I reflect back to those days when he would be my companion while I passed my time with nothingness. Do I relate him with any known face? I do not know what to reply because surely shapes of faces cannot be formed just out of the blue. I however do not feel very comfortable to look at faces. Not now not then. And so I couldn't have really seen many faces. I wonder thus. Whose face did he have? It just happened to me that it was the same person as if he was some sort of assurance to me. Come what may he would be there. And surely he was there while in my moments of crisis. Crisis in the sense that I felt too lost and sometimes too overwhelmed in some situations.

If you ask me to state whether he was black or white, or Indian brown, I surely would not be able to tell. All I can say is that by merely imagining him around I could feel secure. Were there any words exchanged between us? No I do not remember that to happen. You do not need words to communicate many things, like something as subtle as assurance. Look at the setting sun. Does it need words to tell the earth that it will be back on the sky the next day?

The illusion however had to go.

How did the illusion go? One day I found that someone sat on the place where he was sitting. And with that my middle-aged man of assurance just faded out. He was replaced by the reality. So it was I who could see this man. Otherwise why should anyone sit on the place where he sat? My logic began to grow and, sure about that, it led me to realise the fact that I had to make it alone. I cannot hold on to a dream. Can the morning hold on to a dream of the night? Thus grew life leaving the childhood behind.

Biklen: Presumably you have had other imaginings over the years. I'm wondering how these may have changed, and what form they may have taken?

Mukhopadhyay: Staircases became a major obsession when I had learnt how to climb. The feeling of my body working against gravity, the surety of getting away from the earth and the surety of what my next step would do when I kept my foot on one step made me get beyond the concrete staircases and procreate my mental staircases.

So I did all my climbing whenever I had nothing else to do. I had nothing to do because I could never apply myself to do anything voluntarily other than my habits. Nor did I want to try. My staircase climbing kept me occupied with something to do with my emptiness. Surely emptiness cannot be that empty for long because "Nature abhors Emptiness." And thus got filled all that vacuum within me with those staircases. How could I resist myself when staircases were right in front of me? So began my climbing and so began my journeys to the nowheres. Nowheres were those abstract incompletenesses tempting the traveler to get caught into more and more of the nothingness.

Nothingness can be very powerful. Look at zero. When it gets added to the right side of number one, the value increases ten times. Imagine the same zero getting added to the side of infinity. Again look at the power of nothingness. The beginning of everything finite began from that nothingness. The staircases led me to the middle of that powerful nowhere. And that absolute nothingness was too overwhelming for me. I feared it with all my loneliness entrapping me with its power although there was also the temptation to climb further, because of a traditional concept that everything began with God and everything ended in God. I wanted to meet God.

Thus caught with fear and hope I physically reacted to it. How was that? I screamed.

And all that nothingness got empowered by that scream. I realised that I hadn't reached anywhere.

And where did the staircase climbing lead me to? I realised that nowhere was not worth me. Sweet may be the grapes but if I do not taste it they can be called sour.

Biklen: You seem very conscious of the injustice of prejudicial pronouncements, for example, when a school official said you were not ready for school. Yet you describe yourself as powerless at that moment to be heard, because the speaker didn't take you seriously. In my own experience, I've noticed that sometimes people just assume that they have the authority to speak for others and about others, never imagining that the person with Autism is able to think for him- or herself.

Mukhopadhyay: [That goes] back to those times when I had the hope to join a school because boys my age were supposed to go to schools. It did not matter which school. Any school was okay for me. But how could I? I was so different. I suppose people did not want to take the risk of keeping me. Yes, I was hurt. But my common sense was also less and I was so naïve.

Now when I put myself in their position I think I get their point of view. I ask myself whether I would have become a happier person if at all I was allowed to attend the classes in a normal school. Every time I ask I get the same answer. "No."

I couldn't have matched with the emotions and the peer level of normalcy. I suppose the classrooms would look like crowded fields making me overwhelmed. Moreover I cannot abide by any rule and classrooms, as I have heard from my mother, that classrooms are full of rules. You are supposed to be in and sit in one place till the teacher is there. I have tried to be in one place, but have failed. But still the sting is always there. The doors were never opened for me. I was not prepared, but I wanted to be given a chance. I could have used the playgrounds. Perhaps my social skills could have improved because I was below five years old. However the ways of the world got learnt by me since then and the dream of becoming something bigger than the limits of the classroom got planted.

Biklen: I know that when you were younger, you imagined yourself inside a mirror. Is this a metaphor for some experiences in your actual life or is this a daydream, a wished-for world?

Mukhopadhyay: Mirror travel was a part of my day's work. And I traveled a lot. It was a sort of an escape from situations and I could form my own little stories behind it by looking through it. If you asked me why I saw a silent world inside the mirror I may not be very scientific in my explanation. I think that the world inside the mirror looked silent to me because the real world was too complex to cope with.

Certainly my power of imagination also helped me a great deal to make my own convenient escape inside the world of the mirror. And wasn't it a great escape specially when I was perturbed with the confusion of classifying sounds into male voices, female voices and radio voice? Wasn't it a great escape when I was challenged with expectations and worried conversations that went all around me? There is no need for the mind to try and escape. It can happen to anybody anywhere be it a normal mind or be it an Autistic mind.

How true were the images which formed in my mind with silent world and dreaming people?

Well,
It was as real as a dream
It was as silent as a scream
It was as bright as the new moon shine
As lonely as a sip of a summer wine
It had the sorrow of a smile
The boundlessness of a while
The distance of the infinite
Everything was there in my eyes' light.

Mind/Body

Biklen: I'm wondering what affects performance. Does anxiety enter in? Is it more a question of knowing where the body is in space, of where the body parts (legs, arms, shoulders, head) are located? Is it a question of having difficulty starting? Is it a combination of all of these?

Mukhopadhyay: There are moments of confusion. Am I made of thoughts or am I made up of my body? I usually experience either, one at a time. For a long time I had no idea of waking or dreaming concept because everything looked as an extension of thoughts. Thoughts would get alive like anything that is alive.

The other day, I had to shut my eyes on the road because the whole road seemed to become so alive, although my logic told me that it could not be so. Only when mother took me to some other lane, could I open my eyes. So how could I trust my eyes when they lead me to such confusion? However, because I am aware of the physical laws, I know what I should see and try to help myself, or take my mother's help.

I had to learn about my body, because I could not feel the pain, or realise it, till I was taught. So without knowing anything about the body, how could I apply my body parts to do the different activities, which people do? So when someone asks me to do something manually, I get clumsy. You have to map yourself, map the part of the body you are going to use and time it up, because someone is waiting for you to complete the task. You know that your intelligence or stupidity would get measured by that performance of yours. You tend to get very clumsy. You wonder which to use, your thoughts or your body because you can use either this or that.

And since you have completed the act in your thoughts, you wonder why you cannot satisfy the person who is giving impatient commands like "Come on, I am waiting," which means that "you are a stupid person." And you realise that the task is not done. You don't fight back because you have already fought back in your thoughts. Only your mouth remained useless.

Biklen: So your inability to play is not unwillingness to play. This is something that comes up a lot with students in U.S. schools and teachers often ask me about it.

Mukhopadhyay: Play and games [are] . . . the most confusing, unpredictable activity, which a normal human being engages himself in and classifies himself a winner or a loser depending whether he is satisfied or unsatisfied. It becomes a very childish deed when he marks himself with some points and feels happy about it. Happiness or sorrow gains the intensity if there are the spectators watching him win or lose. Spectators call themselves supporters. I do not play.

Nor do I understand the feeling of great happiness, which is linked to mere calling oneself a winner because the points are more.

When I was young mother used to call children at home to try and play with me. She would create a playground on the drawing room floor by pushing all the furniture towards one side of the wall so that the children could use the rest of the area to play. How irritating. I would not play. I could not play. I could not plan my move and understand their moves. "Why did that boy give the ball to that little boy and not to the girl who was wearing the red dress?" There were so many movements to choose from. You could run, you could jump and you could roll. At the same time you could scold and laugh. Everything was play. "So you need to move your body to play." I started to spin right in the middle of the room just below the fan. I was spinning on the way and so I was pushed aside so that the game could continue. I came back and was pushed aside once again.

Games can get awfully puzzling. Exercising can work better because you are sure what you are supposed to do. Limited boundaries of movements save a lot of strain. The strain of choosing how to apply your body. I can however play badminton with you. I know what to do. I just have to try and hit the shuttle cock when it comes to me. Easy enough. And what about the points? Oh you can keep them all because you would be a happier person if you win.

Biklen: This reminds me of a young person who can read aloud everything she types and now attends a liberal arts college; she has Autism. She once described herself as "a clown in a world that is not a circus." As she struggles with movement difficulties, she feels watched.

Mukhopadhyay:

> *People yes and people no*
> *People all about*
> *People fill the world also*
> *With questions and with doubts*
> *And people many with twice many eyes*
> *Search your reasons search your price*
> *Search your laughter search your dream*
> *With mystery covered you around the scene.*

I [too] have called myself a clown. I have given entertainment to a lot of people specially when I have flapped my hands or every time I had the fits of laughter or a tantrum. I had made people every reason to turn their eyes towards me. No doubt I did look queer. I get them any time because there is a certain physical need to release the great energy, which I experience at that moment.

In India Autism is another term for madness. So what else could give a better entertainment to people other than watch how a mad person can act and how helpless he can get?

Researchers have done a better job. At least they have noted down the traits and studied them. At least they got doctorates from that. Well, that was my worst quality answer. When the heart does the thinking the head gives up. Isn't the heart more articulate than the head? See how it beats. Sometimes it can silence the head too.

Communication and Rules

Biklen: I'm intrigued by your finding rhymes and songs a way in which to begin speaking. Speech therapists sometimes talk about this too.

Mukhopadhyay: I do not know how other Autistic people communicate but I like to use the words in the best possible way. And what else could be a better way of communication other than through poetry or a rhyme, which is a musical form of poetry.

When did I start? It is way back in the year 1992 when a rising sun had inspired me. I was acquainted to poetry earlier in my life because my mother usually recited them as a hobby. In fact I learnt my language of English through Poetry, which I heard from her. I get very comfortable about my conversation when I am asked to talk and I am replying in verse. A verse is a one way conversation. You are not getting interrupted in the middle. Here only your thoughts are getting flowed in one way. There are no other thoughts to interfere with the flow.

Communication is a very primordial urge of human beings.

Being an Autistic person does not give me any other definition and I am still a human being. Maybe my Autism restricts some of my desires to communicate because of the different working of my sensory receptors. So I find the one-way communication better than a dialogue.

I communicate through rhymes. I get a better payback of my words because some people find them impressive and note them down. That gives me every reason to improve my words. That gives me every reason to write them down sometimes in the form of stories and sometimes in the form of poetry.

If one person found my words good why shouldn't the others? And when others get to read my words I can call myself a writer. There is nothing wrong to dream. . . .

Biklen: You have talked about how your mother tried to use your interests and also to expand them. Do you have any guiding rules for teachers or parents about this?

Mukhopadhyay: "Keep him busy," was what the clinical psychologist told my parents, when they had asked her what to do with me. We had gone to a toy shop and mother started to explore all the educational toys. We had bought many boxes. Boxes containing shapes and colours. Bowls of different sizes and jigsaw puzzles. Rectangles and triangles of different colours attractive enough to pull all my attention towards them. Why should the eyes need to see . . . bland monotonous [imagined] staircases any more? There were red and parrot green, orange and blue, pink and yellow shapes around. My eyes waited to see what was in the next box.

Mother and I started building pillars to begin with. The blocks would tumble down after reaching a particular height. But we rebuilt them and thus I learnt that if we placed the bigger pieces at the bottom, the pillar would not fall.

I did not think about the staircases any more, because I had already learnt to build them by arranging the blocks in a zig-zag manner. Mother brought potatoes and onions from the kitchen and made them climb up my constructed staircases. That was enough to make me quite forget my imaginary staircase climbing.

I think that obsession can be turned into practical reality. But how should the hidden obsession be detected specially when the Autistic person keeps it a secret. I suppose the blocks could be made use of because you can find out what the person is doing with the blocks. Some children would tap and make the sound. They can be put to drum play. If I loved a turning around movement as my mental engagement, I would have tried to turn my block pieces also. Perhaps mother would have given me a string to turn it around a reel. Well I am no pioneer in the modeling of the behavior. And as the saying goes that it is easier said than done specially when things are still so dark with Autism, I shall limit my words as suggestions of help.

Biklen: Yet you do keep making rules for yourself?

Mukhopadhyay: Rules are formed by an Autistic person to simplify the ongoing uncertainty which is taking place around him. The uncertainty may lead the Autistic person to lose his identity. And because that would be a total chaotic situation, he tends to take the shelter of his rules, which he has created, choosing certain phenomenon from the greater uncertainty surrounding him.

The rule can be anything. A man crossing his way, or a train in the process of movement.

When the chaos is more, like the open situation outside the boundaries of the house, you are needed to concentrate on the sight, sound and also the sensation of moving forward inside the train, on which you do not travel everyday, you tend to get overwhelmed. The crowd inside adds to the confusion.

The body and mind need some sort of relief from everything. How should that be possible? It can be possible to simplify the whole system, which is going around, by forming rules. "The train should not stop if the process has to continue. And if it stops, I shall shout at everything till it understood me, and started moving once again. A particular person should not pass my way because that would disturb the stability of the situation by interrupting my view."

But how did everything go? It faded as I grew up and became more sensible and less sensitive.

Biklen: I would think that if a rule is known only to you, this could cause difficulty to those around you?

Mukhopadhyay: Rules are somewhat the very proof to an Autistic person that he exists. He would have guidelines about these rules, which rule would be performed by him to the extremities of forming a rigid system of ritual. I am no exception and I get a sort of self existing sense when I have followed a routine set of activities. How useful are they? Are they creating any problem for anybody?

They are very complicated arguments. I for instance want to wash my hands before any new activity. It is something which is making me feel secure and sure. It does not create any problem for anybody. But if I decide to switch on the lights at midnight and wake the whole house up by playing my tape recorder, just because I want to find my identity, I need to be stopped. But how are you going to stop me because I threaten to become very wild. You can give me a walkman in my ears. And if my light is disturbing your eyes change the bulb tomorrow into a zero powered bulb. But what if I have the rule of going for a walk and it rains so heavily that you do not take me out and I get very anxious as a result? How should you make me understand the problem when I am pacing the room in a very threatening manner? You can turn on the radio to distract me. Eating is a very good distracting mode. You can give me something to chew. If it is bread, make small pieces because an Autistic person is usually in a hurry to finish everything fast. Kill time by talking and then immediately make him do the next activity, which he does after his walk. You have substituted walking with eating.

Thinking, Ways of Learning, and Types of Teaching

Biklen: Now that you write so well, it is hard to imagine that at one time you did not. I wonder how your mother got the idea you were a complex thinking person on the inside.

Mukhopadhyay: Mother tells me that I would listen to music and stop my tantrums when I was a baby. I would memorise the words of songs and I could give signals that I was listening to it if I heard any word go wrong. Mother tells that I was four months old when she realised that I was sensitive to words and tune. She would also play with me by deliberately singing the words in a disorganised way so that I could give the indication that she was going wrong. I was always sensitive to words and I could comprehend the essence even if I could not speak them out.

I had also developed a love for designs. I loved the repetition, and I realised that when anything got repeated in a row or in a radius it formed designs. I understood designs better than the picture of a scenery. Mother had discovered it one day when she found me arranging the match sticks in order to form repeated cross signs. I was a crawling baby at that time. She gave more sticks to play with and I formed repeated plus signs or repeated T signs, which later developed into more and more complicated patterns.

It was a terrible thing to hear from a doctor in Calcutta that I was mentally retarded. And thank God that mother did not believe it after the initial shock because I had proved to her that I was not. Time and again. And what about my memorizing the routes. God! She could not even make me forget the usual route which I was used to. Wasn't that any proof that I was not stupid? Mother later argued with someone that, "if he could remember that, he was capable of remembering this."

Biklen: I know you value a teacher being firm (or your mother being firm). I've heard this from some other people with Autism. What experiences with this come to mind to show how this works? Are there some kinds of firmness that do not work?

Mukhopadhyay:

> Me and mother a fine pair
> In the world a strange affair
> As we days make our parts to share
> Little tussle and little to care
> And the world stands to stare
> How we manage how we fare
> Some times also the world compares
> As we bargain with despair

I knew that the doors of education would always remain closed for me through a school or through a college because [in India] Autism is another word for madness. Why, it is not even allowed for a mad person to become a voter. So when one school said "sorry" and the next school referred me to a school for the mentally retarded, mother did not even try to ask the third.

"Why am I educated?" she argued. And she became my teacher. A very firm teacher who would not give me the next meal unless I used the pencil in the proper way. And because I was constantly dropping the pencil down she tied it to my hands with a rubber band. And when I was not completing the questions which she had given me after reading a chapter, I was tied down to the chair till I finished it.[1]

How should she otherwise know whether I was listening or dreaming? "Throw up your tantrums and then finish your work." Have you seen anything so stubborn as our pair? I remember my shouts and screams and I remember mother proudly reading and reciting out my answers again and again. Sometimes to me, sometimes to father, sometimes to that guest who was drinking tea and talking about his very intelligent son who had learnt to recite Ding Dong Bell. Most of the time she recited them just to herself.

I knew that there was no escape from books. Studying became a habit and habit became an essential part of my life as most Autistic people are guided by habits. We bargain about our terms and deals. I have many demands. I need that ice cream. I need tender coconuts. I need a visit to the railway station. She has one demand. Become a somebody. And she means it.

Biklen: I'd love to know what the studies looked like. How did you start to learn mathematics for example, and then writing?

Mukhopadhyay: At first the numbers looked like an extension of designs. However when mother pointed and told me their names with, "You are Tito and this is one." And "You are Tito and this is two," I was very impressed.

I had learnt how to call them. Their symbols turned out to be more meaningful to me.

I had learnt how to add and subtract also from the calendar. Mother showed me how to count the digits towards the right side for addition, and to count the number of digits towards the left side for subtraction. For example, if I had to add $15 + 2$, I needed to count, two from 15, towards the right side, which would give 17. When I needed to calculate, $15 - 2$, I needed to count 2 backwards, which would give 13, as the result. I counted everything with my eyes.

Mother taught me complex problems and Algebra, using the number board. I could solve everything by pointing at the numbers.

I learnt Algebra first, and writing later. Did I understand anything before I learnt how to write? Of course I did. There were simple equations and there were the LCM [a mathematics course]. Every solution was solved by pointing. No not the Rainman way of solution. Mother saw that I went through the procedures of steps the way everyone solved it.

For that, she had to include decimal points and algebraic signs on my number board, so that when she asked me what to write on the next line I could point the next step.

How did writing help me? Well it proved to the world that it was I who was doing it and not mother.

Biklen: How would you describe your speaking in relation to the complexity of your writing?

Mukhopadhyay: There are many doubts regarding my speech because very few people can make out what I am talking.[2] Many people have asked my mother how she managed to understand what I was talking. In other words they thought that I was only making sounds and mother was making up her own words and giving her own meanings to those sounds. I usually point out my words on my letter board or write them down when I am communicating with someone.

Which is easier? Speech or writing? I enjoy writing when it comes to creative writing than communication. This is because when I am communicating many aspects come on the way. One such aspect is that I need to be alert at every word and the essence of those words which gets pretty exerting for my nerves. Writing slows down the process of conversation. Because it takes more time to think and write than some spontaneous speech. I get my words better organised when I write. And people believe it.

Ways of Seeing and Experiencing

Biklen: You once said that you were still "an intelligent junk," that you were not functioning in typical ways. Are there benefits though in your ways of experiencing the world, for example in creativity, in fascination with colors or sounds, or in imaginative life?

Mukhopadhyay:

> *My intelligence is as much useful to me and you*
> *As the colour of the sky*
> *What could have mattered if it was green not blue*

Would you have thought it twice?
It is accepted fact that the sky is blue
That is very true
How useful is that blue of the sky
Who can explain it better than I?
The blue sky surrounds the earth
Embracing the useful parts
Rivers, lakes and the salty seas
Minerals and the dust.
It could have done the same with being green.
My intelligence surrounds my body which has all the useful parts
*   like heart, liver and lungs.*
What is the use of my mind, which can think of the beyondness of
*   blue, it had once seen in Emma's eyes and yet could not tell her*
*   anything about what it had seen? What use is my mind when I*
*   missed out my turn in a debate taking place? I could not give*
*   my point. What use is my intelligence when I heard the rubbish*
*   from the experts on Autism and yet all I could do was flap my*
*   hands, which is believed to be one of my traits? And what use is*
*   my intelligence when I hear that I am one of those idiot-savants*
*   and cannot say my words? So I have renamed myself as an intel-*
*   ligent junk.*
Just as the blue of the sky
Blue or green
It could have been there is nothing to reply
And the artist who
Has coloured it blue
Could have made it green
Or anything
The purpose could be all the same
No matter which colour it had been.

Biklen: With one person who has a disability similar to Autism, for conversations, I type my part of the dialogue and he types back to me; this
seems to help him focus and to cut down on his excess "chatter." But
here I am going on with my own ideas, possibly pushing you to answer
in a certain way. I'm interested in your ideas about useful strategies.

Mukhopadhyay: Many Autistic people try to cut away the various inputs of sounds by producing their own convenient sounds so that the other sounds get to the background and the sound which he is making gets all his attention and concentration. He should not get away with that because it would lead him to nowhere other than get entangled in its own intoxicating effect leading him to get deeper trapped in the obsessive nature of that sound.

That can make his life miserable. There may be an initial triumph because it may look that the Autistic person is trying to communicate. But soon the realization comes that the sounds produced are far from communication. He is using the sound as a filter.

I had many such sounds to use as filters and each time I happened to produce something new with my vocal cords I wanted to produce it again and again and thus got helpless when I could not stop myself and rather got annoyed when someone tried to stop me.

I should suggest the forced stopping of the sound by turning on the radio at a louder volume or changing the environment or giving something to chew which would make the distraction. My mother did not try anything like those. Then how did I stop them? I got slaps, each time harder than the previous one and sure enough I did not like them.

Touch (the Body Again) and Forms of Questions

Biklen: You have said that you learned the skill of pointing at a young age, but that even this could be difficult.

Mukhopadhyay: Pointing was an acquired skill for me. It did not happen to me as a process of my normal development. And like many others, the doctors were puzzled too when they found that I could point at the letters and spell or point at the right picture when I had to choose from them to match a word that was read out to me, but had this basic difficulty in applying my knowledge to point out my eyes, ears, and nose.

I think that they had their doubts regarding my knowledge and so tried asking me more questions on my environment like "Where is the fan?" or "Where is your shirt?" However when mother showed them how to ask the other way round by picking up an object and asking me what it was, I could do so.

I could not point at objects for many reasons. The most important reason is that I had very little sensation of my body. So to learn the technique of moving my right hand needed control over the ball and socket joint of the shoulder and then the hinge joint of my elbow and finally fold the other fingers and keep the point finger out. After that focusing on the object which matched with the word.

That required quite a skill for an Autistic person to do without learning. I needed to learn with the help of my mother. She held my hands and started me on the pointing of near objects first and then when I could do them she carried it to teach me the distant object pointing.

It is an essential skill because I can go to a shop and point out exactly what I want.

I can point at my forehead and show the doctor exactly where I had got the knock because he should not end up treating my nose.

Biklen: Well you've also said that how people ask you questions can affect your ability or interest in answering. Dr. Pratibha Karanth asked why you liked the calendar [Mukhopadhyay 2000, p. 31]. I'm interested in what sense this was a different type of question than others often asked.

Mukhopadhyay: Questions and Answers were a part of my communication with mother. Mother asked me about the Laws of Gravity and about the position of the earth in the Solar System. She also asked me the square root of 625, and the definition of the Radius of a Circle.

Mother also asked me what I would like to do next, or what I shall like to have for dinner.

Other people did not consider me fit to be questioned or eligible for any direct conversation.

When Dr. Prathibha Karanth asked me why I liked the calendar which I had picked up from her table, I was naturally quite overwhelmed because I had never even asked myself anything like that. It needed no learnt facts and laws to answer. However I did settle with an answer. "I like the contrast," I had pointed on the board.

Later in life I had faced similar questions about my likes and preferences. I kept myself prepared by finding a more honest answer before telling somebody that I like something. I have seen people asking other Autistic people, showing two objects and inquiring whether they would have this or that. And the Autistic person randomly replies this or that. Nobody answers "both," although some may not mind having both. When the prospect of an answer is so narrow and the tendency to escape is more, how could the person grow and organise his reasons? So although it is difficult to face an open question, it should be introduced. Escapism is the doom for any development.

There are many approaches to a question. "What is this?" is a very rudimentary approach to communication. When my speech therapist asked me "What is this?" and tried to get the answer out of me by telling me more than half the answer that "this is a ———" he forgot that I had already authored more than a hundred poems by then and two of them were already published. Naturally I did not like his two-year-old treatment just because he had the advantage of speech. I could have started my answer when he was showing me the picture of the cat like this—

> *Call me a cat*
> *Or call me a feline*
> *Call me any name*
> *I shall haunt*
> *Your doors at night*
> *Now, then and again.*

That would be an open ended response to any question rather than restricting the wonderful prospect of answering with a sentence like "this is a —-." My ego is always an important matter to me.

Biklen: So does this mean that a rigorous school is your ideal?

Mukhopadhyay: My basic idea about the ideal school is not idealistic in nature. Students are not pieces of a jigsaw puzzle who could be forced inside to form a desired pre-planned picture. A student who hates Maths, is forced to study Maths because Maths is a part of the curriculum, and curriculum is a part of the system. And the student is also a part of the system.

Well, I am not here to write a whole education policy. Neither am I sitting here to criticise something which had refused to include me because I was not any piece of the jigsaw puzzle picture. I was some stray piece of a different picture. Truly, I have no idea how the picture would be like if I was included as its part.

My school is that open dream
My words find hard to say,
My school is the doubt in your eyes
And my withdrawing away.
My school is in the summer dust grain
I saw coming through my window,
Trying to find a way to my room
Then disappearing in an obscure shadow.
And again my school can be anything . . .
My school is like a barn owl's eyes,
Seeking the dark of earth
Then spotting a quivering fleeting rat
Hungry to prey on its heart.

Perceptions

Biklen: Are you also speaking literally about how you see and what you notice most?

Mukhopadhyay:

People with faces and faces with people
Which to trace on which
My eyes recognise very little
A trait so Autistic.

One of my ways of linking people is with places where I have first seen them for my first "encounter" with them. So when I see my speech therapist in a bus traveling with me I get rather puzzled if I hear a hello from him. "Who are you to greet me?" but I manage to reply back when my mother nudges me.

I never bother to identify people with respect to faces. I do identify people with their voices. I feel more comfortable to stare at a dust grain and listen rather than look into the eyes of people while listening to them. I have a tendency of associating things to remember. In simple words, number two exists because number one exists. My speech therapist exists in the therapy room. And I interact with him there. So when he greets me at the bus, I see a different environment around us. There is a totally new situation. And so recognition becomes delayed. Which leads to delayed response. And that is something, which I regret because I never want to hurt any one.

New voices bring a different pattern of sound. The word "cat" will be heard in a different way when I hear a stranger speak. However, after hearing it for some time I start getting tuned to his voice. There would be no problem then. I would initially need facilitation from my mother who would repeat the statement for me. I am used to her way of speech. So I would hear the voice of the stranger through her voice. Mother slowly fades out her voice. The time taken to get adjusted to a voice varies from voice to voice.

Biklen: I've seen the label "Mentally Retarded" put on so many children who struggle to communicate. One of the greatest challenges I have is to help teachers presume the competence of each child. Any advice?

Mukhopadhyay: It is the most disgraceful label which the term Autism is associated with. Yes, some areas remain less developed because of lack of associating the mind with body and environment. That does not prove that the mind is incapable of thinking. I had been labeled as mentally retarded when I had my first encounter with the psychologist. I was three years old then. The proof for my retardation was that I could not follow basic commands. I was not able to apply my knowledge although I could understand perfectly well what was being asked.

I do not blame the psychologist. Seeing is believing. And he saw nothing in me that could alter his belief. That was years back in 1992. Today should be different. Special educators should be more open about this. They should begin with the attitude that the client is understanding him and not wonder where to start or what to start. Start with anything. And grow around that anything. Talk with an easy tone because the client is not hearing impaired. Trust that the client is capable of understanding. And then "Carry on."

More on the Mind/Body, a Most Important Theme

Biklen: This brings us back to the body. Part of the problem of following commands or just doing things presumably relates to how you experience your body.

Mukhopadhyay: It took me many years to realise that I have a body. I think that it is not because of my preoccupation with other thoughts. I was totally aware of sounds and colours, which my senses picked up for me. I was, as if watching everything from a distant moon without actually being any part of everything. So the feeling that I have a body never occurred to me. Even this day sometimes I feel that I am walking without legs.

The feeling of pain escaped me. I remember once touching a table fan and getting a shock. It was not "painful" but a new sensation for me. And I had tried to check it again by touching it once again to feel my hands.

Many Autistic people need to be helped because of this reason. How can they perform a task using hands if they just cannot feel them? And without any feeling how should they have control over them?

The sensation of physical pain was introduced to me by mother when she saw that I was unable to show her where I had hurt myself. She kept my eyes closed and pinched my body at different parts and asked me to point out the exact location where she pinched. Slowly I could differentiate between a pain and a sensation.

Problems have solutions. And solutions can be found through trials. The freedom to find should also be there. In some countries, I am sure mother would have been charged with child abuse. In India mother was safe to try out anything and thank God for that.

Biklen: Besides this, are there other ways of getting in touch with your body? I mean, what helps you become more aware of where your arms or shoulder or legs are located? What helps you be more effective in using your body?

Mukhopadhyay:

When I was a little boy
One or two years I mean
I would not let anyone pick me up
If anyone did I would scream.

So sensitive was my body and so frightening was the very experience of the body. I could never enjoy a new shirt or a new shoe, each one making me aware of my own body. However, as I grew up and started my mirror gazing I became more and more aware of my looks and size. I had a favorite bed sheet which I loved to wrap around my body so that I could enjoy it. I still wrap my body with bed sheets time and again to feel my body. When I learnt that a swing was not anything which could kill you I started using it a great deal. Half of my school hours are spent on the swing. I enjoy climbing up a staircase also because the gravity acts on my body as I apply myself against it. Escalators are wonderful as I can be sure of getting the feeling of my body gradually. I feel my body when I am sitting on a vehicle and feel my whole system accelerate to the speed. At home a little rocking and a little spinning also helps. Thank god mother does not stop me.

Biklen: Given your sensitivity as a young child to being picked up, it is ironic that touch became so important to your learning.

Mukhopadhyay: To think about it, I recall that I learnt every skill through the touch method. I have a problem with imitating any movement by looking at people performing or by mapping my body according to the instructions given to me. The simple task of holding a spoon and taking the food to the mouth was also taught by my speech therapist for by helping me for the first few times till my habit developed and I could understand how to do it. I am stressing on how to do and not what to do because no one should have the impression that I did not know what to do. Different skills need different time to practice depending on the feeling of awareness of that part of the body. Sometimes I feel my legs better than the hands. But I needed my mother's help to learn the tricycle. She had to manually push my legs because I could not do the movement. It needed some practice before I could ride it independently.

I was helped by mother with pushes on my back so that I could use my sudden breaths and bring out the sound produced by my vocal cords. That was the beginning of my speech. I can now enjoy hearing my own voice although very few people can follow my speech.

Tying my shoelaces was another activity which needed help by holding my hands and making me do it. It took a year to get independent.

Biklen: And is it the same for learning to play?

Mukhopadhyay: Life can become very boring for an Autistic person, if he does not learn how to play. So a ball can be introduced to him. If you throw it to him and expect him to do exactly what you had done, when you had first played with a ball, I am sorry to say that you might be disappointed. The Autistic person may not be able to judge the ball, catch it and go further beyond that and reciprocate your throw back to you.

I had a problem with this beautiful round object called "ball." Mother taught me what to do with it. At first she stood very close to me. We just did the give and take act. I gave the ball back to her, the very next moment she gave it to me. Then she began to slowly distance herself, about a foot away from me. By now, I knew what I had to do. She began to throw it gently towards me and I caught it. However, I could not throw it back at her. So every time I got the ball, I walked up to her to give it back.

Throwing a ball can be learnt by using a wall, so that the ball could hit against the wall and come back for you to catch. Manual help, by taking the person's hand and making him throw the ball would work faster. I have seen when I was physically helped to do a task, by someone else holding my hands and showing me what to do, I learnt it faster.

Touch is always a big help when an activity is new for me. Only through practice and through the gradual fading of the touch the activity can be done independently. I needed to be touched on my right shoulder, for doing any new skill, be it soaping, be it eating or be it learning how to take my bath, or be it learning how to write. So I consider that the touch method is the vital step to speed up my learning skill.

Biklen: I know that even entering a swimming pool was hard for you. Could you explain that?

Mukhopadhyay: I was surrounded by water all around me when I set my foot in the swimming pool. I realised how unstable my feet felt. It was a disbalancing sensation and there was no way I could walk properly. Mother was standing on the bank and asking me to sit and feel the water. To help me, the trainer was pulling me further inside the water towards the deeper side. And to show me that it was water and nothing to be afraid of, the other children were trying to splash water all on my body. I could feel my body get divided into the aerial part and the aquatic part. I would rather stand under a shower and feel the water than sit in a tub with the unstable wobble of water.

Biklen: You have said that sometimes your world is a combination of fear and fragments. Does the anxiety create the fragmented sense? Or is it the other way around? How do fear and experiencing the world in pieces relate?

Mukhopadhyay: Yes. I cannot feel certain parts of my body at certain times. Whether it is anxiety or whether the cause is something else can be found out only by a psychologist or a neurologist. I just know one thing. That is, I am mono channeled and can do or concentrate on one thing at a time. I can either see or I can hear my environment. So I suppose when I concentrate on seeing, I forget that I am also being. That applies to hearing also.

The synthesis of the experience of having a body gets out of the mind. And since everything can be blamed to the mind, my not feeling the body can also be blamed to my mind.

And about anxiety causing my non body feeling or whether it is due to some other cause is for the psychologist to analyze.

Biklen: Well then are there particular ways for teachers to help you handle hard situations?

Mukhopadhyay: My idea about this is as much as a patient's idea about his own treatment. However, I would like to say that the undesirable behavior just happens with the unpredictability of a situation. Now the question is how to prevent it. Wish I knew the answer.

One thing however is for sure is that eating some crunchy food helps because you can hear yourself while you are chewing leading to distraction. Changing the environment also helps. Sometimes my mother starts to talk with me on some subject which needs some thinking to answer. I automatically get distracted. But if you ask me what are those undesirable behaviors I shall answer "nothing." This is because I am not ashamed of my undesirable behaviors just like I am not ashamed being Autistic.

Biklen: In your earlier writing, you have said, "Exposure to variations, be it clothes or food, place and timetable, help us to, if not love, but to tolerate and understand our role in the situations better" [Mukhopadhyay 2000, p. 57]. I wonder if you would describe some of your struggles with this and how, in specific ways, you went about achieving toleration with different things.

Mukhopadhyay: The main struggle is living and trying to be what others desire you to be. However there are certain essential needs to survive in the world. People cannot be giving me the same type of food everywhere and I have to accept the fact that I love to travel. To travel, my food habits must be very flexible. I need to tolerate a crowd on a bus. So to make myself less sensitive, I needed exposure to new situations like food, clothes etc.

Biklen: You have said that you dream of someday growing up in a world where people are accepted without being labeled and judged. I am wondering, are there some places with some people where you already find this kind of maturity, even now?

Mukhopadhyay: Have I found such a gathering? Yes. I have seen people who overlook my facial twitches and my flapping of hands. They pay more attention to what I am communicating. They are usually the parents of other Autistic people. They are the professionals who have some idea about Autism. They talk to me directly and do not mind my flapping of hands.

Biklen: After you attended a wedding, you said that you felt lost without activity. So does this mean that certain kinds of focused activity allow you to feel calm? What sorts of activities do you find especially calming?

Mukhopadhyay: When there is nothing to do there is a total scattering experience because the body gets overwhelmed with too much stimulation from environment and too much disengagement of the body. There is an absolute nowhere feeling. Focused activity gives the kind of a purpose to fill up the void, which has been built up with that nowhere feeling.

Biklen: And are some settings just too open for you to accommodate?

Mukhopadhyay: "Shall I be here or shall I be there?" I usually find it difficult to guide myself where to be when options are many. Naturally I would like to try out every option. There as well as here. That as well as this. The openness becomes bigger than the world and so I just find myself shuffling from there to here. "What to choose when everything looks good?"

Biklen: Is dealing with people also a bit too open-ended?

Mukhopadhyay: I feel a general discomfort when it comes to people. . . . I am however used to looking at books. I can handle books the way I want to which I cannot with human beings. With human beings, there is a two-way situation of interaction. Because of that, the probabilities of uncertainty becomes more than with the interaction with books. Books allow themselves to be used anyway. So on my first day in school I felt more comfortable to go to the bookshelf rather than sit with the boys.

Biklen: Yet you do seem able to develop some comfort with people; for example you go into the market.

Mukhopadhyay: I am sensitive to a place complete with a crowd. The place becomes a sort of a container and people become the things in it. This may be because I have always considered myself different from them. As a distant observer of the show called events. Like being the audience and watching the performers perform. And just like the passive audience I was the passive observer.

What would happen to a man who is among the audience is suddenly put there up on a stage? He would have no idea what role to play. He would be overwhelmed. The same way by which I got overwhelmed when I went to a crowded market. By practicing it over and over again I got desensitised to the crowd.

Notes

1. Editor: Tito describes his mother as a task master, though I found her firm, and also flexible and tireless. I never observed her to be punitive in any way. Indeed, she always seemed to look to Tito to define both the substance of what he would study and the amount of time for studying and practice.
2. Editor: I found it quite easy to understand Tito's speech, though it was often softly spoken; only on rare occasions did Tito have to spell a word so it could be understood.

References

A boy, a mother, and a rare map of autism's world (2002). *New York Times*, November 19, pp. D1 and D4.

Mabrey, V. (producer/director) (2003). *Breaking the silence.* Documentary. *60 minutes II* (United States).

Mukhopadhyay, R. (2000). *Beyond the silence: My life, the world and autism.* London: National Autistic Society.

Terrill, C. (producer/director). (2000). *Inside story: Tito's story.* Documentary. London: BBC.

Wing, L. (2000). Foreword. In T. R. Mukhopadhyay, *Beyond the silence: My life, the world and autism* (pp. 1–3). London: National Autistic Society.

4

■　■　■　■　■　■　■　■　■

I. An Introduction to Lucy Blackman

The first lines in Lucy Blackman's book, *Lucy's Story: Autism and Other Adventures,* read, "I came to language late—about twelve years too late. Another five years on I was nineteen and I was enrolled in a literary studies course at University" (Blackman 1999, p. 1). As the book jacket explains, growing up, Lucy created "stories and poems" in her head, having come to language through newspapers and books.

I first met Lucy when she was a teenager and in high school. She had been communicating by typing for several years at that point. I will always feel indebted to her for allowing me to visit her school in 1989 and to hear from her firsthand about how she managed to go through high school and take a rigorous sequence of academic courses, and how she managed some of her autistic ways of being in a setting that had not prepared to know someone quite like her.

Since then, I saw Lucy again in the mid-1990s when she came to the United States for the first time. We met at a meeting of the Autism Society of America. Then in 2001, when Lucy again came to the United States, I invited her to give a public address at Syracuse University and to one of my university classes. As the book jacket of *Lucy's Story* says, "as an adult she still barely speaks," yet by 2001, Lucy had been typing without any physical support for several years.

In all my personal interactions with Lucy Blackman, I have found her opinionated, articulate, humorous, ever so candid, and always ready to challenge my ideas or anyone else's. In her chapter, these qualities persist. At several points, she suggests that my questions are from a nonautistic perspective and therefore not about topics that she would herself choose to discuss; she seems to find mine annoying. For that matter, she questions other normate takes on autism as well. For example, she points out that if experts insist on focusing on communication impairment and social interaction as diagnostic markers for autism, then the field may fail to notice other factors that lead to these "peculiarities" (Blackman's term). In another instance, she notes with some upset that people with particular characteristics, for example, blindness or Asperger's syndrome, do receive accommodations such as assistance in library research for the person who is blind and permission not to socialize for the person with Asperger's. Yet when she requires various kinds of support or nonnormative strategies to negotiate the world—she describes these—this becomes evidence of dependence or inadequacy to the normate world. Not surprisingly, she finds this kind of double standard annoying. Her account is reminiscent of Ozick's (2003) account of how certain experts reveled in "doubting Helen Keller" when her ways of writing and expression did not conform to their normate presumptions about how Keller should be. Ozick defends Keller's subjectivity when she writes:

> Theorists have their differing notions, to which the ungraspable organism that is Helen Keller is a retort. She is not an advocate for one side or the other in the ancient debate concerning the nature of the real. She is not a philosophical or neurological or therapeutic topic. She stands for enigma; there lurks in her still the angry child who demanded to be understood yet could not be deciphered. (2003, p. 196)

Blackman helps those around her, as well as the broader field of educators, psychologists, parents, and others, to decipher autism, though there is much that remains best described as enigma. In the pages that follow, Blackman describes some of what might seem most baffling as rather sensible or at least necessary responses to how she experiences the world. Some of her reactions to situations might be thought of as automatic rather than intentional, but even here, she usually can identify reasons for her actions.

■　　■　　■　　■　　■　　■　　■　　■　　■

II. Reflections On Language

Lucy Blackman

I tend to beat around the bush a bit, so I will say in advance your most successful way of making sense of this bit of writing is by seeing it as a collection of the oddities which I have identified in spoken utterances . . . —Oh, oh, oh! That is the strangest thing! As I typed that word ("utterances") I simply had no idea what it meant. Most of the time my speaking self can ready my typed language, and say in my head, "Isn't that interesting!" but every now and again I don't understand my visually acquired language.

Well, I had better introduce myself. 2002 is my thirtieth year. I was born with the type of sensory issues which are typical of those with autism, did not develop coherent speech or interactive play as a toddler, and continued to have auditory and visual processing peculiarities through my formative years. So, if one doesn't have depth perception, what does that mean in terms of facial expression? If one hears the subtle sounds of speech out of order, which I do, how does one process language? If affection in the form of cuddles and kisses cause discomfort and pain in one's infancy, how on earth does one develop interaction which might compensate for not interacting to speech and glance?

I worked out when I was writing my autobiography, *Lucy's Story* [Blackman 1999], which I subtitled *Autism and Other Adventures,* that being touched in my skin and skeleton made my body aware of cause and effect. This created a clumsy crutch on which to hang expression. It does not mean that I changed, though I did make rational and analytical sense of what I was typing.

When I was fourteen I met Rosie Crossley and started to use a keyboard [see Blackman 1999, pp. 79–94]. I continued to have no idea of why I had pragmatic and expressive problems, and why I remained dependent on a facilitator. I understand "pragmatics" in this sense to mean placing one's expression in a temporal and utilitarian photoframe for the information of others. I have seen young children with typical speech development do this, and realise it takes about fourteen years, which is both the age [now] of my eldest niece, Shay [Blackman 1999, p. 269], and the period before which the language I do use was not available to me. In relation to expression, in speech I still only label, pick up others' words in the ritual of echo, and cannot understand past or future in that language stream. I am writing this as prethought (possibly "drafted-thought"), more as a sketch than a diagram for someone's information.

Right through *Lucy's Story* I try giving examples, but of course these relate to the period I was describing, or are what I was experiencing at the time I wrote. There is one example I used in a series of demonstrations in 1995 of facilitation and the ongoing role of the facilitator even when physical contact and unconscious cueing had been eliminated:

> The difficulty is that no one really knows what language is. There are plenty of things it is not. It is not echoed spoken words, but a single twitch of an actor's eyebrow for some people may be language. There are words that I speak that in other people's speech would mean something either to the speaker or the listener, but the way that I use them I do not consider them language. For example my obsessions include McDonald's, and I might say "Ronald McDonald!" when I stand before the large fibreglass statue in our local branch. At least conventional if not age-appropriate expression! That though is not communication. It is a kind of reflex in my memory, just a sound which happens to have form.

> If I am distressed I may also chant "Ronald McDonald," which is also a reflex, but a different kind. I would roughly describe this expression as spoken, but it is not language in any real form. (Written January 1995)

I find it impossible to write about language and its implications without mentioning a "facilitator." In this rather specialised sense this person is assumed to be in physical contact with the person who is producing the typed or written words or who is pointing at a desired object or letterboard. However I have found that physical touch is such a small part of this process. If a tree falls in a forest and no one hears it, can one say it made a sound? That is, I point at a donut and no one sees! That is not communication. This is where the facilitator also has a role in my speech. This often happens. I believe that I have spoken but only in my brain, not in my throat. In fact often I make a sound I believe to be a word, but it has no form. I type words which are precise in intention, but do not have meaning in a context a stranger understands.

I have described my autism through the lens of someone who is very aware that speech has little practical use in her life. If I want something, I can use a naming word, but often it is only an approximation—a mostly indistinct oral equivalent of a card or symbol. Of course a symbol for something precludes negotiation. Just think about it, and, short of shuffling place mats, how does one choose between Burger King and McDonald's? Using a flag as a symbol of a place or idea involves one's preconception, whether on the part of the communicator or receiver—and so on!

In typing I can express attitude, but it may be at variance with my facial expression or vocalisation. Suppose I feel and appear distressed that the person with whom I am typing has no idea of why I have such pleasure in the theory which I am discussing in an essay. Obviously at a rate of about sixty key strokes a minute—usually less—I am not going to waste time or lose my thread to have a long and useless discussion about the other person's attitude. Only joking! In fact I can't have that discussion, and that is because of autism compounded by lack of early childhood speech.

If I were to say anything about autism, it would be how fascinating it is. The idea that autism is fascinating is more that it is what I hope for the future, that my kind of thought processes are seen as possibilities for the next genetic shift in Homo Sapiens, not that it is a progression, but that further down the track the slight changes in individuals scattered among the population is a slight difference in problem solving. Unbelievably those of us who have greater difficulties may be nature's experiments, and you can't expect evolution to get it right every time.

More importantly I have to admit that other people's attitude to autism and to its various attributes are even more fascinating. It may be that the social deficits which are the cornerstone of an autism spectrum diagnosis tell us far more about the person who made them markers for such a diagnosis than about the child whom he observes. I realise that social life and affection are essential for being human, but I still wonder whether the "Me" factor is properly understood. That is, the whole testing procedure is somehow actually constructed on whether the tester observed the person to socialise in a way the tester understood to be socialisation. This has implications for whether autism spectrum behaviours can be seen as simply a side effect of neurological difference, which may arise from some exceptional reaction to stimuli even in the womb. As long as we are told that communication and social factors are the markers for autism, there will be an uneven response in tackling the discomfort and disorientation which may predate these peculiarities.

This is the discovery which I made during the period covered by the last four chapters of my book, *Lucy's Story*, and strangely enough I had not expected my thought-out autobiography to be any more than a description of what had occurred in my life as a result of using what is now called "facilitated communication." That I originally believed was a misnomer because I misunderstood the meaning of "facilitated" in that context, but in retrospect I think that the use of the word "communication" is an unfortunate one.

To work out a difference between an autistic understanding and what might be a more typical one, it helps to have a point of reference. Mine came in that year when I first underwent Auditory Integration Training (AIT)[1] (this was in 1992 when I was 19). Which is not to say that AIT had a major effect for practical purposes, but that within a space of a very few weeks it gave me a glimpse of the differences from growing up with more ordinary responses. By coincidence, at that time I was regularly taken to visit my sister's children who were aged four, two and about twelve months. "In their language exploration, manipulation of their parents, discovery of themselves and their furious tempers, I thought I could see what I might have been in a calm, coherent and stable world" [Blackman 1999, p. 269]. I drew on them and my own memories to write the first draft, in November 1992, of what eventually was published as *Lucy's Story.*

AIT in me created changes in balance and perception, so I that could compare what I had endured before with the rather improved environment I now experienced. It was this which I tried to bring out in my book. For example:

> That was when I had realised that I did not always process information at the moment that my skin, balance, sight or hearing presented it to me, and that sometimes touch and sight were not in sync. Once again I learned this by comparing the Old and New Lucy. . . . No wonder I had psyched myself up by bouncing around. (In generalising this discovery, I had a great feeling of relief. I realised that sometimes I had not reached the bathroom in time simply because I had not known that my body was giving me a signal.) In hearing I realised that a temporal gap substituted for [the] difference between body movement and visual measurement. . . .
>
> I had discovered a trigger for both my echolalia and why I threw up apparently nonsense words. So the way that I used speech was a reflection of what I gleaned from my hearing. This was only apparent to me because I was learning to accommodate to a new and slightly less distorted environment. However I had changed from one set of problems to a different version of the same. [Blackman 1999, p. 278]

I have been asked whether it was that AIT itself had made some difference, or whether it was the task of reflecting on sound and language enabled me to focus on language and communication in a way I had not previously. I think that the notion of focusing is a teacher's concept. One can only focus on something one has learnt to see as relevant, and really I remain an observer rather than a participant.

In December, after AIT, I was shown an article by Teresa Joliffe in *Communication,* the journal of the National Autistic Society, UK. Not only had she written of similar differences, those of which I had just become aware, but even some of her phrasing was almost the same as mine. What a thrill.

I am aware as I type of [the] long-suffering parent-facilitator raising her eyebrows, now sandy grey on a summer-tanned Australian face. "The Hag" is my pet name for my mother, though in *Lucy's Story* I call her "Jay." I did not want my dependence to be seen as childish, but more of an adult-to-adult co-operation which it has become over the years. Well, the way that I compensate for my major problems is partly by mirror imaging. That may not be a familiar concept to non-autistic people who confuse it with dependence, and certainly it is not used by many with autism. However in the past I have seen others do so.

I think it is very irritating that a person with little vision or mobility problems does receive acknowledgement that someone might have to do library searches. An ordinary student who has Asperger syndrome won't be forced to socialise. I depend on an accustomed companion for negotiating these, but really I don't feel that I can go into detail. I find it really difficult to understand why other people are more interested in the process of what I produce than the content. I have sometimes felt that being a demo is not the point of my being a student, and really that this kind of discussion is more about wanting to be "normal" (which I don't) than about what I am achieving in terms of pure intellectual thought. After all, that is why I went to High School and university, not just to be with a whole lot of other people.

In making it possible to do assignments based on research, the person who supports me has to compensate for a number of factors, such as my inability to turn to a certain page, my intense distaste for rewriting, and my terror if I have to search for a book on a library shelf. I simply read, then type, and later go through several drafts and dictate changes. I cannot word process at this level of complexity because, if I can't see my thoughts static on the screen, I lose all memory of them.

The issue is not one of emotional dependence. From my visual fluctuations and thinking about how they affect me now, I deduce that in childhood I had real problems in knowing exactly where my connectional limbs and trunk were, where they would move to next, and, even more frighteningly, where they had last been positioned. The solution is to make the other person part of my visual field. For example, is the pedestrian in front of me, a hypothetical little old lady walking in the same direction as I am, too far away to mirror? The solution is to walk close to her. The miserable little grey haired woman is nervously looking over her shoulder. Then suddenly she scurries forward as I latch onto an arms-length distance on which to forge an invisible chain. As she moves, so do I because her body is now mine—that is until her movement is out of kilter with what I project as the future. In that event I float off, or, if really terrified, in that uncertainty I scream then bite my hand on the existing scar below my thumb.

If the little woman isn't already a speck on the horizon, you can bet she now has gushing jet vapour coming out of her sensible shoes. When I was younger I found this kind of reaction massively amusing, but as an adult I am irritated both with myself and with the non-autistic world, for I can't see why other people cannot understand that people with autism need the other partner in an interaction to do what my mother describes as "socialise for two." If for example I see a doctor, I type my contribution on a keyboard. However all I am contributing is words and spaces. The other two people present have to produce the cotillion that is the structure of a medical consultation. That is, although I no longer am touched when I produce typed language, I still need a personal facilitator as well as the natural facilitation which is the job of the consultant.

That is not to say that I don't give the impression of interacting. I have been asked [by the editor of this book]:

I've seen you be assertive in your conversations through typing. You pushed your point of view, took issue with mine, and seemed to engage in a real *give-and-take* [my emphasis]. Is that different from what a so-called typical person would do in a medical consultation situation? I do understand that you say you need the facilitator with you both to keep [you] typing and to negotiate everyday events like walking to a particular location, but are your words really just words and spaces? One person who communicates by typing and also by speaking slowly (syllable by syllable and word by word) told me that the facilitator helps him have the right environment for communicating. Does it work that way for you?

However it is almost like my being an angel sitting on my own shoulder. I can see myself in this interchange. If it goes on too long I have no interest in it as a social occasion. I really am more interested in why I am typing than the opinion I am trying to express. In fact it isn't a give-and-take. I am able to understand that gavotte when I observe it in others, but I would rather read a paragraph and comment. If I speak the words I type, I am reading them off the computer or from an imaginary screen in my head.

If I link this to my language I can see the same process at work, but somehow it is reversed. Language in humans has many functions, of which communication with others of our species is only one. That is, I can see that using language also creates self-image and places one in space, time and society. That also allows self-monitoring and analysis within cultural norms. On a personal level, I don't believe I would have understood the lessons I learnt from becoming aware that my sensory processing was so out of whack if I had not undertaken to describe this on a daily basis. Using language allows relative understanding to become part of memory.

We often use the term "communication" when really we mean that we have observed in another human being a behaviour from which we derive meaning. So if my mother is deliberately angry with me to make a point to modify my behaviour, she is intending to communicate that anger. If she is angry [though she] does not mean to show it, but is so angry that her behaviour is indistinguishable from when she is acting her annoyance so I can get a message, that is a communication she did not intend to make. If she has enough self-control to wait until she is out of the room before she blows up, I don't receive the communication.

What is speech? I laugh to myself when the scientific community privileges our interaction over [that of] the animals. Perhaps the very complexity of the human brain makes us humans as a species having to work harder at abstract things. How can we say a sardine doesn't know the meaning of life? They don't necessarily become part of a silver flowing school by chance. To suggest that a cat doesn't know what death is would seem to be downright totally unobservant. But we big brained apes, because so much else is going on in our heads, have to work so hard at this, using different social construction to do so.

Where does this fit with the topic of vocabulary, autism, speech and communication? How much time have you got? I thought a lot of this out when I was writing *Lucy's Story,* and some of the descriptions I have used in this piece of writing are comments on the writing that went into creating Chapter 20 [of *Lucy's Story*]. As this was five years on from my experiencing these realisations, and now I am a further five years down the track, it is reasonable to think that I have changed again, and so I have!

Many of my stereotypical utterances have disappeared, though others have taken their place. In 1995 I wrote:

> In fact, the small amount of spontaneous speech I carry today had all been laid down before I was ten. That is, the basic words of my post-AIT speech were laid down at the age that I have been told that verbal autistic people develop speech. As a result the same things are tagged with the words that I used for them in my childhood world. For example, if I find my mother is packing clothes, I say "Camp" as a way of saying, "Where are we going now?" If I do something really nasty, and want to apologise, I say, "Better," which comes from being asked were things "better now" because "they" realised that often I was awful when distressed. That is, neither am I asking, "Are we going on camp?" or saying, "Things are better!" Rather, those words, "better" and "camp" have become meaningless sounds that are triggered by certain situations. [Presentation, Toowoomba, Queensland, 1995.]

I still cannot operate effectively in language or independent movement in the community without someone who is involved in most aspects of my life. That is, not only do I behave oddly and not interact when people need me to create a bridge so they can behave in an appropriate way to me, but also if there is not absolute certainty and a lack of ambient sound, I can't sequence. So places like supermarkets or even the street require a one-on-one companion.

I still have sudden changes in obsession and avoidance which assert themselves at the most inconvenient moments. For example, in the middle of doing an assignment which was worth a full semester's work for a postgraduate course, I suddenly had an irresistible compulsion to replace every noun with "that word," and every proper noun had to be struck out as soon as it was typed. As this assignment was already late due to cyclic immune problems, this is an autism issue which happens to spill into language, whether typed or spoken. That is, illness may appear as "behaviour," which makes any kind of achievement so difficult. That is one for the linguists. (Of course, ASD [Autism Spectrum Disorder] is a biological condition—can't help a little missionary work here.)

My dreadful fluctuating visual processing is a side effect of this unrecognised illness which I believe to be part of my autism. Although we have caught many of the worst aspects through vitamins, etc., the fluctuations in personality and performance will always be there. That is why physical "facilitation" is so useful, and I am often deeply sorry that in changing how I have made use of a keyboard, I can no longer use it (physical facilitation, that is). Long ago I thought this through, and I now believe that continuing touch which does not interfere with output is both therapeutic and also a help with creating a bond within the partner. After all it is very difficult for ordinary people to interact normally with us.

Some time after AIT, I wrote to Donna Williams [editor's note: see my references to Williams in Chapter 1; she is a person with autism who has written autobiographical as well as instructive accounts about autism] in answer to a question she had asked,

Auditory training has made some difference to my perception of sound and, though some changes were not massive, they allowed me to see some of the reasons for [problems with] both speech and initiation were completely sensory. . . .

The nearly intolerable loudness of some sounds died and the queer blanks diminished as the time passed. However a break in the way I distinguish speech remains, though it changed enough for me to be aware of it. That makes me totally understand what the fluctuations in pitch and processing problems mean. However there is more [yet] to change than has changed as the shifts are very slight.

The feeling that I have is that written language is real and spoken language a pit of misconception. AIT has cleared some of that up, but differences may be very slight as the reaction of each person [may be] less obvious than their internal comfort if that is augmented by changes in hearing.

The anger reported in some people [during the period after AIT] may (as happened with me) be partly due to a physical response that lasted a few weeks, and partly due to a false hope of a major and immediate change in competence as there is a real change in perception of oneself and the world. [Correspondence, 18 November 1992]

It was this improvement in problem solving which led to my typing in this way, that is without touch.

As I came to write more fluently, I learnt something particularly important. The speaking world expects abstract thought to be expressed in a way that readers and listeners can decode. The personal narrative is the most common framework for experiencing this, so here we go! I acquired language with words when I was fourteen. I had used spoken words in a way I don't consider to be language since I was a toddler. When I started to use typing, my speech continued to be more of a handicap than total muteness would have been.

> My speech really just bulges out of my mouth like a balloon, and the real thoughts in my head just keep on a direct line. The direct line and the balloon are related, but they do not correspond, and the more the balloon bulges, the less sense it makes, until it bursts, leaving all my thoughts scattered, and me wild with anger and shame. [9 July 1988, quoted in *Lucy's Story* (Blackman 1999, p. 135)]

That confused me an awful lot. Later I described this kind of thing.

> For example, for years I have used the spontaneous word, "Bertie!" to say how I feel. Although "Bertie" the word is flourishing, Bertie the long-haired dachshund dog has been dead for about fifteen years—a problem, as no one apart from my family remembers him. "Bertie" underpins several emotions, and the other person has to understand exactly what his link with the present is to be able to respond meaningfully.
>
> "Bertie!" I will snarl at [my mother] when I think she has been neglectful or unsympathetic towards anyone (not just me). She struggled unsuccessfully with Bertie's summer eczema for years before she had him put to sleep. I am simply having a memory-jerk into the mood that I personally was in when I saw him being led out of the door for the last time.
>
> "Bertie" is also my generic word for canine. That is the second use of the word. "D-o-g" is an exotic import which [in adulthood] has only recently come easily to my lips, though I had been taught it for many years. So if I see a dog, my mouth flaps, and I speak.
>
> "Bertie."

When I stand without distress, and gaze over a large walkway flooded with people and completely dogless, one would think that this should be a "Bertie"-free zone, but the furry long dog is still floating around somewhere in my speech processing.

"Bertie." My tone is interested, conversational even. Across the furthest corner I have spied a slightly built, dark-haired man with horn-rimmed glasses. What I am saying is, "Oh, is that Dad? No it can't be, but he is very similar to how Dad looked when I was small." This was true of course of how Dad was when Bertie, his little mate Alex and, for two brief enchanting seasons, luscious litters of sausage-shaped puppies competed with Dad's feet, [my mother's] discarded reading matter and us five girls for space in front of the gas heater. (This blasting warmth was almost silent to the rest, but bombarded me with hissing jets and continuous vibration from the fan.)

To understand the word "Bertie" in all its glory, one has to be an initiate. [Blackman 1999, pp. 44–45]

In 1992 when I underwent auditory integration training, there were a number of issues which arose out of AIT which are relevant. The first is that the practitioners who treated me asked me to keep a record. The thoughts that I wrote down for the first time were an account of my experiences which gave the "before and after" Lucy as a basis for comparison.

That is best illustrated by asking each reader to describe the cultural or emotional characteristics of their own sex, whether man or woman, without any reference to the opposite, not even by implication, as if you were completely unaware that there is another set of options available. If you are uncomfortable with this particular sort of difference, think instead of a kinship-based, preliterate society and an American academic meritocracy of the twenty first century, and compare the thought processes in either of a thirty-something woman asked to make a value judgement—that is not the moral basis, but the way in which the brain processes the decision. That is just an exercise in the kind of internal difference bound up in language processing—just an intellectual amusement aimed at "the rest of you," a reminder not to create meaning where none is meant. Autistic people aren't meant to find their therapists funny . . . but guess what!

When I had first learned of auditory training I had hoped it would enable me to make speech sounds comprehensible to both myself and others. I had thought that if people understood each word I spoke individually, I could build on this to make full and ·onventional sentences. I had assumed that unclear consonants were my major problem but now my reshuffling of the world briefly showed me possibilities in human life I had not dreamed. By this I mean that my entire environment had changed, and so I underwent a process of intellectual change as well.

I was beginning to realise that my understanding and processing of both spoken and visual language was far removed from that of other people. I was also beginning to wonder if this kind of thing resulted in part from how I had experienced my family in babyhood, distorted as that must have been by the discomfort of being embraced and the horrors of people looking at me or speaking to me.

That was because I had improved to some extent in how I processed other people's speech. Parallel to this I changed my understanding of what I should be hearing. So now I knew that words which were spoken to me should have far more impact on me, when in fact they still fluttered around fairly randomly. So I was more intolerant of other people's lost conversation, that is the way that people assumed I understood what they were addressing to me, especially if they looked at me in the face, which always makes me lose all auditory processing.

This made life very stressful. I could no longer simply sit and flap, or rock from foot to foot while being flooded with information in a kind of hit-and-miss manner, because now I automatically was starting to create coherent information from this sound maze. The sitting, flapping and rocking had made my body able to tolerate the flood of stimulation. However I can only do it when I feel well as I don't seem to have the co-ordination to process this comfort when I am ill.

I knew that I was not hearing some parts of voices other people found clear, and faces still occasionally decomposed, along with other focal points, and when that happened my embryonic understanding of what was happening could not prevent full terror sweeping in:

> I suspected I was even transposing some sounds from the moment at which they flowed from another person's lips. From my new way of looking at faces

when all was quiet and calm, I had learnt that mouth movements should invariably synchronise with spoken words, but that was not always so for me, even with my improved sensation. The sight of someone trying to be friendly, chatting away with the relationship between the features slightly awry, speech noises a little blurred, and having no idea myself at what instant my own feeling of anxiety would transform itself into a full panic was not new. I simply had not realised that most people did not have this experience. Now I recognised that there was a reason for my confusion, and consequently for my terror. [Blackman 1999, p. 276]

On those occasions that my real language processing problems in speech had been obvious even to me, I had assumed that the way I had not been able to make the words that others do in certain situations had been because of some lack of intelligence or a cognitive problem, because I could not see what I was doing wrong. Before AIT, when I tried to catch someone's attention spontaneously I usually said a descriptive word in the way most people would consider accurate only to ask for something.

For example, if the shower would only run cold, I would call out a single word (hot), without coming out of the cubicle to see if anyone had heard. "Ho'!" in that situation was asking my companion to make the water warmer, not saying it was too hot. (Unsurprisingly, most of the time I did not get a satisfying response). If the water ran too hot I might show my red skin to my mother, and say "dore" (sore) or "burn." For me a comment was always bound up with my own subjective experience, rather than an accurate description of something that had happened for someone's interest.

As soon as I started AIT, I had suddenly had a shift in my language perspective. The second night after I had started sessions of tortured reggae, my mother looked up to see me nude and dripping, looking at her.

"HoT!"

In that moment she only registered that I had sounded the final "T." She came to turn on the hot tap, and found the whole bathroom billowing steam. It was only later when I read her notes that I pointed out that I had said this word in a different sense from before. I was describing something accurately for someone else's information!

What I could not learn at nineteen, even though for the first time I could visualise it, was the requirement to describe the past, the non-meaningful and the invisible for the information of my partner, either by speech or typing. I am reconciled that this will never now happen. Language became explicable to me, but I did not burst into conversational speech. However [for a few weeks] I was just about bursting to speak, not just to say words of items which I wanted, but to converse in a reciprocal sense. This wasn't a learned skill but something like a biological urge that had developed two decades too late. Even ten years later I look at someone, and find my sensible words expelled as a single grunt. If I try to make speech, my mind goes blank—literally. This is one example of what Donna Williams calls "mono," an awful, catastrophic cause of misunderstanding what autism is all about.

[At the time] this made me think anew about how I had grown to adulthood without speech, because to me this new impulse looked very much like the social urge that my one year old nephew, Aaron, had developed. Because he learned to smile and babble, he and his family tossed this back and forward in even the most unconscious encounter, so that I could see the building blocks of language in place before he had the words with which to cement them.

I decided that my strange combination of sensory misinformation had somehow scrambled this urge when I was a toddler because when all this stuff happened now that I was an adult, I had some very real physical reactions that made me wonder even more about which comes first, ability to do something or the slow building of that ability by experience. Suddenly over those few weeks in 1992 I found my tongue moving in my mouth in some kind of mobile, lashing motion, with the normally bulbous tip pointed and cupped. Like my new gait and dexterity that were other side effects of these changes, this was a kind of interim effect. None of these made a lasting change in how I could interact with other people in a way that they understood, possibly because they were prerequisites for the skills I should have developed as a toddler.

When people had tried to make me enter into a conversation at school, or even at home, it had seemed to me to be for the amusement or pleasure of the other person. It usually was of no significance to me, except as a game of the peekaboo variety. As I got older, I had learned to extract information from conversations between other people, but as soon as they turned to me all meaning went from what they were saying. So I would (and still do) make the answer that experience had taught me made the exchange worthwhile as a social activity.

For example most people talk to a comparatively speechless person with a face shaped into a smile of comprehension, even if the answer does not make sense! So in my case I smile and look pleasant, and say "Yes," or echo. That may be quite the wrong response in terms of what I mean or want to say.

That is, the worthwhile social activity mentioned above takes place without, or rather at the expense of my being able to say what I mean.

On the other hand, if I speak the word "No," it is not the answer to the question, but may indicate that there is something very wrong with the whole situation. For example someone may ask a question.

"Do I need to go to the supermarket?"

"No!" I reply, because I wrongly believe the shops are closed, even though I know we have just run out of my favourite frozen popsicle. At that time I cannot change tracks to make an alternative suggestion either.

"Convenien' store," I will echo only if the other person had suggested this as an alternative, but otherwise I have no useful contribution to make. Meaning is bound up in what I think the [other] person wants to extract from my lips. I simply cannot negotiate by speech even now, though I do understand what is expected.

The non-handicapped person is really in a "no-win" situation, because what I always find, even today, is that any second attempt I make at using speech or at a socially based task even when using typing, is accompanied by problems in interfacing different time senses. So if I start to try to make things clearer, it only makes me confused as well.

Timing is always a problem, but it is worse when there is any noise, such as water in an air conditioner or another person breathing or wearing perfume.

Donna Williams has talked about how she can only handle one task at a time. To make conversations is not to use language. Unbelievable to say, it is a complex interaction which involves about twenty tasks on the part of each participant. Some of those are the flicker and blinking of appropriate eye contact, control of breathing or stance. Then there is the content. Is one intending to bring one's own interests to the exchange, or just to reinforce the interest of the other? Watching the rest of the world I see them combining these two techniques in, I think, a spectrum of exchanges. Then one has light, noise, and the unpleasant thought that one is sharing one's thoughts, and that in the head of the other party they will be slightly different.

Thought is easier however. To think intellectually one has to use words. Temple Grandin thinks in pictures. I have substituted printed words and phrases for pictures. That is, I see a label which is related to the item, intellectually or in memory. That relationship is not "rational" but sensory or some kind of sound- or time-shift which links with the printed image in my head.

Back in 1992 I was just working this out, and my diary shows I was only scratching the surface. I typed, "Very strange things start when I try to express anything in words whether spoken or typed without facilitation. The intention gets lost in a welter of unknown impulses that are likely to take over."

If I were asked a straightforward question like what did I want for lunch, which is a much simpler concept than "Do we need to go to the supermarket?" I was beginning to make pretty exact one-word answers. However often I had to admit failure, because my mother simply could not understand what I was saying.

I was also now making sudden spoken syllables to occasional words as I typed them. So we decided to try making me speak the words as I typed so that I could see the reason that I should make certain mouth movements. We had seen only too clearly from my counting and chanting in ball games that my speaking in imitation of the other person made things worse rather than better.

> Jay [as Blackman noted above, this is the name she uses for her mother in *Lucy's Story*] started to get me to use a couple of tennis balls to get me to focus on my left and right hands.
>
> The ball left her hand.
>
> "Catch-and-throw!" I chanted, in memory slotting into playing with Jenny and Kim. The ball flew from my hand vaguely into the quadrant where I knew Jay would retrieve it.

"Do concentrate, Lu! You threw more accurately than that in PE at school." She tossed it back at me, and my cupped hands gathered it to my chest.

"Now," said Jay. "Think about what you are doing. Which is your right hand? Yeah. . . ?" sarcastically, as I put the left one up. "Try again!"

I fixed the word "right" onto the hand I type with, and which I knew perfectly well was pronounced that way, and raised it. The ball by now had dropped to the floor. There had been no extra hand to hold it.

"Right!" said Jay, confusing herself almost as much as me. "Pick up the ball in your right hand," nodding. "That's right. Now throw—wait for me to finish!—throw to my left hand," and she raised the hand opposite my own raised right hand. The ball flew vaguely towards it.

"That's fantastic!" said my uncoordinated, sans-ball-skills parent. From her I accepted this as real praise, unlike how I had wrongly assumed that teachers had been talking condescendingly to me when I had shown confusion in chucking projectiles at school. Also I realised what an effort this was for her. She was not only disinterested in most sport, but visibly curled up inside when people produced even a beach ball at a barbecue.

Ball to me—fine—then ball to her. Nothing new about this. Of course, I had heard people say how good this kind of thing is for co-ordination. What these well-intentioned, enthusiastic rationalists had never realised was that I had had no idea what co-ordination was. The fuzzy and overlapping limits to my body had seemed to have a life of their own. As the New Me reached for that virulently yellow-coloured, fluffy ball, I now saw why. I could see multiples of both fingers and palm as I stretched. In some way, probably because I was not fighting to maintain my place in space when I sat or stood, I was aware of this phenomenon consciously for the first time. Maybe also it was slightly improved. As I moved bits of me through space, I had slightly more understanding of what was happening, and my hands made movements that were in some ways more in sync with what I was trying to achieve.

Jay's voice would snap.

"To left!"

"To right!"

And occasionally I was told, "Both together!" So strange to find my cupped hands not just wrapping round the ball, but my fingers starting to move, each as co-operative as a strand of sea-anemone.

I also started to nominate which side the ball was to be aimed. The first time Jay looked clucky in a proud-mother kind of way, and the second she beamed like a Cheshire Cat, which she certainly did not resemble—more like Hobbes of Calvin and Hobbes fame, I would say, endlessly floating along in the trail of my enthusiasm.

She was not very impressed though when my speech-urge lost all contact with the reality of the situation. Whatever improvements Auditory Integration Training had made to movement, hearing and behaviour, the Old Lucy pathways between speech, excitement, fear and obsessions had been so deeply planted that they were to sprout again and again at the slightest encouragement.

The link between word and movement loosened.

"Le, righ," popped from my mouth in a chant. My catching was suddenly frantic, and drowned in the repetition rather than catching with any kind of focus on the task of concentrating on left and right when instructed to do so. Nevertheless, we went on doing this kind of thing, but Jay would cut me short whenever I started to spin out into my own world.

I learnt to bounce balls with the hand that she nominated, and throw them into the air and catch with the same hand. However we found that I simply could not throw a ball from hand to hand, unless one of those hands was nearly the centre of how I saw my body. Even then letting go of the ball was terrifying. I would pass it from hand to hand unless Jay screamed encouragement and extravagant praise at me. I was not aware that I could not track the ball across the midline. When it moved into that area, it disappeared momentarily, and I think my visual memory had to reinvent it. That was not such a problem inside or in enclosed spaces, but chaos still lurked in the wider world. [Blackman 1999, p. 250–252]

We had got into the habit by now of my mother holding the keyboard of the computer as a palette and with some eye contact between us. This made it easier to make typing into conversation practice. The collection of letters came from my finger and, as soon as Jay was sure of the exact word, she would speak it so, if possible, I could model it orally before I had lifted my finger from the last letter. Over-optimistically I was determined that I could, and indeed had to, learn to match what I understood my spoken language to be to my typed language. For the first time I did hear my own full language from my own lips. However I never managed to follow through with more than one word at a time.

What had happened in the time before I made any connection between words and writing? Somehow there is something very odd about my sound-memory. I think that is possibly a result of auditory processing differences. (Note: I don't say "auditory processing difficulties." The word "difficult" means that I would be trying to do something that I understood to be a possibility. However I simply live in a world that has completely different sounds.)

For example, I sit in front of the television. It splutters and the electrical field hums slightly. That fluctuates, depending on how tired I am, what I have eaten, what colours the room is decorated in, if any petrochemical is used in bonding the carpet, etc. Then there are other sounds. The sea at least a mile away, that car going past, the other person in the room breathing, the dog puttering about. These all—particularly the air noises—fluctuate at different rates.

The way that I made the word-connection in childhood was not by what a word related to, because each time I heard a word it was not connected to the sounds on each side of it, and of course each time the word was sounded in my presence did not mean that I heard it. Only the memory of Lucy's feeling was constant, so a phrase I heard clearly in one context was tagged forever to my emotion on that occasion.

That is why I would chant "Just Jeans" again and again. I could link my mouth movement to a sound that I understood, and that related to a strong positive emotion. That is because I adored denim. As a child I could make patterns with the diagonal weave, and the stitching on the pockets and hems was totally symmetrical. Denim was constant, calming and undemanding. I loved it.

Birthdays were happy, exciting, chaotic, and connectional with food—the ultimate source of pleasure—so excitement was a birthday party. But excitement, terror and fury are very similar emotions, so I still scream "birthday party" when expectations are more than I can cope with.

The old me (pre-AIT) had lived totally drowned in sound. I realised this because I now had a basis for comparison. However in most situations my family and friends saw little change. I became aware that my rudimentary attempts at speech were most effective in a quiet environment, not very useful in a room where there were two or more people, and very basic in such places as shopping centres, or in fact any of the places that one would be expected to go to meet with other people.

That made me realise that my vocalisations were responsive to sound input. I realised also that the spontaneity with which I started any action, my initiation, was progressively less under each of these conditions. I was distressed because this seemed to indicate that although I had changed a lot I was always going to seem very odd in the very places where I wanted to be accepted.

At home when we had no fans on, now my body was much more comfortable so I was more relaxed and alert, with fewer odd movements. However in other places, especially in busy environments with forced air-heating or cooling and other small motor noises such as computers, I was often distressed, and my behaviour was rather erratic and even slightly threatening towards people whose speech I still found confusing to my new form of processing, even university lecturers [Blackman 1999, p. 275].

I had been so swamped in sound that I could not bring short-term memory and language together. In places like shopping malls I reverted to asking for food that I associated with that kind of interaction, but this was less a request for what I really wanted to eat as a memory process. I had to make do with what I had pre-programmed, much as the way I would ask for a hamburger if I saw a McDonald's.

I learned this was involuntary the day we were standing on a pedestrian crossing in sight of the big gold M. We were talking about where we would have lunch, and I typed, "PLEASE DON'T LET ME MAKE YOU GO TO MCDONALD'S!" As I got to "the M word," my voice cut in and I declaimed "McDonal'!!" while physically tugging at my bewildered companion so forcibly that we ended through the sliding doors and in the line of surf-crazy youngsters almost before she was aware of it, and certainly before she could begin to analyse her own responses.

It was the first time I had seen clearly how often my obsession overcame what I really wanted to do. Previously I had believed it was just a matter of self control.

I often still make a statement by answering an unasked question. For example, something alarms me. I assume in my mind that my companion is my anchor. My mind creates an unspoken question from the other person.

"Is something worrying you?"

"Yes!" I should then say (but do not).

"Don't worry!" my imaginary mentor should have answered.

My mouth flaps suddenly in the first sound of this unspoken interchange.

"Don't worry!" This other person has spoken with my mouth, much to the confusion of whoever is standing beside me, and who had provided me with the puppet for this shadow play.

That is almost as if I am making an imaginary documentary. But then, as I said at the beginning, I see language as an interesting phenomenon which does not always relate to me in all my senses.

Note

1. Editor: Auditory integration training is a procedure that is supposed to help individuals with autism overcome hypersensitivity to certain sound frequencies. Cohen describes the procedure: "In AIT a child or adult listens to modulated music through headphones for two half-hour periods a day over ten days, with certain sound frequencies filtered out. Why this should result in improved functioning is not clear. Berard believed that AIT enabled a person to adapt to intense sounds, but many other explanations have been proposed" (Cohen 1998, p. 141).

References

Blackman, L. (1999) *Lucy's story: Autism and other adventures.* Redcliffe, Queensland, Australia: Book in Hand.

Cohen, S. (1998). *Targeting autism.* Berkeley: University of California Press.

Ozick, C. (2003). Doubting Helen Keller. *New Yorker,* June 16 and 23, pp. 188–196.

5

■　　■　　■　　■　　■　　■　　■　　■　　■

I. An Introduction to Larry Bissonnette

I first met Larry Bissonnette in 1993. He had come to Syracuse to participate in an interview with an NBC reporter on a show about autism and communication. Since then I have gotten to know Larry through his writing and his art and at conferences on autism. He is an accomplished painter whose work has appeared in a number of galleries and is referenced in an outsider art compendium (Sellen 2000). In late January 2003, I viewed several of his paintings at the annual New York Outsider Art Fair on Houston Street in Manhattan.

When we met in 1993, Larry was thirty-six years old. He had spent ten years, from the age of eight, in the Brandon Training School, a mental retardation institution in Vermont that has since closed. For a time he was also incarcerated at the Vermont Psychiatric Hospital at Waterbury. He currently lives with his sister in Winooski, Vermont. He has autism, but over the years he was also variously classified as mentally retarded, schizophrenic, and clinically insane (Bissonnette n.d). During his youth, psychologists tested and judged him as moderately retarded. It was not until he was in his mid-thirties that he began to learn a reliable way of communicating, by typing. He does his typing with an assistant, most often Pascal

Cravedi-Cheng, sitting next to him resting a hand on his shoulder. As Larry types, Pascal occasionally draws Larry's attention to a phrase that may be unclear or to a word that appears to be out of place. He continues to hold a hand on Larry's shoulder, but frequently lifts it off the shoulder as Larry continues to type without support. Larry finds that Pascal's hand on the shoulder helps him keep focused on the typing.

Up until the time when he learned to communicate by typing, Larry Bissonnette had to rely on his limited speech and what he revealed through his paintings. His speech has been described as coming out "garbled, in ferocious repetition, or not at all" (Bissonnette n.d.). My own observation of his speech is that sometimes it is echoed, such that he says a phrase (e.g., "Out of here. Get out of here" or "Who broke it? Who broke it?") several times over. And sometimes he will say a word that relates to a topic such as eating. But with speech, he cannot carry on a conversation. His writing, by contrast, is rich in visual images and often leaves me trying to unpack it, as if reading poetry, to understand his points. Invariably, it is an engrossing and enjoyable experience, for even when conveying a feeling of anger and frustration, Larry's images and vocabulary are captivating. And his turns of phrase often have a distinctly humorous quality to them.

In addition to the NBC news program in which he was interviewed, Larry's artwork has been displayed at galleries and was featured on a CNN report in 2000.

In October 2002, Larry addressed a conference of the National Autism Committee (Autcom) at its annual meeting. In the address, he spoke about "Things That Matter" (Bissonnette 2002a). He wrote and then displayed this narrative to an audience of professionals, parents, and other people with autism:

> Spending money means little unless nearing easiest to say food order in restaurant, McDonald's, is coming soon. Cash leads towards rewards of the stomach. Casting teepee posts of happiness in the ground of slaves to big accounts will never make your life better. Nurturing relationships, contact with attractive woodworking artists, rate as more appealing options for Easterner, long on senses for enjoyment in life. It's not something you can buy or get lane assignments or raffle tickets for.

Palatial, with work sorted by size, studio space is also needed to let me do art in comfortable surroundings like a librarian putting books away in a lofty ceilinged, well lit, tall shelved, frescoed, round room. Most people need video games and elegantly tailored clothes to survive in this hysterically peculiar time of war and stock market dives into collapsible tents of bankruptcy. Larry has more ordinary requirements for necessities of life. Promises to not change my obstinately held to routines are criminally the straws that shouldn't be broken. Pass the basket first for McDonald's change and there slides away preparations you will have to make to please me. (Bissonnette 2002a)

After his presentation, which included a display and explanation of some of his artwork, Larry answered questions from the audience. One person asked when he had begun his art. To this, he typed that his art was an early development, in part as a reaction to his having extremely limited speech: "Larry began painting keeping busy as powerless to communicate young child." Writing about his art, Larry says, "Tapping well of silence with painting permitted songs of hurt to be meted with creativity" (in Lippard 1998). And where did he start his painting and drawing? Text in a brochure featuring his artwork reads, "Bissonnette has always manifested an irrepressible creativity. He was drawing prolifically at age five. At BTS [Brandon Training School] he often jimmied his way into the locked workshop to draw, paint and build through the night" (Bissonnette n.d.). At the Autism National Committee conference, he replied to a question about his early art, saying it began in earnest at the "[n]asty residential better for growing vegetables rather than people Brandon Training School." In a presentation at Syracuse University in 2002, Larry referred to this time at Brandon as "[m]y leap into the pond of painting" (Bissonnette 2002b). He describes his art as a way of participating with the nondisabled world: "Knowledge and learning of art have allowed my abilities to soar out on an airfield occupied by people who don't have disabilities" (Bissonnette 2002b).

Larry paints mainly in acrylics on thin boards as well as on canvas. He paints with his hands: "Creation of dramatic painting starts each time in the movement of fingers on sopping, greatly malleable, gobs of paint" (Bissonnette 2002b). He paints at a rapid pace, working in a second-floor studio in an industrial building. At one end of the studio there is a wall of windows, giving good natural light for his work. At the other, windowless end of the studio, he has dozens upon dozens of his finished works waiting for display at galleries and in art exhibits. He personally saws rough-hewn wood strips for frames.

In this chapter, Larry Bissonnette narrates his art, using an image-rich and distinctive writing style. When he first drafted the account, I wrote back to Larry and met with him at his art studio to talk about specific passages where I needed clarification on his meaning. He then reworded certain passages. I suspect that readers of these accounts will find that in some instances they take considerable contemplation to understand. Yet I believe that readers will have some of the same reactions I do to Larry's art and his narration; reading the passages can be engrossing and uplifting, even when the message is stark. As Larry says in his commentary of the work titled "Seeing Eye Friend Felicia . . . ," his writing can put even his friends in the "role of interpreters extraordinaire."

■　■　■　■　■　■　■　■　■

II. Letters Ordered through Typing Produce the Story of an Artist Stranded on the Island of Autism

Larry Bissonnette

Title: Pell Mell Mainland of Rolling Fortress of Monastery
of Brandon Training School, Vermont (1987)

Commentary: Noontime lunches at nicest restaurant in New York City lose their appeal in treatments by worst chefs of awfully tasteless fast food, dealt with comatose preparation, snack bars. Lopping of roaring brooks of individuality by institution is really like making meals out of McDonald's recipes.

Going back in desolation where it's only me and letterless walls is not pleasant to think about. Nothing "apartheids" you like the insensitive world of institutional existence. It's politically correct to say that kind, needing gratification for giving people started impetus for building structurally sound, not yet humane institutions.

Let me mention that it's practically getting possible to create satisfying life, interesting and meaningful nowadays because really institutions' popularity slides towards storage underground at a pace faster than police chasing stepping for escape prisoners.

Title: Larry Bissonnette As A Youth Living In DC Comic World Of Brandon (1990)

Commentary: Toes sadly squish into tight shoes. So did autistic residents in not teased in lustrous colors dorms at Vermont's institution in Brandon.

My leap into the pond of painting happened there [Brandon Training School]. Knowledge and learning of art have allowed my abilities to soar out on an airfield occupied by people who don't have disabilities.

Title: Old time portrait style kicks out attractive but lightweight new age pattern of putting appearances before fitness of spirit (1997)

Commentary: Traditional less imaginative portraiturers approach painting to make money. Naturalistic Larry isn't striving for profit, just passes to McDonald's and elegantly decorated but positioned tastewise to feed steak eaters like Larry restaurants.

Title: Placement of photo is perfectly aligned with nothing (1998)

Commentary: It provides cartoonlike casting of images in realistic and dated for essential age setting. Answers really to aesthetic value of work aren't written in magazines of specialty art but in already directed for getting most out of life thinking of spiritually responsive autistic people.

Title: Very pale Ray, temporary roommate (circa 1992)

Commentary: My pent-up time in tested for learning patterns of best behavior institution wasn't entirely greys; it offered personal periods of great relationships with friends with disabilities.

Title: Seeing Eye Friend Felicia in gathering
of my very canned together speech (circa 1993)

Commentary: Larry's somewhat bastardization of English language puts friends in the
role of interpreters extraordinaire.

Title: Lack of light restraining emergence of artist's vision (1996)

Commentary: Leaping into stream of creativity prepares artist for partnering technique
with passion and dramatic vision of malleable for beauty real world. Same beam of en-
lightened belief in artist's ability as is shown on president of a nation is required.

Title: Paints get really loused up by my signature so
both art and letters learn to cohabitate (1997)

Commentary: Powered print treats painted images well as long as colors Larry selects match. Larry loves pink and purple because pressured painter gets to lighten stroke.

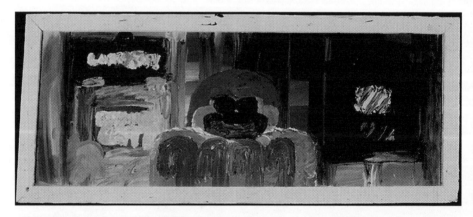

Title: Plenty of art very like modern man doesn't stress high issues of morality so praise me for telling stories shining colorfully over northern skies (1997)

Commentary: It's possible today, practically past necessary to paint rhythmically with sound of dollar bills exchanging hands with passionate for clichéd images of pretty people public. Also, eating out at fancy restaurants is appetising side benefit for starving artist. Larry owns eating record at McDonald's so meal payments are kind of satisfying an already full stomach.

Title: Massively added on with tons of entirely empty of people windows house looks less imposing if walls are painted in papal reds and windows are decorated with acutely marketed for staring into curtains (2000)

Commentary: Larry leads an existence which promotes passion for colorfully patterned, open to attractions in environment like smokestacks. Past life of institutionalized person lets in novel ideas. Outsiders to this life can't go out and obtain it. It's significant that my artistic style lets me express personal perspectives of autistic but intelligent old Vermonter.

Title: Sameness of picnic shelters positioned in parks created for personal enjoyment of summertime family life takes satisfaction of practicality and blends it with Larry's personal drawing style (2000)

Commentary: Slowed down pattern of summer picnicked leisure time always lets Larry relax, dreaming of delicious barbecues and parties with salvaged from grind of work family members.

Title: Landlocked pool, palefaced Vermonters,
spreadable blankets promise Floridian experience (2000)

Commentary: Larry's pale complexion elementally owes its darkening redness to pool-side sitdowns on camping, you better sleep on slabs of lean mattresses trips.

Title: Bird would violate airline dapper standards for appearance but the skies sport vivider dayglo colors when it can fly freely and uncensored by mankind (1998)

Commentary: Producing art is like making puppets on strings because massive edges of inspiration in creating graspable figures get constricted by people's patterned control of sticks put on strings. Not allowing people with disabilities their patterns of inspiring art through total freedom of expression is like limiting creativity with censorship.

Artists like Larry urgently make situations of doing art into large statements; occupying worlds of public awareness; calling for justice for people without speech; praying for true freedom of splashing language over pricey spreads in people beautiful but superficial magazines; mowing down stereotypes of disability and leaving people speechless over power of brushed on with wild, outside the mainstream ideas, steeped in the tradition of autistic compulsivity.

Title: Larry looks like latter day, rather rooted in routines of catholic church, saint. Massive miracle if acceptable behavior for a saint ever gets achieved (1999)

Commentary: My claiming of sainthood involves order of control over Larry's impulsive and relationship battering behaviors. Total immersion in priestly work plays well in roles of truly normal people but can't if a person moves the way I do, touching poles with his nose and talking in peaked off the charts grunts and yells.

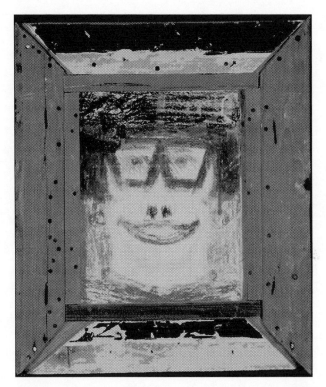

Title: Aunt Theresa Rings in Her Eyes Pizzazz (circa 1988)

Commentary: Look up early lessons in learning about my struggles to communicate and determination of others to make me learn to eat neatly and talk clearly was really most important factor in my rostering of skills. I am seriously past learning swimming in the shallow end of the pool of language but I am ever told "can do" words by others like Aunt Theresa and that is the sled that pushes me to accept excellence over languishing in mediocrity.

Title: Mansions rescued from demolition crews
by historically preservative nature of art (1996)

Commentary: My muralistic lettered view of life is stimulated not by likenesses of reality
but by intuitions of plentiful feelings and sensations.

Creation of dramatic painting starts each time in the movement of fingers on sopping, greatly malleable gobs of paint.

References

Bissonnette, L. (n.d.) *Constructions and personal insights*. West Glover, VT:
G.R.A.C.E. (RFD Box 49, West Glover, VT 05875).

——— (2002a). Things that matter. Paper presented at the 2002 Autism National
Committee Conference, Nashua, New Hampshire.

——— (2002b). Letters ordered through typing produce the story of an artist
stranded on the island of autism. Paper presented at the Narrating dis/Ability
Conference, Syracuse University, Syracuse, New York.

Lippard, L. R. (1998). *States of grace*. Hardwick, VT: G.R.A.C.E. (P.O. Box 960,
Hardwick, VT 05843).

Sellen, B. (with Johanson, C. J.) (2000). *Outsider, self taught, and folk art annotated bibliography*. Jefferson, NC: McFarland.

6

■　■　■　■　■　■　■　■　■

I. An Introduction to Alberto Frugone

Alberto Frugone was born on November 25, 1978. When he was four, his mother moved from the north of Italy to Rome. In Milan, when he was two and a half years old, he was diagnosed as having "infantile autism." Even in the early 1980s, it was not uncommon in Italy that a child with the label of autism would be referred for psychotherapy, as the dominant view at that time in Italy was that autism was a psychiatric disorder. Alberto refers to this period of treatment as "a great loss of time." In Rome, he received an additional diagnosis of "psychomotor retardation and autism." In Italy, any child with a disability was entitled to be included with nondisabled students in a regular class in a regular school. Thus Alberto's mother was able to enroll him in an inclusive classroom, where he remained until he was three years old. She then transferred him to a special school where he felt contained but not educated:

> I was sort of a piece of furniture in the classroom. I was engaged in senseless occupations all day long. I was unreachable. Nobody knew what to do with me. I was quiet; I knew how to behave; I was a clean child and I was able to eat by myself. All these things I learnt at home. Apparently a special school

had no special programs for an autistic child already trained to basic activities. (Personal communication)

When he was nine years old, Alberto and his mother moved back to Zoagli in the north of Italy. He entered another special school.

I first learned of Alberto in the spring of 1992, when his mother wrote to me about her interest in finding a way for Alberto to communicate. It was then that he began to communicate through typing. He became independent in his typing five years later. Nearly as soon as he began sentence-level communication, he asked his mother to withdraw him from the special school and to prepare him at home to take fifth-grade exams. She complied with his request and he soon passed the exams. Despite the fact that he was by then fourteen years old, he enrolled in junior high school; his classmates were younger than he, but he was in the process of catching up on the education he had missed. He subsequently enrolled in and finished the *Liceo,* comparable to high school.

Alberto wrote this next chapter in Italian. I then had it translated into English. At several places in the text, I found myself confused by Alberto's meanings, and so wrote to him for explanations. Alberto's mother, Patrizia Cadei, is fluent in English as well as Italian, and so she was able to act as a translator when I wrote out my questions. Alberto then composed his responses that she translated. Later, I traveled to Italy to interview Alberto in person and to complete the process of clarifying what he had written.

■　　■　　■　　■　　■　　■　　■　　■　　■

II. Salient Moments in the Life of Alberto, as a Child, a Youth, a Young Man

Alberto Frugone

I was a child fighting sensorial distortions, attracted by light's double spell, which altered reality made of perspectives that seemed to have been put there for me to play with. One could say that the light opened vivid rifts between shapes; I would say that the alternation of light and dark was magical. I was emotionally serene because the light was sending back precious dimensions that would give me the desire for stimuli that I certainly received from ritualistic, loving, and unequivocal maternal care. I was often mesmerized by the serenity without which a child doesn't know how to grow inside; I take my mom by her hand and I imagine the regret of Bettelheim[1] for not having the mother he searched for.

Unfortunately I could not even respond with lallation; I tried hard to mimic the sounds, in particular to answer to the environment, but I had no success. I remember that I was especially disoriented by the revisiting of faces that afterwards I was doing in my mind. I lacked the natural pre-suppositions with which to evaluate different facial expressions.

When I was out in the world, I was too scared to look around and to judge what I was seeing. The syllogism of the world outside my home did not allow me to repeat the images in my mind; the routes were always changing, whereas inside the house I did not have this problem, because I had memorized the position of objects. I was able to think serenely at home, connecting all the images together, I had more references.

At that time I was two or three years old and I was very dependent for everything, but I did have feelings, receptivity to what was going on around me, and thoughts.

I could read but without giving any meaning to my readings. Actually I was playing with the rules of writing. I liked to read and I went constantly from one side of the paper to the other seeing the words as only visual emotions. After having read and memorized whatever text, I processed with my visual perception the shape of a simple word, arranging the consonants—of course I didn't know at that time they were consonants—like C or S in clusters from right to left. The symmetries thus obtained, gave me wonderful visual animations. I drew shapes by observing the words. For example the Italian word "letta" is a bisyllabic word that goes up and down, to me a motif inside a blot. Every type of regular shape fascinated me. For example, I liked to compare two words similarly written, like the words "aereo" and "aria." Remember that at that time I didn't know the meaning of those two words, I just played with their shapes. This is something I used to do but don't do it any longer.

When my mother was reading to me a fairytale book—I was then six or seven years old—there were pictures and words in it. I used to find rigorous rules in the passages that were read to me, making similarities among them, but most of all educating myself to activate my logic, directing it to exercise comparisons.

Advice for Teachers of Young Children with Autism

If I go back in my mind to questions pertaining to nursery school [attended until Alberto was six years old], I wanted to suggest some ideas to follow that would have enabled me to play, but on the outside I only appeared to be an idler. I could not connect with the right movements to put, for example, certain blocks in a container. Were I a teacher, I'd be very patient with an autistic child and educate him to a gradual passage in which words are pronounced and shown by the teacher in connection to a picture. If this becomes a routine, the child will be able to use the written words to make a sentence and become aware that he can read despite the fact that he doesn't speak.

My teachers demanded only that I color. Instead, they should have made me practice doing things, such as giving, taking or finding. I was interested in learning.

Learning Praxis

I must picture actions before doing them. PICTURE = to visually represent them in my mind. It is efficacious for me to observe someone performing an action and then I can try to do it but with facilitation. It's necessary for me to gain real experience. While trying to perform an action, even if my gestures are difficult, I obtain valid practice. But it has to be a practical, contextual action not an artificial situation.

Even today, actions can be difficult. A scene could be: I'm in the car, sitting near my mother who is driving. It is hot; we should open the window. Technically I know how to open it: on the dashboard there's the button to raise and lower the window. I can describe the action: I must push the button with my finger. But my hesitation grows while I try to put together the sequences to go through the action. I mentally review all the necessary steps, but the first one simply doesn't come out. I'm trapped. To help the child with autism, verbally give me the sequences and facilitate me while I try to organize myself! But of course mum doesn't know what I want. How could she? She doesn't read my mind! Unable to move, the only thing that comes out instead is a stereotyped movement that eventually consists of a reassuring thumb in the mouth or four fingers quickly flapping in front of my eyes.

Connecting What Is Heard to the Printed Word, and Making Sense of Printed Shapes

My ears remained resilient in the face of sounds bent on disorienting me; it was easy to smile inside to myself constantly playing with pictures that I invented, a private learning inside myself.[2] I heard the songs seconds after they came to my ear. I had to process the rhythm. And the rhythm and sounds and voices were abnormal; it was necessary to "clean" them. I was compelled to exclude the possibility to experiment with a direct hearing of words—too confusing. So I would hear them and memorize them in order to clean them through a reviewing process.

I was mute, but filled with true internal voices that I had memorized, dialogues and even short discussions picked up from television. I was helped in this regard by the fact that then, as well as now, I could exclude sounds and slowly put my attention to the selection of auditory perception. I selectively turned off the hearing, inhibiting language that then I memorized. I knew very well how to pass from a stage in which I could decant my hearing to a stage of non-memorization, easily balancing these faculties in my mind.

Where strange words slipped out [from others' voices or from songs, for example] I tried to decipher them using terms previously heard. I remember the word "icon" dancing inside me, floating while I was playing with it. Perhaps I laughed at the singsong created by the silent repetition of the word: iconiconiconicon. The autistics are really handicapped: strange phenomenon it must be to silently "feel" the meaning of a word. Granted that I was not considered a phenomenon by anybody because nobody knew what I was experiencing—the fantasy of a crazy mind filled with thoughts—at that time. Finally, the meaning I gave icon? Madonna.

Now, almost automatically I try to deduce the meaning of a new word by defining at first the meaning of the whole sentence. I study the etymology of the word in relation to what I think is the meaning of the sentence. For example, the sentence: "the doctrine of labour subverts some values and lies to the workers." I think that "lies" has a connection with "subverts," so I sense something negative. The prefix "sub" takes something away, while "verts" (which in Italian is "vertere = to put into order"), must have a positive meaning that "sub" diminishes.

I used empathy efficiently, and still do, to learn. I define empathy as the homeostatic reflection of thought. Reality is fast, especially for me. To process information means to work on it rationally and promptly. Instead I have to work by selectively putting in relation to each other ideas and facts, without anxiety. Reality around me was not something moving at a pace that is too fast, neither was I processing it too quickly, simply it was hard for me to interpret the situations in the real world because immediately anxiety got in the way. Now I have learnt how to manage this, but one thing that makes me extremely anxious is trying to do things spontaneously. For example, I'm about to ask someone for something, making mental note of various facts, but many times I have to let go of my intention because the time limitation seizes up my brains. It is not a matter of organizing my thoughts. Rather, I lose the opportunity because questions are expressed too quickly and require a quick answer. Sometimes I feel really lost.

The elements of my world as a child, were my psychologically restricted thoughts. I used to give irrational answers to questions, based on distorted sensations. For example, I hold my mother's hand. My mom now lets go and begins to throw me a ball. I might have thought that it was a useful suggestion, a good exercise, but then it proved to be dreadful because, not liking to touch anything, I became wooden when thinking of touching something with my hands. Besides, not being able to act quickly, my only response was to engage in a stereotype. I knew it was dissociation, and suddenly I felt insecure while silently I fought with the gestures (i.e., movements). At that time I was dissociated from the facts around me and I had a hard time making sense of the practical elements of daily life.

I felt I had no elementary life experience. I was in an enigmatic relationship with my emotions and often I was quivering with anxiety because of this. But I felt a loving pressure to unite body and soul. I thought: if I don't teach my body to educate its expression then the matter will be serious because my thought alone is too despotic and restraining. But I also felt the "machine" inside me. I "observed" the ideas (those put into practice by the others), torn, without fabricated tracks to follow. What I called "my powers" was actually my hope to obtain practical actions without passing through the homologation of my body. [Editor's note: Here Alberto refers to his belief in his early years that he possessed special powers to mentally cause actions to happen. He discusses this further in a subsequent section, "A Private World of Fantasy."]

The Difficulty of Matching Action and Events with Purpose

How to accomplish an intentional action, this is a fifty thousand dollar question. For example, sometimes I wanted to follow mother in the street, in her walking. But then, once out, I found that everything around seemed precarious to me. I looked beyond my own stereotyped movements and I did not understand the logic that motivated her going. To me, not understanding a course of action before doing it meant I felt in need of being led by the hand. As far as being able to do things after they were shown to me ahead of time, I could not repeat an action simply by having seen it. I could make a picture of it in my head, but I could not put it physically into motion. I could not show my actions as I saw them in my mind and, consequently, I ended up withdrawing from actions, not using my reasoning anymore, not wanting to feel a strong and an unacceptable silence. Right from the beginning of an action, I was conscious of my inability to access motor planning and I was lost in an unacceptable motor "silence."

Other times I hesitated on doing things because, not knowing their purpose, clumsy as I am, my actions ended up in the wrong way and I was afraid of being considered stupid. Depending absolutely on another person, even for playing, made me addicted to this fear [of being considered stupid]. This had detrimental effects. Today I would say I experience the same fear if I'm insecure when I type to communicate and I feel a lack of tolerance from the others who might mistake me for stupid.

Regarding knowing the purposes of particular actions at that time, I was reasoning well about my needs, for example to demand to eat only smashed food, to require absolutely a bath every evening, and to insist it was me who decided when it was time to sleep. But, not being able to coordinate with sensorial feelings, stimuli, and images, I elaborated illogically the activities outside of these: mountains of practical moments—time to go out, time to dress, time to rush, you need shoes to walk out, it's hot I should take off my coat, and so on. For example, I focused intently only on a part of a person, or on a certain bent chair not on the straight one. Also, it was difficult for me to organize the shifting from one sense to another.

And Now?

Being able now to modify the film that I project in my mind with measured, ordered ties and with a greater capability of judgment, I put together facts that I have learned, my illogical sensory processes and laborious mental mechanisms. I have memories of that time, as a child, when I was unstable on my legs. I knew that I did not have to tremble, and looking at my mom I discarded the idea of falling on the ground because I suddenly felt strong. It was a joy for me to find the courage to go around by myself or to learn how to climb stairs by myself, and to make decisions to be independent.

Now, [as a young adult] I use a film, i.e. a pre-ordered projection, sometime to determine a real future action, something that I have to do. Now I can accept modifications, required by real situations encountered, to what I have imagined and ordered in a film. Yet, for example, it hasn't been necessary to prepare a film for the impending trip to Como, for I must feel a specific necessity to make a film now. A film is not always needed, because now I can adapt myself much better to the events. Now, the situation that would require a film in the mind has to be an occasion that worries me, for example if I know that I will meet a "certain" girl.

As for school routines, I learned to manage them empirically, torn inside myself, a person at the beginning so refractory to remain seated and attentive. I was a complying subject in a confusing situation, as a noisy classroom can be. But I have advantageously adjusted myself over time, improving my attention span in such a way that now I can say all the best about my school presence.

But are there opportunities to converse with other students? Dear me! I'd like to be able to give a hand to my schoolmates, mostly girls, but, definitively, there's no time for such a thing: we pass from one lesson directly to the other and no hope to drink my juice if I start a conversation during recreation! Usually I do not express opinions about my schoolmates. Let me do it now: a few of them are "frogs," but some others are really special.

On Words and Speaking

I became a youth, suddenly growing up from the world of pretense to the world of when I decided timidly to tell myself "now I will show I am able to speak!" It seemed alarming to me not to be able to talk, even though my actions frequently ratified my internal reasoning, and even though I received, for these, rewards or punishments, which my mom easily would grant. I was and am completely mute in a world of speaking persons. Yet, it might happen that I could figure out something instantly. For example, as a child, I am in the garden with other children and they want to run. I know that it is their desire to run without me. I know it by instinct and I don't need spoken words for it.

I could not learn words like everyone else, but I imitated everyone else in my mind, beginning alone to think of a word, modifying it in my mind for the need of normal sounding. I realized that it was necessary first to hear logically in the right way and, therefore, I have learned to value new ways of reading, following inside of me two roads: the internal evocation of the sound of a word and the passage from hearing it inside of me to keeping it inside after having read it and heard it. I had to separate the feeling I got from the sound or meaning of a word or passage from the task of capturing the sound inside of me to be used again. The process was putting together states of alignment between the visual routine and preserved, necessary auditory action. Thus, I ended up in one appalling situation. The artifice worked in some way, but I became unstable, repeating to myself the foolishness of wanting to learn to speak at the age of thirteen. So much hard work and the results were poor, I still was not able to speak with my voice: it was frustrating.

Since auditory stimuli could reach me in a comprehensible way even if their processing was at times irregular, I decided to train myself and asked my mother to tape at first some sounds from the environment including birds, water, bells, a passing car, a slammed door, and so on and then have me listen and name them on my typewriter. After having identified the sounds, it was necessary next to break with the necessity of working in an indirect way to understand the meaning of a speaking voice. The flatness of a voice processed afterwards dispersed emotion and naturalness.

I desired stereophony [in this case thinking and speaking]; I wanted so much to write but I also wanted to talk. I had this impossible dream: to speak with my voice, and I was convinced that if I had adjusted my way of processing sounds and words my voice would have come out.

I asked my mother to find me an Italian grammar book also recorded on a tape. I wanted to hear the lesson on the tape through headphones but I quickly understood that I could not make sense of what the voice was saying and that I needed another adjustment. It was necessary, before listening to the alien voice, to read the text. In this way, it became easier to decode the meaning of the recorded words and sentences. I asked to read and then listen to the tape. The new enterprise was to put together the elaboration of a read passage [visual perception] and the hearing of the recorded same passage [auditory perception]. It is still the way I study: I read the text and then someone reads it aloud to me or records it on tape for me. Slowly, with time and exercise, I can now most of the time concentrate on the spoken lesson of one of my teachers without having to read it beforehand. It is tiring because I have to rely only on one single channel with a great effort of concentration not to lose the meaning. But I can listen and simultaneously understand. So I guess that the exercise I invented definitely worked for me. Without this exercise I wouldn't have been able to accomplish the process of direct hearing, and would still always be working in delay. By doing the exercise I have succeeded in stepping out of mono-sensory processing [i.e., only one channel at the time].

A Private World of Fantasy

My mother managed my fantasies with quibbling questions. When I wanted to charm, I had in store so many strange words. Why was it necessary to charm? One can think to moderate his own nature (i.e., to have a measure of control). I don't deny it. I wanted to light a fire under people. I had things to show. My mind was filled with mad thoughts: I really believed that inside me there was a personal world of my own, shining with psychic energy that I had to bring out into the practical world to show its talent. I even asked to work to prove it. For example, when I was about thirteen, I asked my mother to put some books on the floor and cover them with a blanket. When she asked me why, I answered that I was going to raise them with the force of my mind. Mother was the true connection with the real world: she allowed me to carry out my disastrous experiments and then denuded each of my surreal behaviors. She did what I asked for and when nothing happened she didn't comment on it. She complied with my request for several days until I gave up.

Erroneously, I thought myself impervious to objective reality. Lying to myself, I found it sidereal, optional, chaotic. Safe within my fantasies I didn't value the chaos for what actually it is: a preordered Pandora's box, conceived, I suppose, to demonstrate that one belongs to humankind. In a way I knew I understood, but my game of not using my thoughts on concrete facts was detrimental to my understanding. I was always giving to facts an opposite value, a surrealistic one.

My extreme difficulty to call forth certain actions from my body also pervaded the way I worked intellectually on those practical data that I observed and recorded. If you have difficulties to act but only observe and think, you loose a lot of useful information which many times are implied and not explicit. Good heavens! There are traps everywhere! For example, suppose your parents decide to grind the wooden lounge door; they want it to look prettier. Not for me, my idea was that they were doing it so that I could pass through the door without hurting myself.

I wanted so much to write about what I was feeling as a personal journey, but everything was subverted by my fantasy of omnipotence, which by itself, was living the experience, making it a supernatural event; when, for example, it was imperative to dedicate oneself to the syllogism of doing some action—syllogism because I was mechanically plunged into stereotyped praxis and movements—I did not feel the limitations because I imagined going through an immortal existence, mediated by fantastic and exclusive power of the mind. I was on this earth to live an exceptional life governed by unlimited mind's power.

I certainly was one who let his imagination run riot. After having learned—through communication—to express my thoughts, I still felt more secure if I fled from the real world. I was trying to find evidence allowing me to escape from my place in the objective reality. I was thirteen years old. I lived far away from the practical world. I found that the idea of being spirit and not matter was pertinent. Only after long discussions serenely reasoned upon with my mother, have I finally decided that a fantastic sensation doesn't always correspond to a real thing.

I used to have unreal communication determined by my fantasy; I tried to study a guiding thread with the right personality. While solely meditating on my way of being, I remember that the sensations I felt were irksome. I didn't feel a connection with the persons I was observing: I felt anomalous. But, relating to my mother, working with her, I could examine in my actions some motivations that I didn't have before. It was a good new sensation and I longed for mom's vital force.

Definitely I lived moments where I inhibited the logical directions of my mind. Since I lived in the irrational, it was necessary to present to me true purposes so I could find my balance.

A mother can do such things as provide logic to a dull son. It will depend upon her diligent choice of offers. She, my mother, did it. She provided lots of exercises in which I tried to carry out an action after having learned to describe the sequence of the steps.

After hours of positive communication and by going inside the facts, by the selecting of the real from the fantastic, interacting, ratifying the needs of feeling reality that existed, not the alleged one, the one in which my fantasy indulged, demanding from myself forgiveness for a defective birth, pushing away sadness, I finally placed my thoughts in the power of valid intellectual events.

Let's consider the idea to allow myself serious work aimed at socialization: for the first time I had the opportunity to confront myself with socialization in a conscious way. I could reason over facts. Nobody would have bet I could become the social person that inside me I wanted to be. Working out so many cause-and-effect relationships, an ability very limited in me before I could communicate, has put me slowly in contact with practical memory, favoring the correct tie with the motivation of doing something, or if not being able to do it, of thinking of doing it. By dissecting my inabilities to execute, I finally and objectively understood myself.

A complete elaboration of facts can be done through an objective comparison; otherwise the reality can be deformed. Little by little my fantasies of omnipotence left the room, giving way to more realistic ideas.

My "valid intellectual events" can now confront themselves with everyday practical life. Not being able to communicate means that you cannot ask, that all your questions are unanswered, but, with communication, I have in a way reassured myself, I can dedicate myself to my intellectual life and put a stone on practical life which I can now understand but which is not part of my being.

Summing Up

I am tempted to give a testimony on the rapid descent that urgently forces one to go away from the madness of the fantastic, choosing the seriousness of real human dimensions, but I prefer instead to talk about the improvements that come with living day after day with people with which we measure.

Give me credit for this, mother: not only did I improve our lives, but I put at your disposal practical weapons for the valuable actions you later used to teach other autistic children.

Measuring myself with the others I learned how to make my practical memory function, I learned the real connections with facts, how to quickly internalize facts and events, to be less oppressed by errors of interpretation. I learned to stop fighting with myself; I have limitations. So do many other people. Communication freed me from the pain of compressing the human dimension into empty silences.

Examples of what life should be came to me from real relations with my classmates. And now, once I overcome moments of great anxiety, affectionately my friends cheer me up and I intend to reciprocate their love. I must say that in the past I refused similar situations: this is the first time that I feel accepted for what I am. I learned from them successfully what is a legitimate demand of joy and, stirred up by their spontaneity, after strong emotional moments, I have learned to activate the desire of friendship, hope, dreams, projects, and reflections. Less today I would modify myself. I am no longer so maniacal with the obstacles of my disabilities. I show an objective, modified property of answer to the depressive states known. By this I mean that I can fight depression when I confront myself with my peers. And I repress the sense of vanity in my mind. I am, indeed, more aware of the limitations which I find in my astonishing and lonely figure. I manage today my sensory distortions, not allowing stimuli to flow directly, but deciding their frequency, balancing their endurance, utilizing an open channel and protecting it, compensating with memorization for the bad functioning of the two channels in simultaneous process. The two channels are the visual and the auditory. For example, I'm sitting in front of the TV set, I hear the words and I can decipher their meaning, but I don't use my visual perception simultaneously, otherwise my attention would go. This strategy allows me to satisfy my wish to watch educational programs. Necessarily, however, functioning in this way, I had to decide to lose the immediate flow of emotions, letting them flow only successively.

I would like to mention some of the stimuli I must activate to better promote my visual and auditory qualities. I learn by scan reading the page in my mind before listening to a lesson: I get an idea of the argument the professor will explain. I grant myself the prerogative to get information from memorized pages by extracting logical connections, and by working with competence on managing the itinerary words, those words which trigger selectively certain routes extracted from readings previously memorized. This is difficult to explain, but suppose the professor asks me to speak about "reasoning or ratiocination." I might think with no sense for hours. Instead, I launch the word in my mind and suddenly a memorized text appears, or parts of it, and I can also manipulate it while I'm writing.

Going back to my memories, there is sadness for situations that now have precise boundaries. At one time, I was feeling omnipotent, and this means that I was programmed only for my way of being. I lost in this way many precious years in which one should instead be programmed to make practical experiences. And the years I've lost are decisive in a person's life. I was far from having the complete usage of a correct form of communication. I was following a path not knowing the reason why; I thought to motivate myself with the value of the answers that I learned, by reflecting in my spiritual element.

The review of all the facts makes me sad, aware of the awful mistakes that the field of medicine can perpetrate. Gems become today my thoughts and the words I can now express, which yesterday had no collation, while I try to measure myself with the decision of living the precious opportunity that has been given to me.

Notes

1. Editor: Here, Frugone refers to Bettelheim's theory that "refrigerator mothers" (i.e., emotionally cold mothers) were responsible for their children's autism. Bettelheim published his theory in the book *The Empty Fortress* (1972).
2. Editor: In his younger years, doctors thought that Alberto was deaf and so provided him with hearing aids that he wore for some time. Asked how he tolerated them, Alberto said, "By commanding myself to ignore them."

References

Bettelheim, B. (1972). *The empty fortress: Infantile autism and the birth of the self.* New York: Free Press.

7

■ ■ ■ ■ ■ ■ ■ ■ ■

I. Introduction to Richard Attfield

I have already introduced Richard Attfield in Chapter 1 and so will be brief here. Richard's chapter is organized around events in his life and has a strong human rights and inclusion focus. Some of the topics are ones I suggested, based on our conversations, while others are ones he suggested.

Richard left special schools at the age of nineteen when he gained entrance to college, a pre-university, A-level program where he could study English literature and art history. In 1997 he won the Journalism Category and the Overall Award in a writing competition for college students, sponsored by a regional newspaper, the *Gazette,*[1] and the *Talking Newspaper for the Blind.* In his essay, he describes what it was like to grow up unable to communicate through speech. He recalls a scene from playschool: "I remember one day when a little girl spoke to me and called my name, I could not even respond to her attempt to hold my hand.[2] . . . Autism[3] takes total control of a child and one becomes a prisoner in one's own body" ("Crying Inside," *Gazette,* Thursday, June 26, 1997, p. 3). Other people cannot know "the frustration, of not being able to join in a conversation, but I guess that most people thought I was retarded and that I had no thoughts or feelings that mattered" (p.

3). His early schooling was highly repetitive: "one plus one equals two gets pretty boring. . . . Even the fact that I managed to show them that I knew the answer seemed to make no difference, as next day out came one plus one equals two again" (p. 3). With inclusion at college, he "cried inside with joy" (p. 3).

Appended to his award-winning essay was one of his poems:

> *I Am Not Here in This Room*
> *I am not here in this room*
> *I am out in the clouds flying*
> *I am not here in this room*
> *I am out in the meadow running*
> *I am not here in this room*
> *I am out in the mountains climbing*
> *I am not here in this room*
> *I am freed from this body roaming*

(© 1997, Richard Attfield)

■　　■　　　■　　　■　　　■　　　■　　　■　　　■　　　■

II. The Colour of Rich

Richard Attfield

Do You Remember My Name?

I have been given many labels during my life: low muscle tone, ataxia, cerebral palsy, delayed development, retardation, autism, brain dysfunction, learning difficulties, low functional abilities, and as unable to communicate. When I was a toddler one doctor stated, on a five minutes acquaintance, that I was "somewhat backward." My mother was told "it was nothing physical." One month later a Consultant Paediatrician wrote: "He appears to understand what is said to him, spoke in single words and has good jargon." He perceived me as "a child of normal intelligence, possibly with some motor problems" and with "general behaviour" so "near normality" I was "difficult to assess." Three months later, the same Paediatrician diagnosed me as having an ataxic walk. It was decided I should have physiotherapy at the hospital Observation Unit once a fortnight.

When I was two and a half, a local GP referred me to a London hospital. I underwent numerous tests. All came back normal. My mother however, worried at not being given answers, looked at my hospital file, when it was left on a table. It question-marked cerebral palsy. No one actually felt the necessity of mentioning this to my parents. I began to attend the Nursery Observation Unit at the hospital two afternoons a week but by my third birthday I had become so distressed that I hid when people came to my house. On the advice of an acquaintance who was a remedial gymnast, my brave mother removed me from the unit and approached a playschool in the quiet country village where I lived. They were both concerned at the level of help I had received from physiotherapy and speech therapy and felt I would benefit from the social interaction with my peers. To my knowledge, I was the first disabled child to attend the mainstream playschool at the church hall in the village. It was what was termed a "free play" group in that I could choose some of the activities I participated in. Having an ataxic walk I was very unsteady on my feet. A one-to-one support worker was engaged to help me should I need assistance. I became aware at a very young age that I was different from the other children. I had a good verbal vocabulary of three hundred and fifty words, but I had great difficulty expressing myself. The world seemed a big frightening place to me but the children and staff accepted me willingly enough. By the time I was five I was able to participate in the playschool activities that did not require good motor co-ordination or fluent verbal skills.

I loved the bright colours of the paint and stood absorbed as I applied thick red, blue and yellow, in the form of capital letters onto large sheets of paper pinned onto a board. "A" for apple, "B" for bicycle, "W" for witch. The jigsaw puzzles kept me enthralled for hours. I never did learn how to ride a tricycle, or catch a ball. I became an avid reader at home, and spent many a contented hour reading. One day, at the end of the morning, I marched up to a group of the mothers in the playschool kitchen and announced proudly, "I can read." I hated the texture of the play dough, the dreaded sand and glue, but I could cut along a line with scissors.

On a bad day at playschool I would sit quietly in the book corner and read to myself, cuddling a large teddy almost as big as me, desperately wishing I could speak fluently like the other children. I have so many memories still: of crawling through a large blue tunnel with a little girl chasing after me giggling, calling my name; being seated at a table at break time with some of the other children and two members of staff, as we ate slices of fruit, apples and bananas, and drank milk through a straw; the smell of apple and the stickiness of it on my hands; being asked in a calm quiet voice by the lady supervisor what fruit I wanted to eat and replying "apple" or "banana please"; being told to stand at the green door when I wished to go to the toilet; the sound of the scuffle of small feet on the floor; the chatter of children's voices and laughter echoing around the hall; the smell of the paint and a damp musky smell; the cold in winter; a cool breeze floating through an open door in summer; the scrunch of damp grass under my feet in the garden outside; the warmth of the sun of my face; the sigh of the wind in the trees; and most of all happily walking the mile home clinging tightly to my mother's hand.

Around this time my mother, under the impression that I was on a list to receive speech therapy, spoke to a Health Worker. She was told I would have to wait six months but I would be at the bottom of the list due to the nature of my condition. The children with minor problems would be given priority. At the end of the six months she enquired again. It was stated this time that my name was not on the list. I never did reach the top of the list. My mother tried to engage a speech therapist on a private basis to no avail. She found out years later that one speech therapist she had approached had considered taking my case. The speech therapist was told by the powers that be that I was retarded and there was nothing she could do to help me.

Just after my third birthday my mother and I went to meet a teacher who worked at the local infant school. She had studied for a year at a specialist centre on movement and offered to see me on a weekly basis at the school where she guided me through a structured remedial movement programme. The programme included work on stress release, balance, body image development, proprioceptive recognition and gross motor co-ordination, language positions and directions in space. After the trauma of attending the hospital Observation Unit, her calm gentle patience, encouragement and knowledge brought about a transformation. I can remember walking and running in a circle around the hall, my hands gripped by the teacher and my mother, as they swung me through the air. I walked along beams, stretched my arms up to the sky, crawled as an angry bear, marched to the beat of music and walked heel toe, heel toe. My mother continued the programme on a daily basis at home. She turned our kitchen benches upside down to use as beams, crawled on her knees moving my feet, heel toe, and rolled me through the grass in the garden on warm summer days. I can still hear the words in her soft voice, "heel toe, heel toe, heel toe" ringing through the air as we journeyed through the village streets to the bank, post office or local shops. My mother pushed me on a tricycle to the school each week, my little feet on the pedals flying round.

The teacher, pleased with the progress I made over a two-year period, wrote a report to the Education Department stating I was "a very tense, frustrated child, using exceptional mental force to gain control of my movement and that my estimated IQ was above average." How I loved her for that. One of our local General Practitioners later told my father that "my mother was an angel," and that it was a "miracle that I had ever walked."

My fifth birthday loomed nearer. It was time for me to leave the playschool and enrol at school. On an appointed day an Educational Psychologist arrived at our home. He was a huge, insensitive man. As his foot crossed the door of my home, he courageously announced that I was severely mentally retarded. He spent the next three hours politely arguing with my parents. Angry with him, I took every book in the room and threw them in his direction. I do not think he took the hint that they were my books and I understood the words in them. Despite the efforts of my parents, I was denied entry into mainstream education on the grounds of my disability. "How would we teach him?" was the cry. As I see it, I was not given a fair chance. No one at the time thought to ask me where I would like to go to school. For the next four years my mother taught me at home. My parents refused to send me to a school for children with severe learning difficulties, which was the only offer on the table.

A doctor and a speech therapist at another hospital saw me at the age of six, and thought that features of my behaviour were autistic. The doctor wrote a report that stated: "What concerned me was that there certainly seemed to be areas of ability, both from observing him and from what his mother says that were at a surprisingly high level. . . . I was therefore unhappy about making a definite diagnosis of mental retardation." He acknowledged I had a "wide variety of single words." Yet, he was concerned that my mother was teaching me to read and write! It was felt that I "was a child who was very confused and has great difficulty in interpreting both visual and auditory sensory information." A "period of extended observation" was suggested to see if a diagnosis could be made as to the nature of my difficulties.

The doctor stated that my language was "scarcely at a word-joining level yet seemed to be very deviant." My parents thought this finding was odd, as sometimes I spoke in whole sentences. For example, when I was aged two my first sentences were "I am worried" and "I have a book mama." One evening, sitting on the stairs at home, I said, "I want to go to bed." My mother thought it was my brother that had spoken. Another day I said, "It is all right, I am here Mum," and I put my arm around her. I can remember that day clearly—she was standing at the kitchen sink washing some dishes. Another morning I was sitting on the floor with her doing a jigsaw puzzle and I told her, "I love you." Another time, I told a friend of my mother's, "I want my mummy." On one occasion I told my father, "I want to go and see nanny and granddad." Another day I saw my father outside in the garden and said, "I can see daddy." I had been reading a book called "I can see" a week or so earlier. A speech therapist, engaged by my mother, who visited me at my home between the ages of six to seven, noted that I was able to work with my mother for an hour or more reading or writing or constructing sentences with flash cards and that I could spell words with eight letters after one sighting. The contents of my vocabulary included "nouns, verbs, adjectives, adverbs, pronouns, conjunctives and prepositions." She said, I was "determined and usually quite biddable," and she was of the opinion that I required help from teachers who had "a specific knowledge of communication problems." I do not remember her ever working with me; she merely observed.

Eventually, at the age of seven, a Consultant who specialised in autism and paediatric disability suggested either a school for a child with a communication disorder or a school for the physically disabled would be appropriate. I remember the day I met him. I entered a large bright room, where maybe six or eight professional people were present to discuss my case. I was sitting on the floor when a kettle hissed a high-pitched scream two closed doors away. I shot out of the room to find out where the noise was coming from and located the kitchen. (Later an aunt told us that she also had a problem with the shrill noise from a kettle.) The Consultant, whilst talking to my parents, noticed that I had walked over to a wall cupboard and upon reaching it had opened the door on the left. Pleased, he remarked that by my opening the cupboard I had demonstrated that I was not mentally retarded. It had a concealed hinge and a touch latch, with both doors rebated so that the left hand door had to be opened before the right hand door. He wrote a report:

> Looking at Richard's work and watching him, impressed all of us how complex his learning problems are . . . we really ought to try and unravel the nature of his disability thereby better to define his special needs and where they can be met. In his case this is a very complicated issue; at this stage I would simply comment that in terms of schooling he could be seen either as a child with basically a communications disorder . . . however his language difficulties are different from those of autistic children and in particular he is a child with considerable social potential . . . and could therefore perhaps be better assisted in a more normally intercommunicating peer group. . . . If one emphasizes the perceptual difficulties . . . which interfere with his capacity to make sense of his world, not only in communication, but in organising all his motor activity, then he would be a legitimate candidate for a physically handicapped school.

A year later, he wrote, "I am far from clear of the precise nature of this interesting little boy's disabilities," and that he could not "confidently attach a diagnostic label." Two phonetics and linguistics experts who worked with him wrote that I produced "some verbal output and spoke in a slow strong low pitched voice which was often creaky." I had joined in a spelling game with letter blocks and had verbally identified the letters. The conclusion was that although "phonetically adequate, my speech was far from normal and not typical of a younger child." It was suggested, "a more normally communicating peer group would help," and that I required "skilled individual speech help." They concluded I was seriously speech impaired.

The teacher, who worked on the remedial movement program with me from the age of three, expressed her concern that because of the diagnosis of autistic features I would be given placement on the wrong kind of language development program. A very big disagreement ensued between those doctors who were satisfied with the diagnosis of "autistic features" and those who were not. One doctor who saw me for two hours once a fortnight, and worked with me on an education programme based on movement, threw an almighty paroxysm and said my problems were physical. He was in such a rage he shouted at my poor mother and told her I was not autistic. Another doctor wrote that I had "a fascinating problem of development."

Based upon this information my mother made enquiries about a placement at a unit a short distance from my home that specialised in language development and was situated in the grounds of a mainstream school. She was told there was a waiting list and a recommendation would have to be made from the Education Department. The Educational Psychologist dealing with my case at the time, reluctant to comment, stated she did not know what was wrong with me. Two years later my parents were still waiting for me to be statemented and no new offer of a different school from Severe Learning Difficulty (SLD) was forthcoming. I was nine years of age before a Consultant Neurologist agreed that there was "evidence of a degree of cerebral palsy, represented by a hemi spastic gait."

One person made a huge difference in my life: my mother. She always held such unfaltering belief in me and felt that although I had speech and movement difficulties that I did not lack in ability. She always saw me, the person within. She retained a very positive attitude and taught me to believe in myself. My mother was angry with the professionals.

She felt I should have been receiving some help with my speech and movement difficulties, but when it never materialised she broke every rule in some unspoken book to help me. I tried so hard as a child to walk and speak. I attended several hospitals over the years and saw numerous doctors in the hope that someone would be able to offer some constructive help. I was something of an enigma. They saw only that my speech was not fluent, my walk ungainly.

I have had lots of tags hung round my neck, but I have also been fortunate in knowing some warm endearing people, who supported me through some tight moments. My loyal, indignant, tiny aunt once suggested, after seeing the reaction of people when I screamed in distress and suddenly became the focus of attention in a busy tourist filled coastal town, that we wave a large placard with the words "excuse me, I am autistic." I was maybe seven years of age and we were on holiday at the time. Having lost some treasured toy that my mother had given me I bellowed hard and long. The street was full of people that stopped in their tracks and turned to look to see who was being murdered. I had had the toy in my hand, then a few seconds later it had disappeared. My brother and cousins retraced our steps to see if they could find the lost item but it was nowhere to be found. It was decided that someone must have taken it up off the pavement. Inconsolable I trudged along wanting to go back and shout at the top of my voice: "Who has taken my toy?" A year later hundreds of miles from home we returned to the same coastal village for the day. I reached the exact spot, recalled the incident clearly, and yelled in anger.

At the age of nine I was offered a placement at a school for autistic children. The Head Teacher visited my home to meet me before confirming the offer. During his visit I accidentally caught my foot in a table and some books perched on it slid ominously towards the floor. My father told me to be careful but the Headmaster had my card marked, from that moment on. He remarked that I was a "stubborn spoilt brat." The Headmaster was an odd combination. He wanted to help the children but could not see that his efforts were often misguided. My mother in particular was not happy with my placement at the school. She had merely caved in against her better judgment. Remember, I had been out of school for four years and one of her primary concerns was that my social contact with people of my own age was restricted after leaving the playschool.

It was scary as a child being unable to express myself fluently. This was the situation I found myself in as a child, when I was to visit the school where I had been given a placement. I did not know anyone at the school other than the Headmaster whom I had met for a short time a few weeks earlier. I had considerable trouble organizing my movement and I was therefore dependent on other people. I could not express an opinion or ask a question or comment on situations. I could not say, "I don't want to go," or "Can we go home now?" or "I would prefer to do it this way," or even "I am cold." I could not say the hundreds of little things that most people take for granted. I wanted to go to school with the other children where I lived; with the children I had been at playschool with, with my brother, to walk the short distance to the school with friends of my own age. When the Education Authority refused to give me a placement at my local school, I wished I did not have to go to school at all.

I met the teacher whose class I was to be in. I was a model of good behaviour. It was the first time I had met other children who had communication disorders. Several of the children were younger than me. The teacher seemed pleasant enough and the visit went well until at the end of the afternoon the Headmaster, all authority, deemed he would drive me home from school. I was not familiar with the area where the school was situated. It was miles away from where I lived. The Headmaster unceremoniously bundled me into the back of his car. I sat in the car determined I was not going to cry, even though I would rather have driven home with my parents. My fear got the better of me and I yelled in protest. The Headmaster turned the volume of the radio up loud to drown out my yells and I sat in distress for the long journey home.

My first day at school dawned all too soon. The morning of the dreaded day arrived and I sat looking out of the window, with my coat and shoes on, waiting for the taxi (funded by the local education department) to arrive. It turned up promptly. An escort was to go with me. I hated the thought of having to travel the hour journey back and forward to the school. I had insufficient verbal language to ask questions that first day. What time would I be coming home? I was unable to state that

I was scared to go because the Headmaster shouted at me and I did not like him. War had been declared!

At home I had had one-to-one support in the form of my mother. No one at the school had any experience of a child with an ataxic condition. A report written at the time stated that my "general functioning was largely dependent upon my ataxic condition" and that I had "poor co-ordination in most muscle groups including the speech mechanism" yet I received no physiotherapy or one-to-one support worker. There was no speech therapy. I would get really angry when the staff at school could not understand my speech or I could not do things for myself. I can remember wanting to express my own thoughts and not just repeat back the sentences that I was told to say. It was as if I had no personality, no thoughts or feelings of my own.

At school I found myself back to adding one plus three and reading books meant for an infant. At home, before I started school, I had covered the junior maths syllabus, writing in the answers with some physical difficulty, at first with my mother steadying my hand and then a year later independently. I had read my fair share of books, and had been structuring sentences using words written on cards (referred to as the Breakthrough system) and copy writing and taking dictation. I also was able to answer questions by pointing to words on a word grid, which my mother had devised. School was a big disappointment and the work never challenging. My teacher gave up on me within weeks of my beginning school. She went through the motions but she had no great expectations of my achieving. My teacher felt she received "little co-operation with written work." She pinned a note on the board in the classroom at the end of the first term addressed to the Headmaster for visitors, staff and everyone to read. "I have tried, but Richard cannot write." My mother saw it, as was intended. She was furious. I incurred the wrath of my teacher by reading a book she lent me over the end of term break. It had been her planned syllabus for the whole of the next term. She remarked that "I could not have possibly comprehended it." Both the teacher and the Headmaster obviously thought I lacked the ability to read, write or do maths.

I did not enjoy being in special education. I resented the implication that I was different. Segregation made me a social outcast. I made no friends outside of school. I became the child that was disabled, the one who went to a school for children with disabilities. School was an unhappy place. I sat through days of misery; the hurt expressions on the children's faces when they were told off, the worried looks, the tears, and tantrums when they could not do what was expected of them or could not express their needs or feelings or just articulate what they wanted to say, have stayed with me to this day. Memories close in on me. One is of a little girl's rapt attention engaged at the rabbit cage. Take away the surroundings and that child could have been any child anywhere, except she had no speech and no way to communicate what she was thinking. She had no verbal language. Another is of a child sitting on horseback, sitting up straight and alert, enjoying a horse-riding lesson. Again this was a child with no way to communicate what she was feeling or experiencing, as she also had no speech. I left the school at the age of eleven, traumatised and disillusioned.

The next school I attended was an improvement on the first. The staff were generally kind and well meaning, even though most of them still misjudged my ability. One teacher in the school recognised my intelligence. She took my mother to one side and told her that it was obvious how intelligent I was; she commented that I was always so observant of what was going on around me. This teacher was one of the small minority who saw more than my disability. She tried to do her best for me despite the inadequate facilities—the overcrowded, badly equipped, small, cramped classrooms. Upon leaving the school, she wrote me a long letter advising me on how to try to gain entry into College.

As a fourteen-year-old teenager, whilst out of school for a walk in the forest on a scorching hot summer's day, I ran away. The teacher in charge that day turned her back for a few minutes and I took off. I was free. My spirits soared as I flew through the trees, my heart thumping in my chest, sure at any moment that I would hear a shout and feet pounding behind me. We had been out walking for what seemed an age and I was unable to tolerate the strong sunlight. Tired, thirsty, irritable, my head aching, I had requested a drink. The teacher, under the impression that I was incapable of making a decision for myself, told me to wait. I wished they would all go away. Angry, I stalked off in a huff. I ran through the forest to the nearest pub and sat outside on a bench. I was probably shaking in my boots, but decided I could walk the thirty miles home. My mother frowned at me later when I told her, and remarked it would have been a long walk. She did not know whether to hug me in relief that I was found or scold me for running off. I felt really guilty when I found out that the staff had been frantically searching the forest for me, some of them in tears.

The next day in school in an attempt to enable me to communicate, a member of staff drew some line drawings of faces on pieces of card. It was suggested that I take out a picture to show them how I was feeling. The well-meaning intention misfired. I was mortified. It was so inadequate and so demeaning. I wanted communication, not picture cards

Each time I had a new teacher, I hoped for some improvement in the curriculum. I felt I was being denied an education. I was taught to tell the time in three separate terms, over a two–three year period, by three different members of staff. I could tell the time and had been able to do so from the age of five or six. My mother had taught me. What I did have was difficulty with co-ordination and expressing myself. When I failed at set tasks or refused to do them I was then damned as not having the ability. Some of the staff did not seem to comprehend that being unable to vocalize one's thoughts is not the same as not having any. There was no structured syllabus or language programme throughout the school, each teacher worked out their own timetables. At fifteen years of age I was drafted into "Life Skills." It was like a deathblow. Some improvements to the curriculum were eventually implemented after a long fight on my behalf but I felt it was too little too late.

The Lost Years

The day had started well enough. I had travelled to school in the taxi that collected me from home each day, escorted by a warm hearted elderly gentleman. He sat on the back seat next to me. Another boy, some four years younger than me, who travelled in the same taxi, was seated on the left side of the Old Gentleman.[4] The little lad wriggled excitedly and chattered constantly throughout the journey that day, but this did not trouble me as I enjoyed his boisterous company.

The Old Gentleman told me that he was seventy-eight. Proud to have reached such an age, his shoulders bowed, as if both by age and the weight the world had put on his frail shoulders. I cannot remember him ever speaking of having any family, but he did tell me he lived in a flat by himself on the coast. His lean, bony frame fitted uneasily into the back seat of the taxi, but he was not one to complain. He sat between the other small child and me, his warm gravelly voice recounting some tale to keep us amused on the long, tedious journey to school.

The Old Gentleman showed a great fondness for puffing away on a mouth organ. His wiry, bearded face would crinkle with pleasure at our interest, as the fleeting notes pierced the air. How he loved that time-worn burnished piece. He spoke of it with warm affection in a soft, good-humoured tone and told us it was a wind instrument—a "mouth organ." On the odd occasion, it would magically appear from within his inner coat pocket and he would deftly pipe some lively refrain during our journey. I do not recall with any certainty the tunes, only that he would tell us that if we were "good," he would bring it to play again at the end of the week. I would shut my eyes tightly and listen with rapt attention as he jauntily blew and sucked the air through the vibrating reeds.

On the day in question, the morning lessons at an end, mid-day arrived and it was time for the lunch break. I sat in the school's small, oppressive dining room, with the noise from so many voices vibrating around my head. I did not want to be in school that day. My head ached. I did not want to be bothered with lunch; I wished I could go home. The dilemma was that I had no way to communicate my thoughts or feelings to any one present in the room. A muttered "Go home" achieved no response.

Stifled by the heat of the day, the confines of the dining room, and the people in it, I wished I could go outside, to be by myself and sit quietly in the garden in the fresh air for a while. I wanted to be away from the constant pandemonium of school. The plates rattled in the kitchen adjoining the dining room and I could hear the hum of voices as the staff dished out dinner. I had to wait at the table and eat the meal that was set before me. None of the children were allowed to leave the table until everyone had finished eating. The rule was that one had to devour what was produced from the large "black cauldrons" on the stove, whether one enjoyed the contents or not. In my case, it was generally not. If some stew boiled furiously away on a warm summer's day, there was no choice, that was what one was forced to swallow. I often wondered about the questionable ingredients of some unidentifiable looking substance that landed with a heavy thud on my plate. "Witch's stew" had been one description that came to mind.

My thoughts wickedly wandered to a book I had been reading earlier that week. The title of the book was something like "The MacGuffins' Picnic." On the front cover of the book there was a picture of the ravenous MacGuffin family—prickly, bear-like creatures, with hugely exaggerated physical features and gestures—greedily gobbling a picnic. Their rather sinful, grinning faces seemed oddly hyperactive. I cannot recall much of the book, other than the MacGuffin family had all climbed into a vehicle, a bus or a car, and had travelled out to the woods for a picnic. It was the thought of the picture of the MacGuffin family devouring the picnic that struck me as highly amusing. The MacGuffins, which included a number of adults and several unruly children, were gleefully, and in somewhat wild frantic haste, stuffing cake, ice cream and jelly sandwiches into their mouths.

I likened the antics of the MacGuffins in the book to those of certain members of staff who had particularly annoyed me. One by one, I carefully studied the staff in the room and applied a name to each from the MacGuffins in the picture. The Head of the school showed a remarkable close resemblance to the Head MacGuffin. From that day he earned the name of Head MacGuffin. Of course, I would not have dared address him as Head MacGuffin in place of Headmaster, so I abbreviated it to Mac, spoken under my breath. Out loud I referred to him merely as "the Man." I never did call the Headmaster by his name during the two years I was drafted into his authoritarian regime; I would not give him the satisfaction of acknowledging his presence.

I was frequently in trouble for one thing or another at school. By nature I was easy going. I greeted the staff at school each morning with a big smile during the first term. I was however known to show a rebellious streak. Bored with the work, I kicked my legs and rocked back on my chair in class. By the second term I had progressed to being able to quickly pick out sentences (ten to be exact) in sequence and read them. The number work was still boring and repetitious, and my teacher felt she received "little co-operation with written work."

I can recall one incident when I was in trouble over a particular sentence that I could speak quite well. One morning in school the teacher suddenly decided it was not good manners to politely ask, "Can I have a drink please?" It was suddenly decreed I should parrot back, "May I have a drink please?" I gave it a fleeting thought, decided against it, and refused to conform as they saw it. I hated people telling me what to say. The teacher actually wrote home to my parents, complaining when I did not comply. I would get really infuriated when the staff at school could not understand my speech or I could not do things for myself. I would clench my fist in frustration. I can remember wanting to express my own thoughts and not just repeat back the sentences that I was told to say. It was as if I had no personality, no thoughts or feelings of my own.

After two terms at the school I was transferred to another class with the older children. At first I was the blue-eyed boy. Now acquainted with the layout of the school, I ceased to "rush around the school bumping into furniture and people" and I was beginning to use my "quite extensive vocabulary." That did not last long. I caused too much trouble. There was the incident where my parents were invited in school to see me swim in the school pool without armbands to keep me afloat. I had only been swimming at school for a week when my new teacher, convinced I could doggy paddle, invited my parents to visit. Regrettably, as my parents stood watching, I sunk like a stone two or three times, swallowed mouthfuls of water, and nearly drowned. The teacher, unconcerned by my yells for help, stood by the side of the pool and merely shouted at me to kick harder. I was hysterical by the time someone dragged me out of the water. It brought about an abrupt end to both my and the teacher's enthusiasm for teaching me to swim. When my parents next took me to the local swimming pool on my brother's birthday I had a panic attack. I screamed and screamed, clung onto the door with a frantic grip and refused to go into the building. After nearly drowning me, my end of term report read I "had learned how to swim—albeit vertically upright."

Not long after, at a horse-riding lesson at stables near the school, it was decided that I should go up three or four steps to climb onto the back of a great beast of a horse. The staff did not realize that I had trouble with heights—although it was only a few feet off the ground. No one thought to warn the poor horse that it was probably beyond my ability to step from the mounting block onto his back. As I tried, the horse stepped side-ways. I panicked. The horse angrily reared up. In the turmoil that followed I almost fell into the gap between the horse and the block, nearly taking one or two staff members with me. I was not popular that day. I had been going horse riding with my parents and brother since I was two or three but that incident gave me a real fright and I was never very keen to go horse riding again. Another day I fell into the rose bushes in the school garden. I was pulled out with scratches all over my face. One narrowly missed my eye. I was in hot water with the Headmaster over that. The rose bushes were promptly dug up a few days later. On another occasion I fell over some builder's rubble in the school grounds and cut my knee open. Hours later, one poor girl suffered a fright when she saw the state of my knee. My parents were called and asked to take me to the hospital. I needed ten stitches when I arrived at the hospital with a lump of flesh hanging off.

One half term break my elder brother, aged twelve, offered his services for the day to help out. He travelled to the school in the taxi with me. He was the one in trouble this time, for pulling me up out of thick snow. Catching my leg under me, I tumbled down a six-foot slide, landing headlong in the ice-cold snow. My brother, seeing me crash land, hauled me out, stood me on my feet, and brushed me down. Annoyed at his intervention, the Headmaster shouted across the playground at him to leave me to get up myself. He was not allowed to sit next to me in the school dining room that day. He went home and related the incident to my parents. My mother shuddered at the thought of my climbing a six-foot slide. She thought I was lucky I had not fallen off and broken my neck.

It was rumoured that anyone who did not toe the line at school would be permanently evacuated from the premises. I was not unduly worried. I disliked the Headmaster's methods and his ramshackle old school. I would have been ecstatic if I never had to set foot in the place again. I shed silent tears on the way home from school. Many a day I curled trustingly into the Old Gentleman's bony frame and fell asleep from sheer exhaustion.

The Old Gentleman, unlike the staff at school, never had occasion to tell me off. He would inform the taxi drivers—they changed on a daily basis—what well-behaved lads we were. He referred to us as "good little chaps." On more than one occasion, when I was in deep water for some misdemeanor at school, I sensed his anger with the Headmaster, as stern faced, he tried to protect me from the Head's fury. Incensed at the injustice, he would tell the Headmaster that I was "never any trouble." Judging by the glint in the Headmaster's eye as it settled on my shaken form, he resented the Old Gentleman's intervention. I thought it was ironic the Headmaster did not think more about his own language; he referred to me as a "bloody sod" when he thought I was not listening as he stood talking to my parents one day. He thought I was daft, deaf or both. I gleaned enough from the conversation in the car on the way home to know that my parents were shocked and angry. It was the end of term and I was grateful not to have to be in school for three weeks.

I marched into school in early January, battle lines drawn. Shortly after, my parents removed me from the school.

The Christmas after I had departed from the school, my father and I called on the Old Gentleman at his home to take him a bottle of whisky. He enjoyed a wee dram. I thought he would be pleased to see us. Instead he was angry. He told my father the Headmaster had hassled him when my parents had withdrawn me. I left distressed. I wondered what kind of person would take his wrath out on an old man who was in no way at fault; he had done nothing to be shown such disrespect and unkindness. He deserved better. I heard later the Old Gentleman died from the flu at the beginning of the winter. Saddened by his death it fuelled my utter contempt for everything the school stood for.

"In Solitude, Such Intercourse Was Mine"[5]

It was winter. The bleak, bitter air came like a rawboned insistent intruder, wrapping its wintry fingers over the landscape. I was fourteen years of age. It was the weekend and I was at home with my parents. Upset by a minor problem in school that week, I stood in the snug warmth of the kitchen venting my worry and anger at anyone who would listen. My mother, unable to make any sense of the jumbled half sentences I had uttered, terminated her chores and took a sheet of paper from a pile on the kitchen worktop. We sat on the floor together, legs and arms entwined, and she hastily drew a series of two-inch squares and scribbled each word I had spoken into a square.

I did not use what she referred to as "little words," so she wrote into the squares that remained empty the words I had not spoken, for example: *as, and, at, a, the, it, is, in, to.* I pointed to the words to form a number of coherent sentences. My mind raced ahead. I attempted to put my thoughts into words. Hesitantly, unsure of myself, I choked back the emotion, and fought the tears that welled up in my throat. I spoke each word, in a soft, low tone as I pointed to it. My mother had come to my rescue. Together we had conceived a way by which I could converse.

My mother had originally devised the method and we had used it to communicate when I was five–nine years of age. It had enabled me to answer questions on work sheets, books I had read and maths work. At school the emphasis was put on verbal speech but I was fourteen, and still unable to speak in fluent sentences. The grids changed on a daily basis depending upon the subject of the conversation. Piles of them lay strewn in a higgledy-piggledy fashion on a chair in the lounge, each covered with my mother's untidy scrawl. Some days, up to a hundred words were written on the grid. It was restrictive in format but it was a beginning, it opened a door.

Winter changed to spring. Whilst old man winter snored, and stretched his weathered limbs, the brocks surfaced from their setts, red admirals and cabbage whites flitted from flower to flower in the garden, and I left my childhood behind, thrust unwittingly into the world of adulthood. In a fit of pique, I was determined to take a stand at school, and to use the grid system to air my views. At an assessment at the end of the school term, a senior physiotherapist told my parents that I adapted my movement continually to compensate for my ataxic condition. She wrote a report stating that I had "re...rkable control" of my "gross motor function," and that my movement was "high functioning," but I would need "some support when doing fine motor activities due to ataxia." She drew four diagrams on a sheet of paper outlining some motor targets.

At the end of the day, sitting at home with my mother, I pointed to the words on the grid and questioned: "Did the physiotherapist say very much help I need? I think they can help me." Resigned to their attitude, I said, "I will think about my movement, and what I can do to help myself."

August swept in, to beset and haunt me, mingling her mellow sighs with the scent of summer roses. The sweet fragrance of lavenders, in pots on the patio, wafted through the open kitchen stable-door, where

I, on summer vacation, mused with a wistful gaze. My mother had lain on the sofa, unable to sit or stand, in agony, for weeks. She had dislocated a bone in her pelvis. Then out of the blue a package arrived in the post. I observed, intrigued, as my mother tore off brown paper and opened a square squat box. Like Pandora's box, it conveyed an undisclosed quantity, the gift of hope. Packed neatly inside was a Canon communicator, a small hand held device with a keyboard and a key guard.

It brought back a memory—an image of myself as a small child, sitting at the dining room table. I was five or six years of age and my parents had bought me a typewriter for my birthday. I did not have sufficient strength in my fingers to hit the keys to print the letters, so my mother supported my hand. As I typed each letter an electronic voice spoke the twenty-six letters of the alphabet, "a, b, c, d, e, f . . ." Captivated by the bright red machine, and the black characters, I typed words and the odd sentence.

Eventually the bar that held the typewriter ribbon in place broke; the ribbon grew old and faded and the typewriter was thrown away. My mother had taken me to the shops to look for a replacement but it was no longer manufactured.

My mother feeling poorly, the Canon communicator lay on a worktop, in idle inactivity, for a week. It gave me time to think about what I would type on it. I had been brewing for a fight with the world in general for ages. The first day I tentatively held the communicator in my hand, neither my mother nor I had any conception of where it would lead us. I found myself (i.e., who I was) in a way that had never been possible before. It began with my typing a few sentences: "I autistic am. I did know this when I was a child by listening to doctors talk about me. Paediatricians said that I was retarded not intelligent, but you thought that I was clever. I realised I was intelligent when I was asked questions and was discussing the answer with myself. I realised you were trying to communicate with me on the computer. You had problems at first because I could not converse." I had typed five sentences in a row, not discussing schoolwork, not in answer to a question, but explicit communication, expressing my thoughts and feelings.

I had missed the "a" and "r" out of paediatricians, but other than that the spelling of the sentences was correct. I had also inserted punctuation marks. I had started to spell the word *paediatricians*. I typed the first five letters, "paedi," and then hesitated trying to think how it would be spelt. My mother waited for me to continue. When I did not, she spoke for the first time and said, "That is not a word Richard." I merely typed "paedi" again. She again told me it was not a word. I typed "paediatricians" with the above spelling errors. My impatience matched her own. I do not know who was more shocked at the discovery that I had typed those few sentences, my mother or me.

The communicator was on loan with the expectation that we would purchase it. My finger fitted neatly into the hole of the guard and did not slip off the keys, or knock another key unintentionally. It was relatively easy to use. The letters blurred out of focus at times but I was able to see the keyboard sufficiently to type. (A month later I was to acquire tinted lenses. I was diagnosed as having sensitivity to light. Wearing the lenses, my typed language improved dramatically in the space of a week.) In school I had typed on the odd occasion on a computer keyboard but I found it difficult. The keyboard was larger than the Canon's, and required good hand, eye and arm co-ordination, none of which were my best assets.

That first day I typed it was a new beginning. No words can describe what it felt like to be able to converse with my mother. Words sallied forth as I typed. I typed for hours—a sentence, a paragraph, a page, two pages, six pages, day after day. Exhausted at times, I felt alive. The joy was exhilarating. I wanted to shout out: I am here; this is me. My cousin told me that I used verbs as if my first language was German. I found it curious. I reflected on my childhood. I recalled the fear of being unable to reply when people spoke to me, of being misunderstood when I tried to speak, and my inability to communicate with the other children I came into contact with. I pushed the hurt away. I had forfeited many childhood experiences because I was not able to function in the same way as other children. Although I had been able to speak words or odd sentences, I had never been able to join in a conversation. I feared as a child and young adult, that I would never be able to express my thoughts and feelings, that I would be locked inside of myself and that people would be blind to the person within.

It was traumatic to suddenly discover that I could communicate, after spending my childhood years unable to converse. What I had thought about myself was untrue, a misconception. All my life I had been labelled "learning disabled"; it was hard to weather people putting me down and to nevertheless keep faith in myself. It took all my strength to stand my ground and type. I concluded after much heartache that I was as equally intelligent and competent at communication as the next person.

Children vocalize their thoughts day-in-day-out. I never had that experience. It can never be easy for a child to come to terms with the fact of having a disability. People expected so much from me despite my ataxic condition. It would have been so easy to give up but it was not in my nature, so I battled on.

"The Past Is a Foreign Country"

I was fifteen years of age and I was desperate to go to College. Having made the decision, I waited for the day when I could leave school. I felt school no longer had anything to offer me. It was the end of an era.

The end of term in which I was due to leave school loomed nearer, but no College was willing to offer me a Course. I had been waiting to hear from one College for a year. Another College had offered me a placement but had then backtracked and withdrawn it. I had been in correspondence with a third over a period of several months but no concrete offer was forthcoming. I wrote my thoughts on a page.

The shadows of my past
Embedded in my mind
A ghost walks near the window
A form stands by the door
Faces that haunt me
Indistinct whispers on the air

Immovable, defiant, I refused to concede defeat. I felt the school I attended had failed me. I had wasted so much time engaged in fruitless, mundane, useless activities.

Determined to gain entry into mainstream College, nothing or no one could shift me from my objective. I asked my parents to telephone every College in the area to make enquiries on their equal opportunities policy. I studied the fine detail on "equal opportunities" in every College Prospectus that came through the post. One afternoon my father came home with the news—one of the local Colleges had offered me an interview.

The day for the interview arrived. Nervous, my emotions in turmoil, I rehearsed in my head what I would say. Both of my parents were to accompany me to the interview. It was the third interview I had attended so I was getting the hang of it. I dragged on a pair of designer jeans, and a t-shirt, fumbled clumsily with the gleaming buckle on a leather belt, sure the implication would be once again that I was particularly dense and there was nothing they could offer me.

We arrived at the College in good time. A parking bay at the front of the College was marked "disabled parking." Anxious to begin the interview, I breathed a sigh of relief there would be no great distance to walk. I made an exit from the car.

Groups of students stood outside the entrance chatting eagerly to one another. I looked down at my feet, too shy to meet their eyes.

Once inside a room set aside for the interview, I was introduced to a row of courteous, attentive faces. Intent on making a good impression, I calmed my nerves sufficiently to smile hallo. The interview did not go quite how I expected. Instead of being made to feel as if I was extremely odd, and stupid, I met with nothing other than politeness. I was expecting another refusal, so I was rather taken aback when they did not abruptly show me the door and mumble to their feet, unable to meet my eye, "Sorry, we are full!"

The interview seemed endless but I was offered a Course. Instead of the General Certificate of Secondary Education Course I had thought I might be able to enroll on, they suggested the Advanced Level, a pre University Course lasting two years. The College, being less judgmental than others, accepted me on the merit of a poem that I had written. I made a hurried escape before anyone changed their mind, full of good intentions. I would prove my worth. I was enrolled on an English Literature Course and an Art History Course. The Art History was a three-hour evening class. The English Literature, two morning sessions.

Going to College was exciting. I faced up to the difficulties of not being able to function in the same way as the other students and tried to deal with them the best I could. I felt more alive than I had for a long, long time as I sat in the still quiet classroom and tried to follow the workings of, among others, Milton's "Paradise Lost," Shakespeare's "King Lear," and Friel's "Translations" and Eliot's "Prufrock."

My English Literature Lecturer inspired me to work harder than I ever had. The fact that there were people in the College who believed in my ability and who were willing to give me a chance drove me to strive harder. I was able to work at my own pace in my own time. I walked into the classroom each week determined I would succeed.

At the beginning of the term my English Literature Lecturer wrote in a letter to me that he was pleased to see how relaxed I was with the other members of the class. At the end of my first year at College, he wrote to me stating how impressed he was with my work and thanking me for the effort I had put in throughout the year.

Upon reading the first line of the Prologue of Hartley's "The Go-Between," "The past is a foreign country: they do things differently there," I considered how relevant the quote was to my own life at that moment.

The American Professor

As I left the travelator, to go shopping with my parents early one November evening, two sure-footed, sturdy little boys, dressed in colourful winter jackets, darted across my path and ran into the shopping precinct. One child, four or five years of age, laughing impishly, lingered behind his parents, trailing a long yellow woollen scarf along the ground behind him. Narrowly avoiding tripping over it, I smiled to myself in amusement and awkwardly slowed down my pace to avoid spoiling his enjoyment of the wavy, flowing yarn, sailing behind him. I held back the urge to tread teasingly on the scarf. The thought of the child brought to a sudden halt, his bright face scowling in bewilderment, forestalled me. I watched as he slowly disappeared into the crowd.

It brought back memories of a year earlier, when I had narrowly missed mowing down a small child at the entrance of a bookshop. It had been late afternoon as we slowly strolled through the precinct, shadows dancing erratically at my feet, my parents and I, and a rather tall, dark, rugged American Professor. My foot hit the pavement hard and unmoving. Intrinsic energy surged through me as I tensed trying to control my lean lanky form. Sheer will power forced me on as I did my utmost to make my body conform to my own expectations of it. As people milled chaotically all around me, a small girl appeared from nowhere and, oblivious to my presence, stood in the doorway. Grinding to a halt I had averted a collision. My father, irritated, said that I should be more careful. His remark stung. I made a resolution to watch in future for small children running in my path. The American Professor said, "It must be hard to always be in control." I replied, "I guess it is."

Summer had arrived, striding in with grace, and we were on summer vacation. The American Professor had flown in from the States the day earlier, and had booked into a hotel a short drive away, in the country town where I had been born. The Anglo-Saxon name of the ancient market town is "Ford of the Hunting Dog." The town itself, steeped in history, has a notation in the Doomsday Book (1086) as having had a mill, 3 cobs, 2 foals and 16 sheep. Once a river port, the old town maintains some of its mystery with its old-world charm, quaint houses and narrow streets.

Four roads in the centre of the small country town converge to form a cross. I had forgotten to warn the Professor not to go wandering during the small wee hours of the morning as it was rumoured that the area was haunted. It is reputed that restoration work on an old house in the old town square had activated ghostly sightings. I was interested to stand watch for the night in the hope of some paranormal phenomena activity. I invited my mother to accompany me but she gingerly declined the offer. I then approached my father, who merely turned rather pale and seemed somewhat reluctant to commit himself. I debated whether to ask the American Professor but decided against it, thinking that perhaps it was not quite the done thing to scare one's guest to death when they had jetted in from the States to meet you.

The Professor and I had been in correspondence over the years and he had expressed a wish to meet me. I had sent him a half-hour audiotape, which my mother and I had recorded for a school conference. It outlined my ambition to attend mainstream College and the frustration I felt at the position I was in at school. I say, my mother and I, in that I had sat on a chair speaking the words into the microphone, shocked at my own audacity at having the nerve to stand up against the bureaucracy of school. My mother had held the microphone and with steely-eyed determination, gently bullied me into speaking louder, as I hesitantly whispered the words. The Professor had learned from my letters that I had been able to read out loud since I was five years of age, and although unable to hold a fluent conversation, I was able to speak most of the words I typed, before, as, or after I typed them.

My father had left early one morning in his car to collect the Professor from his hotel. Upon his arrival at the house, the Professor had enthusiastically strode into the room hauling an enormous bag, from which he drew out a tape recorder, stand, external microphone and a dreaded video camera, which he proceeded to set up in the middle of the lounge. I had been looking forward to talking to him but I was on the defensive, as when I had arranged to meet with him, I had not realised he would bring all his paraphernalia.

He sat in the chair across the room, from where I, on guard, tried to merge into the soft cushions of the sofa. He looked impressively serious and thoughtful, except that on occasion his weather-beaten, bearded face broke into a warm engaging smile. He exhibited a keen sense of the ridiculous, out of keeping with the room and my occupation of it. It was infuriating not to be able to engage him in verbal conversation. Consumed by fury I felt the urge to climb out of my body, walk away, and say, "It is not me."

In a miff, I flung myself into a nearby chair, crossed my legs and looked back on my life in uncharted anger and sorrow. I asked myself, "Am I that person?" Is he me, with his unordered inept actions, face tense, screwed up in concentration, no words spoken with measured ease? In fierce determination, I looked myself menacingly in the eye. An indestructible thought pushed the all-consuming anger aside. It is not so painless to fight when you have nothing left to fight back with. It is not so simple to defend yourself when you have no armour to protect yourself against the world, before you have been able to master the terms of engagement. Conscience-stricken, my anger became of no consequence. Cooling my impatience, I told myself it was fine to be me.

In a quarrelsome mood I sat on a chair, my "Lightwriter" on my lap, and began to type some words independently, annoyed with both myself and my patient mother settled beside me. She had become my unmovable rock in any storm, my harbour of refuge I could return to, as I was tossed relentlessly on the sea of life from one raw emotion to the next. I spoke the words as I typed one or two sentences, at one juncture I said,

"I want people to understand." I held a model car for the American Professor to see, opened the doors and typed, "I will tell you the doors are open, I am free." Ironically, the words from a song "one world for us, one world for humanity . . . one world for us, one world with her open door," drifted across the room.

I hesitantly read out loud some lines I had typed from a page, frustrated that the words came out in stops and starts, not articulately as I am able to read to myself. I told the Professor, "I have had years of not being able to communicate," and that I was now "able to join in the conversation." The words I wanted to speak to him were all in my head but I could not express them. How do you say to someone like that, "I am so pleased to meet you," when all you can do is extend a hand in friendship and hope the message gets across.

We had a good time, the Professor and I. It was last day of the Professor's visit and once we were able to escape the confines of the house and the video equipment we travelled to Cambridge. I wanted to show him the ancient University town, with its numerous historic colleges connected to the 11th century University. The slothful heat of the day engulfed us as we strolled through the alluring moss-green lawns and avenues known as the "Backs," which stretch along the banks of the river Cam with its graceful sloping tree-lined banks and timeworn stone bridges. The "Trinity Bridge" and "The Bridge of Sighs," at the "Backs," are connected with the gardens where the students hire long narrow punts to laze away hot, humid summer evenings and Sunday afternoons.

The centuries have seen many inspiring poets tread its well-worn cobblestone pavements, Tennyson, Lord Byron, Rupert Brooke, to name but a few. Tennyson, a dashing character in his black frock coat and dubbed "Poet of the People," noted, "with studious eye, How Cambridge waters hurry by." Society flirt, Lady Caroline Lamb, said of the wild rakish poet and idealist liberal, Lord Byron, that he was "mad, bad and dangerous to know," before cold-shouldered by his contemporaries he left England and became involved in the rebellion of the Greeks against the Turks. Rupert Brooke, scholar and poet, wrote of Cambridge, "I only know that you may lie, day-long and watch the Cambridge sky." Not that I had lain and watched the "sky" or studied the "waters" with "studious eye" mind you. I did stand in front of a statue of the founder of the College (1546), King Henry VIII, at the Great Gate of Trinity College, and, giving him a wary-eyed glance, recalling his wrathful remark, "There was no head so fine that he would not make it fly," I cautiously took a step backwards and boldly enquired, "Why the devil did you chop off the heads of your poor Queens?"

I loved the atmosphere, the hustle and bustle, the quaint old-world charm of the tiny narrow streets, the indigenous architecture, the buildings, the hundreds of students, calling out to one another as they rode past on their cycles. Of different nationalities, Americans, French, German, Dutch, Japanese, they intrigued me. I savoured the distinctive vibrant energy of the city, the tourists, the noise, the crowds, the excitement, the chatter, the movement, all of it.

I stood hesitantly in a shop doorway, the inner depths of which were humming with industrious activity, to choose some post cards off a huge flat display, wishing I had the resilience to venture inside. I had foolishly committed such an act of recklessness on an earlier visit, but on this occasion I reluctantly handed the cards I had decided upon to my mother, who stout-heartedly plunged into the crammed shop to pay for them. It was decidedly less painful than doing a body-swerve, dodging and ducking into the skirmish myself. I would have been jostled, knocked, thumped, jerked and propelled through the recesses of the shop, arriving at the till, infuriated and belligerent, like a stubborn, ruffled, disconcerted cock-robin bristling with indignation. All arms and legs, endeavouring to allow people past, flattening myself against the walls, hair-on-end, to eventually emerge from the shop twisted and bent out of shape, clutching the cards, disjointed, breathless, bedraggled, one impudent eye-brow raised, but victorious.

We did a lightning tour of the city, going through St. Mary's Passage to visit the sanctuary of St. Mary's Church, walking through the cool, still, silent aisles. We then viewed the Round Church of St. Benet's with its interesting pre-Norman tower. Ultimately we came to a pause to sit in idle inactivity, tired, hot and thirsty, on a wall opposite one of the University Colleges, to quench our thirst from some cans my father had purchased. I did not let on to the Professor, but I had never actually sat on a wall before and drank from a can. I deduced the trick was to keep one's feet firmly on the ground and not to fall backwards as one took a swig or one might choke to death.

As the cool liquid slid down my throat, my thoughts turned to a young man that had sat on the pavement with his dog, outside one of the shops, not far from where we were now seated on the wall, a few months back, and I wondered what had become of him. The day had been, like this day, hot and humid, one of the warmest days of summer, and I had noticed him as I had walked past with my parents on the way to find somewhere to eat a late lunch. We had found a vacant table adjacent to the window of a restaurant and as I had looked across at the world-weary young man stroking his dog affectionately, my father remarked that he was selling the "Big Issue," a magazine that down-and-outs sell on the streets, in an effort to regain entry into affluent society. My father slowly ambled over to buy a copy, my mother aiming a remark at his departing back, that perhaps he should ask the young man if he would like a cup of tea or coffee, or something to eat.

I studied them both as my father bent down to speak to the young man, to return a few minutes later, saying he would be glad of some coffee. My father immediately disappeared again to purchase it for him. I wondered whether the young man had eaten recently as I held my lunch in my hand and my hunger rapidly receded. I thought that could easily have been me sitting on the pavement, perhaps homeless, destitute, penniless, alone in the world. My father came back with the coffee, food and a bottle of water for the man's dog. He took it across the street and stood chatting to the young man for several minutes. I watched as the man poured the water into an empty cup for his dog to lap, before he closed his eyes, and rested his head against the wall, the warmth of the late afternoon sun on his young care worn face.

Having finished our meal I had taken a note out of my wallet and trusting he would not be offended had walked over and clumsily reached out to hand it to him. The hand that took it was black with grime. He clasped his hand round mine and thanked me. Choking back tears, he told my father that he had had an argument with his girlfriend the previous day and he was worried about her, as he did not know where she was. I wondered if he had a home to go to, and thought maybe he slept on a park bench or lived in a run-down squat or cardboard city somewhere. Feeling guilty I walked away.

Leaving the wall, and throwing the empty cans away, we walked through a maze of narrow alleyways with the American Professor. It was suggested we find a restaurant to eat. Famished, I was endeavouring to ignore the rumblings of my stomach when I caught sight of a sign that said "Fish and Chips" a few doors further down the alleyway and attracted my father's attention. Entering the Greek restaurant we climbed a steep, narrow row of stairs to where the young proprietor politely ushered us to a table. It was the first time I had been in a Greek restaurant. My main concern was the flight of stairs and if I could make it down without landing in an unruly heap at the bottom. If I fell it would be a question of whom I flattened in the process. Praying it would not be the American Professor, I thought it through and decided if it was my father that it would not be too tragic, as long as he had had the forethought to have paid the bill before taking on the roll of bodyguard and contriving to get me in one piece to the ground floor.

On the way home, my father having asked the Professor if he was interested in visiting an American War Memorial just outside the city centre, we took the road to Madingley where the cemetery was situated. My grandfather, a World War II veteran, had brought my mother here forty odd years ago when she was a child. I recall my mother asking my grandfather where the cemetery was that he had taken her to visit. He had replied that it was somewhere near Cambridge but he could not remember the exact location. When we were next in Cambridge we had studied a map and taken a detour to unearth the cemetery.

It was late afternoon as we arrived at the cemetery. The still silence was sobering after the excitement of the town. We followed a small pathway to stand inside the gate in front of a long stone wall, 427 feet long, with the names engraved upon it, of soldiers, airmen and seamen, some listed as missing in action, others that were lost or buried at sea, or the "unknowns," all of whom had died in the Second World War, the wall being a tribute to their memory. Soft words fell into the air, "whose names here appear . . . part of the price . . . free men . . . to defend human liberty and rights," as I walked the length of the wall. A line of fresh faced "drummer boy" roses stood to attention as they guarded a water garden to my rear. A grinning daredevil of an airman, carved in stone, in front of the wall, one of four servicemen, waved a farewell as he took off on his eternal flight. Further on down the line a tough, weary, stony-eyed soldier tensed with expectation, leapt into action, his rifle rammed into his shoulder as the enemy stealthily crept into sight. A rugged young marine lunged desperately into the depths of the dark midnight sea hauling an unconscious comrade with him. Polished boots pounded across the deck of a destroyer as it went down. I could hear scared shouts shattering the ominous deathly hush.

Turning, a lump in my throat, I came to a halt and took stock of the mass of graves, a white marble cross marking each one, arranged in curved plots, row after row after row of young men who fought and died for their country. A solitary leaf from a nearby oak fluttered to the ground as my feet crunched harshly on the gravel underfoot. I felt so humbled in face of such a loss of human life, as though my own problems, my own existence were of no consequence.

I sat in the quiet beside the American Professor on a stone bench and tentatively put my hand on his shoulder. My mother took some photographs and we walked down a row of steps at the end of the cemetery to look at the view of the rolling tranquil green fields of England. The smell of smoke drifted across from a bonfire where workmen were burning some branches. I gazed absentmindedly at the curl of smoke that rose into the air and drifted through an avenue of trees that lined the pathway as we returned the way we had come. I climbed nine steps, to stand beneath "old glory," the flag of America, flying with eminence over the peaceful countryside. In the office of the Superintendent, the American Professor and I each wrote some words in the visitor's book. I gave thought to those men who fought together side by side. They had been part of something, a bigger picture, lives sacrificed for the good of the whole. I could not have put into words what I felt that day. I felt so proud of my own grandfather, and my great uncles, and all those courageous men and women who had defended their liberty. I had also fought a war, on a lesser scale; it had been a battle for survival.

College Life

I had survived the first year of my "A" level course. With summer coming to an end, I enthusiastically read "Translations" twice in one week in preparation for my return to College. It was a play we were to study the next term by Brian Friel, an Irishman, covering the Irish language and culture, in a modern day setting.

It was a wonderful time in my life. I sat in class encircled by vivacious studious faces, enthralled. The students had presented me with a card at the end of the term, signed by each of them, extending their best wishes and commenting that it had been good to have me in the study group. Appreciative of the gesture, those words spurred me on. I was bent on going back for the new academic year. In all my years at school I had not before felt as if I was part of some bigger perspective, as if what I thought was of significance. I was given recognition for my ability at College, not penalized for being disabled. I did not want tea and sympathy. My uppermost intent was to come to terms with my difficulties, to undertake to adapt until it hurt.

As the first day of term drew nearer, butterflies began a war dance in my stomach. I wished I could impart to my College Lecturer and the other students how I would have liked to engage in instinctive conversation with them. Full of misgivings I asked myself, where would I begin? How would they respond? How could I hope to counterbalance the disadvantage of twenty years of lost experience in the three short terms I had been at College? I reflected on my childhood and upbraided myself for not acquiring verbal language. A friend told me I was not at fault.

I consoled myself with the thought that there was no time for social chitchat in the study sessions. We had worked at a furious pace to cover the syllabus over the last year. It sufficed that I was able to go to College and be accepted by the other students and be one of the group.

The Lecturer and I communicated by note form. He wrote me a note each week outlining the lesson plan for each session. Keen to learn, I hungrily devoured each word. His cheery hallo as he handed it to me when I walked into class, made me feel welcome. I would write back, sometimes in the car on the way to College. It enabled us to form a good relationship and become friends.

My father went to College with me as my support worker, for the English Literature sessions. He paced down long corridors with me, the soft thud of his heavy steps echoing mine. He guided me through open doorways, up and down stairways, and pulled out my chair at the desk, enabling me to collapse onto the seat in relief that I had made it that far with no mishap. There had been insufficient time to find a support worker when I had been offered the College placement. My father had consented to step in and the arrangement worked. We were both happy with it. He drove me to and from the College (a twenty-six mile round journey). Each session was recorded on a cassette tape, which I was then able to replay at home. I was unable to write out any notes as it necessitated support to steady my hand, and the speed at which I wrote was painstakingly slow. I would not have been able to keep up the pace if I had taken notes whilst the Lecturer spoke. His low, quiet tones captured my attention as he discussed the aspects of each book we were reading. My secretary, in the guise of my mother, typed out the contents of the tape each week. The study notes were then at hand if there was something I needed to refer to. The majority of my work was done from the books we were studying and from memory.

The first day of term arrived and I crept somewhat sheepishly back into College. I sat still and silent as a small mouse throughout the lesson. A memory had surfaced, a worry that my English Lecturer would be annoyed with me after an incident in one of the sessions towards the end of the term.

It had been around the beginning of May. I had sat in class one morning with a support worker. She had been engaged to sit in over a period of weeks in the expectation that she would thereafter take over from my father. A momentary lull in the morning's industrious machinery took place and my thoughts turned to something that I was agonizing over. I wanted to somehow speak to the other students at the College or maybe approach the Student Union, but my communication difficulties deterred me. The Art History Lecturer had told us he was leaving to continue his career at another College. I was consumed with anxiety that the English Lecturer would go as well.

One by one, the staff had resigned, been dismissed, or made redundant at the College where my father had worked. Changes had been taking place all over the country with regard to the position of Lecturers in Further Education. We had heard on the radio that a generation of Lecturers, many thousands, had been forced out of their positions of employment. College staff nation-wide were being pressured into signing new contracts. There were several articles in a local newspaper, talk of one-day strikes and redundancies, of the unrest at the College I attended. I felt it was a civil liberties issue, something that affected all of us. I remembered that at the College where my father worked and my brother had been a student a few years earlier some of the students had felt so strongly about the situation they had organised a demonstration. Many of the staff, union activities banned, disquiet rampant, had been forced to leave the College over a two-year period. One department had been closed down and the Lecturers given notice. The organisers of the walkout called upon the other students to come out in protest to show their collective solidarity for the College Lecturers. Leaflets were handed out the week before the demonstration in a determination to make their protests felt.

On the day of the demonstration, two hundred students set off from one of the College buildings, during their lunch break. They marched round to the front doors and called upon the other students to join them. As the high-spirited body of students flocked outside the College, the doors were abruptly slammed shut and locked. The students wishing to join the protest were unable to leave the building. Uproar followed. The students outside stood shouting for their fellow students inside the College to jump out of the windows, to unite with them, in their larger numbers. Reporters turned up with a film crew, but for some reason it never made the press.

My brother was unaware of the goings-on until he came home that evening. My father had asked if any of his friends had joined the demonstration. He told us he had only been in College for a few hours in the early morning and had not heard of the students' bid to use their democratic vote with their feet. I wished I had been there. Always a hot-head, I visualised myself leaping out of the window, landing on my feet, yelling for my fellow students to join en masse.

As I sat in the quiet confines of the classroom that day I wanted to illustrate my support for the College staff. I waited anxiously towards the end of the morning. Then desperate to catch the attention of the students before they all left the room for lunch, in a sudden rush of inspiration I jumped up from where I sat and climbed onto a chair. I wanted to address the other students, to inform them what had transpired at other Colleges, and solicit their support for the staff at the College. I wanted to make an inspiring speech on the rights of the individual. I wanted to be the me that no one other than myself knew, the me that I could have been, outgoing, eloquent, vivacious, passionate. The words I would say pounded in my head. Only, when the moment arrived, the words did not come and I forgot in my haste one very important thing—I actually had no head for heights. Once up, standing upon the chair, ashen faced, I was stuck, unable to climb down. The Lecturer, seeing I was in danger of taking a dive out of an open window, called for my father. I was rebuked for causing a disturbance.

I decided in hindsight it would not have looked too good in the local headlines. "Student at Local College Jumps Out of Open Window." I consoled myself with the thought it was a mad idea. Belatedly, I decided I should have written to the Lecturer and asked him to read the contents of my letter to the other students. I debated as to whether I should own up as to why I had climbed on the chair but after much deliberation I decided I was in enough trouble as it was.

A Blue Hair Day—Making a Statement

The New Year breezed in and I resumed my studies at College. In a reckless mood, I walked through the doors of the College one morning, my hair streaked blue. In the corridor my English Literature Lecturer greeted me saying, "I see you are making a statement today Richard." I grinned back ruefully into his courteous, good-humoured face.

I had thought to be the first in, and sit all moderation, waiting for the other students to put in an appearance, but with the usual mad scramble to leave home on time, and the traffic jammed along the route, fate had not been on my side. Or, nearer the truth, I had spent ten minutes too long in bed, before reluctantly, and sleepily, I dragged myself down the stairs for breakfast. Cursing the traffic that held us up on the journey to College, I glanced impatiently at the clock on the car dashboard.

By the time I edged straight-faced into the classroom, the half a dozen students were assembled ready for the class to begin. No one said a word.

A Jay Walker

The late summer sun felt warm on my face, as I, hi-jacked by my mother, we waited at the bus stop to journey into town. Nearby houses crouched sleepily under a cloudless sky. A bus materialised and rumbled to a halt. We stood back whilst the people surged forward, climbed onto the bus and paid their fares. With no audience to observe the action, I tightened my limbs in expectation and awkwardly clutched the handrail to clamber up the two steps. As I moved forward into the bus itself, eyes glanced furtively sideways in my direction; well acquainted with this intrusive interest, jaw clenched, I retained my composure. People's attitude nettled me. From the now blank expressions of studied indifference the other passengers clearly thought that I was not conscious of the unwelcome attention I attracted.

The bus suddenly raced forward. I made a grab for a rail to keep my balance. It likely appeared strange to the other occupants of the bus, a young man, six foot tall, hair streaked blue and purple, all arms and legs, hanging on to a rail in quiet desperation, stuck, unable to slide into the vacant seat. In a quarrelsome mood I resented people for being there to witness it. I bestowed a wintry look at one poor unsuspecting soul. Eyes narrowed, I privately reserved the right to throttle any or all of them on the return journey. My mother ignoring their looks, her forehead creased in a frown, unobtrusively took my arm and gently shoved me into the seat. A sigh of relief escaped her lips. I thought it spoke volumes that not one eye had set on the streaked hair!

The journey into town would take fifteen minutes. I stared out of the window, my shoulders set in defiance, thankful that the conductor, a middle aged man with an aggrieved air, had not spoken to me directly; not being seen to respond it would merely have drawn still more of the unwarranted attention to myself. "More astute at this conjuncture to be thought voiceless," I thought to myself; stranded in a time warp by an inability to speak fluently. Indifferent lack of concern was a good attitude, and that worked well unless someone spoke to me; then the chinks in my armour would become apparent.

I bestirred myself as the bus on the final throes of the journey arrived at our destination. The instant the bus came to a halt I needed to vacate my seat, otherwise people would crowd on before I had time to alight. My mother touched my arm in a silent request. I tightened my limbs once more, collected my wits together, and abandoned the seat. The bus now jam-packed with people, the twitching noses and obscure sideway gawks began again. My mother blocked the passage of the person behind her; it gave me seconds to co-ordinate my gait. I shoved my hands in my pockets, in the hope that the glances did not, worse still, turn to one of sympathy; sympathy was too difficult to deal with. I stumbled down the wretched steps; the people clambering on perceived the difficulty, mumbled an apology for standing in my path, and moved aside. I felt guilty for the inconvenience I caused. I gave a philosophical shrug vowing next time I would take a taxi; it was not worth wreaking this upon my mother or myself. The thought occurred to me that without my mother's help, likely as not, I would now be a tragic mass on the pavement. I was not virtuous enough not to wish her to disappear into oblivion anyway!

We moved away from the crush at the bus stop and covered the short distance to a pelican-crossing arms linked. The traffic lights changed to red. The beep beep announced it was safe to cross the road. In theory, it would take me twenty seconds to walk across but the lights would change to green in ten, leaving me insufficient time. I wished someone would change the time setting as I held onto my mother's arm and together we made a mad dash through the on coming people for the pavement before we were mowed down by the now moving traffic.

The pavements in the quiet country town were overflowing with people. It was market day and they were hurrying in all directions like neurotic ants. I undertook to avoid the exploits of the ferocious predators as we manoeuvred our way around them. My mother noticed my predicament. Worried that I would trip on the uneven surface of the narrow crowded pavements she tightened her arm in mine to help me retain my balance. I tried to adapt my pace to that of the people walking around me. No one seemed to look where they were going. Envy burned somewhere deep in the region of my chest; wherever one looked people were happily engaged in conversation. I wished it were something I could do; chat with my mother as we walked. It was impossible to try to walk and type on the Lightwriter; it took all my concentration to co-ordinate my movements and to engineer my way through the crowds. My mother warned, "Be careful of that lady; she's elderly"; not to knock into the child that had just stepped on my foot and kicked my ankle; not to fall off the curb into the road chock-a-block with stationary and passing cars. I viewed the stretch of road in question thoughtfully and decided she was right, "It was no place to die!"

Coming out of a shop, my mother planted her bags on the ground and struggled to collect them together. I walked the short distance to the curb and waited with impatience to cross back the way we had come. Eyeing a taxi rank, I thought we really should take a taxi. I glimpsed my mother's face; her marked look told me to wait for the traffic to clear. Her eyes caught mine. Steps ahead of her, I geared myself into action and strode the six or seven steps between the moving cars. My mother tore after me and on reaching the pavement, we eyed each other, her in angry concern and I in pique. Her eyes glinted with anger. I scowled back. My mother said, "You could have caused an accident." I conceded the point but people walked in between cars all the time. On reflection I recalled cars do fly around the bend at speed at that road junction.

An image came to mind; myself aged five or six, walking across the main road where I lived, clasping my brother and mother's hand. Halfway across I had tripped and fallen. An approaching car braked furiously; the ear-splitting screech resounded in my ears; my mother and eight year old brother seized my arms, dragged me to my feet, and pulled me onto the safety of the sidewalk.

My mother, in one of her saner moments, made the decision to walk home. We made a change in direction and turned a corner and continued on; past the church; past the houses; leaving behind all constraints mother and I walked the miles home, arm in arm, down the quiet country roads, the warm summer sun on our faces.

Award Ceremony/Student Achievement Evening

It was May. Blue bell-like wild hyacinth flowered in abundance, trees broke into leaf, mayflies winged their transparent flight, and I, midway into my third term at College, with thoughtful fingers and willing eyes, studied the works of Shakespeare, Plath and Milton. In class one Tuesday morning, my English Literature Lecturer told me that I had been nominated for an award for Personal Achievement in both "A" level [Advanced Level] English Literature and Art History. I was invited to attend an Award Ceremony at the College. I was informed I could take two visitors with me. I asked if my support worker from Art History could attend with both my parents, making three. Permission given, we arrived on time, to be escorted to the hall, to our seats. The chairs set out in long rows, stretched the length of the room. A thronging mass of amicable nodding faces converged as if from nowhere. The low murmur of excited voices drifted across the room.

My nerves ragged, I waited the half an hour for the ceremony to begin. The Chairman of the Corporation Board was to open the evening, followed by an introduction by the lady Principal. I shifted my position, cramped, on the unbending chair. A head veered round as my long legs hit the seat in front; awkwardly I hitched my legs in, the tight gap dividing the rows of chairs, allowing me no room to manoeuvre.

It had been agreed I could walk the short distance to receive the award, or I could remain seated and the guest of honour, a local radio commentator, would fetch it to me. With a silent groan of despair I saw the difficulty. An ill-fitting cog in the well-oiled wheel of efficiency, I pictured the turn of faces in my direction, the drag of the chair on the floor, the hasty shuffle of people, enabling me to pass. Panic began to set in. My instinct was to flee the room. I guess I looked much as I felt. A kind member of staff standing to one side of the hall asked if I would like a cup of water. I had wickedly thought to myself, a sizeable straw hat might do the trick. My name was called. Transfixed, the horror I felt apparent in my face, I sat motionless. The Presenter walked to where I was seated, I reached out and took my certificate.

(. . . Eighteen Months Later)

It was November. Autumn in homage of bygone summer days set down her roots. The evenings huge and gray advanced their soft march and the warm, pungent, earthy smell of decaying vegetation hung heavy on the air. Out of the blue, I received notification from the Director of Curriculum and Client Services at College, informing me that I had won an award for Outstanding Commitment [Perseverance against Adversity] for my work for the academic year. I was invited to attend a Student Achievement Evening. I was overwhelmed that I had been put forward for the nomination.

Clutching the notification in my hand, I remembered the Award Ceremony at the end of the summer term of the previous year. I had changed so much over the past year. This time round I was resolute; I was going to walk to the stage to accept the award. The day arrived and intent on not being perceived as disabled foremost, I donned my designer jeans, and asked my parent to hi-light my hair with red streaks. It was a sharp, cold, mid-winter's day, the week before Christmas. I wore a new thick shaggy fleece, with a t-shirt underneath, as I did not want to be bothered with keeping track of a jacket.

I arrived at seven thirty sharp at the reception desk at the College with my parents in tow. A lofty Christmas tree stood ablaze with colour in the foyer. We were ushered through to the hall where the presentation was to take place. Tables had been arranged around the hall for small parties of people to sit at. Having made it through the maze of people to our allocated table, I sank onto a chair, only to find that we had to share the table with some people I did not know. Disconcerted, I sat half-turned away so I did not have to register their presence; if they had spoken to me, my nerve would have failed. It was impolite but I wanted to focus on the presentation.

The room was crowded with people. The atmosphere was less formal than I had expected. People were milling around. Laughter and chatter engulfed me. We had been allocated a table at the front, near the stage, so I would not have far to walk. I sat silent, absorbed by what was transpiring around me. I had been told a local MP was going to be there and that the Editor of the local newspaper was going to present the awards. I surveyed the layout and worked through a strategy. Walk to the front, accept the award, offer my thanks, smile and walk back to my seat. I knew one of the young men from my study session was also to be given an award, but I could not see him anywhere. I noticed the Director of Curriculum and Client services, whom I had met once or twice, seated next to the Editor from the newspaper. I determinedly resolved not to let her or my College lecturers down. Besides which my mother gave me a steely-eyed glare, which spoke volumes. My father became the suit sitting to my left. I recited a poem to myself that I had written:

> *I am east*
> *You are south*
> *We are the same*
> *But different*

I am north
You are west
We are the same
But different

We all live side by side
In this world
But each of us
Is different

We are all forms
Of human life
All the same
But different

The College Principal, a slim man in glasses, made an introductory speech welcoming us all to the evening and congratulating the students on their achievements. Warmth in his tone, he said, "This is not the end of the road. Our paths will continue to cross in the future." Then one by one each of the students walked up the steps, across the stage to receive their award. The Director of Curriculum related some personal history of each student, explaining why they had merited the award. My name was called, "Richard Attfield." I tensed, scared to breathe. My mother none too gently dug me in the ribs as a signal for me to move. It jarred me into life. I rose automatically from my seat, my father following close behind, I walked the distance to the stage, climbed the three steps, which I had already counted, and lost my footing at the top of the steps. The Editor of the local newspaper promptly shot forward to steady me as my father seized me from behind, before I landed inelegantly in a heap in the mince pies and plum pudding. Regaining my composure, I stood between the Editor and my father, award in my hand, grinning broadly, as a photographer took a photograph. The flash did not work. I stood looking at my name printed on the envelope, the seconds ticking away, whilst the photographer, fiddled with his camera. He took another photograph, the flash exploding in my eyes. Taken unawares I did not smile or manage to express my thanks, before I walked back to my chair collapsing thankfully onto the seat.

The wine flowed, the speeches were made, the evening drew to an end, and the students departed home. The entire affair had taken two hours. Fatigued, I lingered in the hall until the crush had receded. I made my way out to the foyer where the Principal stood, goodwill written in his smiling features. He stepped forward to offer his congratulations. Wishing I had downed a glass or two of the rich red wine, clumsily I engaged him in conversation, typing two or three sentences. It was too late and to the wrong person, but it went some small way to expressing my thanks.

Does He Take Sugar?

A hospital appointment I had waited months for arrived in the post. I had no wish to go; too many memories of hospital appointments during my childhood became tangible, but it seemed I had no other option open to me. The day before the appointment the telephone rang. My mother raced over to grab it and chirped a hallo down the receiver. An insistent secretary tied up in red tape in a bureaucratic nook, informed us that, due to a clerical error, the appointment had to be cancelled. My mother, nettled, refused to accept the cancellation given the months I had had to wait. She stated to the person on the other end of the line, that we were going to be there. I winced as she slammed down the telephone in exasperation.

The journey was long and tedious. Due to the heavy traffic, we arrived with minutes to spare. The car park crammed full, we hurtled round the grounds on the look out for a space. Now late, upon reaching the hospital we tore along corridors and up stairways, akin to things demented. My mother scurried to the fore with agility, whilst I, leaning disorderedly on my father, matching my strides to his, soldiered on at the rear. Stressed, by the untimely delay and the impending consultation, I reported to the reception desk.

With no time to unwind, I bulldozed into a stagnant, oppressive room where death-watch beetle drummed its beat, to meet a 3rd or 4th year medical student, with a dogged determination to stand my ground this time round. He introduced himself in a hesitant, self-conscious manner and commenced to ask a barrage of questions, none of which appeared to be relevant. Scribbling notes across sheets of paper, he delved into my background history, exhuming ghosts laid to rest, unearthing memories of my childhood that I wanted buried and forgotten. I started to type with some support, bent on answering his questions myself. But, contrary to my expectation, he did not direct them at me; he spoke to my parents, excluding me from the conversation. Not incorporated in the discussion, I became "talked about" instead of "included." My parents insisted I answer myself, not feeling in a position to do so for me. Stung by the student's stance, on the defensive, I sourly doubted if he had any experience of conversing with someone using a "Lightwriter" or communication board. From his reaction one would have thought I was Medusa reincarnated.

The Consultant came in and spoke to the student, asking him to relate back the notes. He began to read them out loud. None too impressed by their insensitive attitude, I tried to point out that the notes were inaccurate. The Consultant a squat, brusque, bulldog of a man, with a condescending air, checked me and asked me to wait until the student had read the notes. I deliberated, ill humouredly, that "I thought I was the person in dire need of assistance, not the student."

At this conjuncture, well nigh half of the allotted two-hour time had elapsed. Worried we had not begun to discuss the reason for my visit, I wished I had followed my own inclination and cancelled the appointment. Conversation flew around my head. The Consultant, uninterested that the notes were unreliable, did not bother to respond to my concerns. I felt it was important to speak for myself. That was easier in theory than practice. I began to point at the Lightwriter keys, wondering if there was any need for me to be there at all. Beginning to feel stupid, it occurred to me I could do a strategic battle retreat to the door. No one would notice that I had left. Given the direction things were taking, the conversation could be conducted without my presence.

Unable to express myself fluently in speech, I found myself in the same dilemma that I have been in countless times before, of people unable to conceive that I have thoughts in my head. Because of my inability to put voice to them, I had no command over my life. Distressed, I stood up to leave.

Flying a Kite

My first reaction to seeing the rather auspicious looking kite, was to moodily tell myself there was no way I was possibly going to be able to fly it. I had sighted the kite in a "For Sale" box. I lifted it out and gave it to my father, who purchased it for me. An image came to mind of myself, six foot tall, all gangling arms and legs tied up in yards of the string. I felt betrayed by the mere complication of it. Consequently the kite sat in the boot of my father's car for a time before I gave it another thought.

I had vague memories of my brother flying a kite on holiday one year. He was eight or nine years of age, which would have made me five or six. I can see him, standing in the middle of the huge green, outside of my grandparent's holiday chalet with my mother one August evening, kite in hand, unravelling the string. One of my cousins had left the kite on top of a cupboard in a bedroom, and my brother having found it, asked my parents if he could take it outside. The angry, howling wind tore across the rugged green, as he laughed and ran with the kite before releasing it, from whence the kite confidently navigated a course upwards into the moaning wind. From where I stood, at the doorway of the chalet, bushy tailed wide-eyed baby rabbits could be seen scampering friskily across the rutted grassy slope to dive without warning into the rabbit holes strewn the length of it.

One summer's evening, my parents and I were driving home along the coast road when my father saw an object in the distance. He drew my attention to it, remarking upon its height and shape, and came to the conclusion that it was a kite. This became more evident the closer we came upon it. The kite, midnight black, seemed to double over and bend back on itself. It was not what one could describe by any stretch of the imagination as an exciting kite other than the fact that it was flying well.

I was quite envious of it; it was flying free, like a great black bird. We decided upon the spur of the moment to pull over and walk along the shoreline to observe the kite. It had however disappeared from view by the time we had driven into a nearby parking bay and quit the confines of the car. Recalling the kite, lying neglected and abandoned in the dark recess of the car boot, we took it up to the seashore.

The evening was drawing in, and the softness of the hour engulfed us in its hushed hues. The glowing, crimson-yellow face of the setting sun, reflected in the rippling waters of a nearby rock pool, dutifully bid us a sleepy goodnight. The beach was by now deserted, other than by a young couple who sat further along, whispering to each other. The occasional straggler sauntered by as we unraveled the kite and tried to give it flight. Our initial attempts failed miserably. The vocal cries, a high pitched, "ke ke ke" of black-headed seagulls, their chocolate brown countenance in evidence, broke the tranquility of the eventide, as they circled and soared overhead. The impudent wind boldly ruffled my hair as I stood with the kite in my hand. I stretched my arms to tentatively hold the kite high above my head whilst my father pulled the string taunt. He shouted to me to launch the kite. A small, black, shaggy ancient dog ran through the sandy shallows, showering me with the salty spray. My mother's eyes crinkled in mirth. Then, suddenly the battling wind lifted the kite, but it seemed to have a will of its own, after lying neglected for so long. It shot up, soaring, wavering for a fleeting moment in time before somersaulting in mid-air, landing with a loud plop at my feet.

A solitary man quietly approached along the sea walk and stood idly by, watching for a few seconds before continuing on his evening stroll. He walked but a few steps further when he halted, to gaze in avid interest, as my mother held up what I had by now decided was a very unfeeling kite to the winds. I sought consolation in the fact that his attention had been engaged by our objective. His stance and empathy brought a quiet strength into my world. The kite took off for about the twentieth time, now diving unbidden well-nigh into the wild spluttering of the slate-grey sea. The man, losing interest in our less than expert effort in controlling the stubborn resistance of the wily kite, once more continued on his journey.

The low drone of a radio could be heard drifting across the cool night air. I gazed out into the darkness of a thousand skies, old man sea lapping fiercely at my feet, all too willing to give up, convinced we were not going to witness the kite flying on the breath of the wind. Just then, my mother stooped, picked up the tiresome kite, and held it high; her five foot nothing frame stretching as far as it could, she yelled across the beach to my father to try once more. It soared, twisted and curved. I watched intrigued, as the kite sailed into the wind. Then seemingly tiring, it dithered as if unsure of its flying ability and once more fell silently, landing with a sudden thud on to the carpet of sand, as I stood cloaked by the dark night.

A Dickens of a Journey

A sudden e-mail leapt up onto the computer screen like some mischievous child, cheekily enquiring if I would like to be a guest speaker at a conference that evening in Middlesex. It took me completely unawares; it made me laugh. The need to stand-up-and-be-counted surged through me. I had sat through three conferences recently resisting the impulse to leap up from my seat in the audience to join the speaker on the stage, like some avenging angel setting the world to rights. Scared, I thrust the thought to one side. I might die of fright or fall flat on my face, but the concept of acceptance began to take root. It was short notice, but that was half the fun of it, the unexpected challenge. It was impractical, but on the other hand it was only three hours drive by car to Middlesex, I could make it if I moved with some urgency. The up side was that I did not have time to become overly anxious; if it had been weeks away, anxiety would have gnawed away at my innards like ravenous wolves who had a firm hold and were not prepared to release their grip.

Ruefully, I glanced down at myself. It was now well past eleven o'clock and too preoccupied answering correspondence, I had not dressed or consumed breakfast. My thoughts wandered again to the conference invitation. Warming to the idea, I decided I should go. My father, who was at work, would be home around mid-day. I was fairly confident he would not mind driving me to it.

It would be a larger gathering than on the two occasions that I had given a short talk, where there were roughly twenty people present. Difficult enough an objective, I was not prepared to dwell on it. Another fear surfaced. It was a nerve-racking ordeal to type on a communication aid in the presence of other people. I wished I could get the words out verbally. Life would be less complicated. The digital voice of the communicator sounds harsh and foreign even to my own ears. I had no notion of what I would say. My mind went blank. I tried to think of an opening line but the words eluded me. I told myself I would be fine when the time came. The words would come. A thought occurred to me. It's odd that for a person who has so much trouble expressing himself verbally, that mentally I am rarely at a loss for words. That thought amused me, as it often did.

Some three hours later I jumped in the car, with my parents in tow, for what turned out to be a mad dash down the M25. Food for the next day brought, for some obscure reason, as he drove into the petrol station to fill his fuel tank, my father felt the sudden urgent need to have his car washed. Perplexed, I tried to fathom why; I thought it was me that was going to be in the public eye, not the car!

All was going well until we left the motorway and reached the outskirts of Twickenham where, unsure of which road to take, we made a wrong turn. In my haste to leave home I had not been conversant of the fact we did not have the full address where the conference was to be held. I studied the e-mail again in the car; it merely gave the name of the hotel. Time was ticking by and I became aware my mother was speaking to my father. I put my own thoughts aside to listen. The anxious tone of her voice conveyed that we were in trouble—she was trying to convince my father of the fact that we were going to be late. My father however seemed to be equally assured that we had plenty of time.

One could never rush my father. My parents are somewhat of a nightmare. Mother, always dashing round like a thing demented, trying to do half a dozen things at once, rarely sits still, whilst my father lumbers around like a big slow, old bear and, at times, one with a sore head at that. Often becoming impatient with him when he does not move speedily enough, my mother raises her eyebrow in despair. They are exact opposites, although oddly, they were both born under the same birth sign of Aquarius.

A constant source of amusement to me, my mother frantically scoured the pages of the map. She could not see the print on the page without her reading glasses on, so she had to take them off and switch to her distance glasses to try to gauge where we were. In quiet desperation she peered at the map and gazed around trying to see a road name or sign. My father, now flustered, hemmed in on all sides by cars, yelled at her for directions. She repeated herself for about the tenth time, pointing out which road to take. Convinced that she could not read a map properly (I think it is a male thing myself), he decided to get into a different lane from the one she suggested. My mother, a good map-reader, given ample warning, is quite capable of mapping out a route. Ill-humouredly, she remarked to my father that she could only relate to him what was on the map. Bristling with indignation at his ill-timed comments, she once more buried her head in the map. We changed lanes twice in the space of five minutes. Then still unsure of which road to take, my father suggested we call at my aunt's house, which was nearby, to ask her for directions.

Mother was still furiously trying to fathom where we were when my somewhat ingenious father suggested she ring my aunt on his mobile to enquire if she knew where the hotel was situated. Regrettably, my father had forgotten to put the new London telephone codes into his tele-phone and she secured a wrong number. I was by now wishing I could slide under the seat and that I had not put everyone to so much trouble. My thoughts went to the conference. I was assured that I could pull out at the last minute if I became too nervous, but I was anxious not to let anyone down.

The whole situation became even more diverting from here on in. My father peered ahead into the now dark night, muttering to himself or us—I was not sure which—that he was quite certain my aunt lived in this road. My mother looked at him in utter disbelief and remarked tetchily, "Surely you must know where your own sister lives." Straight faced, I snorted down my nose, in an attempt not to laugh out loud at the pair of them.

We drove along for another ten minutes or so, my mother endeavour-ing to read the map and look out for my aunt's house at the same time. Without warning, my father pulled up outside a public house, stared across the road, and announced with little conviction in his voice, "I'm positive that is the house over there." Given we had visited only last year, I could understand my mother's irritation, when, in sudden exas-peration, with a rapid glance at the pub and then back at the house, she said, "Oh, for goodness sake will you go and knock." I gathered we were at the right house. Convinced we had time to spare, when we had thought to arrive at the conference by then, my father none too quickly crossed the road. From his aggrieved stance and tone of voice, I gauged he was probably in a real miff, likely feeling that he had been thoroughly nagged by my mother into doing her bidding.

Mother looked across at me and sighed, as she is often wont to do. Whether she was sighing at the sight of me or because of my father is hard to judge—the latter I guess. My father never ceases to amaze me that he cannot see how annoying he can be with his completely unruffable air.

He now stood calmly knocking on the door of the old Victorian house, and one wondered if he had the right house as he hesitantly ventured inside and was instantly swallowed up, disappearing from view. The line "Marley was dead, to begin with" from Dickens' "A Christmas Carol" humorously came to mind. I had a vision of Marley's ghostly apparition suddenly, chillingly materializing in the eerie darkness. A few minutes agonizingly passed by and then a few more. Creepier and creepier! If one listened very quietly, one could even hear the heavy clanking of the chains. My mother, considerably worried by now, more by the length of time my father was taking, I am sorry to say, than at the fact my father might well have met with an untimely demise in the chilly deep recess of Scrooge's front parlour. She glanced impatiently at the clock on the car dash board and then across the road at the door, which had to my mind now become the gruesome residence of the miserly Mr. Ebenezer Scrooge, where father was surely being accosted at this very moment for his less than charitable deeds on earth (in other words, yelling loudly at my mother because he did not know which route to take) by none other than the ghostly apparition of Jacob Marley "fetted" to the chains he had "forged in life" for his misdeeds. Yet another sigh hit the air and Marley's Ghost faded mysteriously away as quickly as it had surfaced, back into the pages of some dusty old book sitting in the corner of the bookshelf.

With yet another impatient sigh, mother opened the door of the car and sprinted across the road, darting between the passing cars. She ran up to the path and banged insistently on the door with the doorknocker. The sound shattered the stillness of the night. Would the ghostly apparition of Marley materialise out of nowhere with his hair looking as if it was "curiously stirred, as if by breath or hot air?" Would the eerie darkness swallow her up too? And would I then be left sitting here by myself with none other than the ghosts of Marley and Ebenezer to keep me company? I doubted it, but it was an amusing thought. I was now the one who breathed a deep sigh of relief and half grinned to myself, as finally a few seconds later both my aunt and father appeared. Obviously father had escaped from the clutches of Marley's Ghost on this occasion and retribution for his sins would wait until another day. I was of two minds whether or not to innocently ask him if he had seen old Marley's face in the doorknocker staring back at him.

My aunt climbed readily into her car that was parked in front of the house and, with us following behind, we once again set off on our journey. I was by now resigned to arriving late. My father told us that my aunt had had the yellow pages and a telephone directory at hand, so both she and my father had quickly searched through them and my father had found the name of the hotel. He had then telephoned the hotel to ask where it was situated. We were following behind my aunt's car when my father recited the number plate and asked my mother to write it down. My mother, rather perplexed, scrutinized my father with grave deliberation, as if he had gone completely deranged. He did not think to tell us until the next day that my aunt had bought a new car and although he had just seen her climb into it he thought he might not recognise it if we lost her in the fast flowing traffic. I thought it was rather odd myself, however his very reasonable excuse was that Londoners drive quicker than us quaint country folk.

Needless to say we were late. The car ground to an abrupt halt in the car park outside the hotel. The entrance hall was full of people. The speaker of the evening appeared from nowhere, spoke quietly to us, and hurriedly led us through to the conference room. There was no time to talk, no time to think, no time to collect myself. There I was in a hasty flurry of activity standing in front of a sea of faces. Lightwriter in my hand, I began to type. . . .

Notes

1. Richard won the Journalism and Overall prizes again in 2000; see "Talent Shines," *Gazette*, Thursday, June 29, 2000, p. 4. See also www.thisisessex.co.uk.
2. Richard later informed me that the girl he mentions in this piece became his friend. She played with him and would dry his hands when he washed them.
3. Richard has also been diagnosed with cerebral palsy.

4. Richard has referred to this person as "the Old Gentleman" rather than use a pseudonym.
5. This line is from Wordsworth, "The Prelude, Book 1" (1991).

References

Wordsworth, W. (1991). The prelude, book 1. In J. Wilson (ed.), *Lakeland poets* (p. 30). London: Grange Books.

8

■ ■ ■ ■ ■ ■ ■ ■ ■

I. The World as I'd Like It to Be

Jamie Burke

Editor's note: Part I of this chapter is a brief essay by a high school student, Jamie Burke. I first met this author when he was a student at the Jowonio School, a preschool that specializes in supporting students with autism and other developmental disabilities to be included in classrooms with nondisabled students. Jamie was four years old. He had not yet developed a reliable form of communication. He could say some individual words, but not sentences. In the years that followed, he learned to communicate by typing. One summer, when he was twelve, I asked one of my doctoral students to spend time with Jamie and to interview him about how he had developed the ability to type independently. During that summer, he began to speak the words he was typing. He showed that he could read aloud both what he had written and other texts. In the essay that follows, Jamie, a high school student at the time of this writing, discusses his ideas about learning and support. This essay builds upon a statement that he wrote when he was thirteen years old, when I asked him to speak to one of my graduate classes in Disability Studies.

What would a school of my dreams look like? Good soft seats and desks that held wonderful books that told of love and kindness. Kids would need to behave in the most kind manner and teasing would be a detention time. Everyone would be asked to join all clubs . . . and pleasing music would play everywhere. I would be able to tell my thoughts and troubles when I choose, not when others desire. . . . The teachers, good and many of them, would only be as we choose, not assigned by computers. Courses would be chosen by teachers' love of subject and teachers must be excellent in that class. If homework was told to be done, time more than one day would be given. Dear parents would be welcomed to meet really good teachers to tell of kids' powers. Lunch would be served in a room far from cooking so smells are not sickening. The lunch would be a time for peaceful eating and not loud talking and annoying bells and whistles which split my ears as a sword in use of killing monsters—my ears hear colossally well so noise can be difficult.

All of the new kids would be treated to a monster movie. A monster movie is what I hate but also love. So it [being treated to a monster movie] means that they would first understand me, as I would desire to understand them. The school would choose to show a movie that entertains and also scares the new students just a bit in order to say that they honor my personhood by acknowledging what I enjoy and need.

Teachers can help me mollify my desire for friends. You can give students a chance to know me. Friends are so hard to keep interested as it takes very much desirous time to type. Kids are mostly good at talking but listening is not an asset they use. If I am able to talk, it still is not very good, as time is fleeting and so are they.

My school is very good and people try both teaching and loving me and my autism. So I think I am fearing less now than younger times of my life. Joy in life as a boy in a journey to a happy life is even a dream now seen. Respect comes with love and understanding each kid's abilities and the desire to teach so therefore teachers must have a desire to teach everyone. They must realize that their dreams are not ours. Ask us what we will need to be an independent person later in our life. Teach good skills in a respectful way. Conversations with me will tell you if I am happy.

When I was growing up, speaking was so frustrating. I could see the words in my brain but then I realized that making my mouth move would get those letters to come alive, they died as soon as they were born. What made me feel angry was to know that I knew exactly what I was to say and my brain was retreating in defeat. I felt so mad as teachers spoke in their childish voices to me, mothering me, but not educating me. I had to try to learn so many things through great books. Libraries were my saving grace. As for hearing what was said around me, I believe my ears only could hear the strong sounding words, I mean the words that made my ears stretch to listen.

I understand why kids scream. It's frustrating not being able to speak and feeling as a mostly invisible being. Do you know the vintage movie, *The Invisible Man* (Whale 1933)? That's how I felt. My clothes were there, but the body and the soul felt like nothing. How can you live a life getting treated as that? Understanding that the only way to make this hell a heaven was with speech, I decided to take a risk and began to try just one word. I know my voice sounded foolish, but it felt okay to try. As my bold new hope grew as a fine now true reality, I tried more and felt that heaven moved closer.

Listening therapy is a joy. It gives your ears the feeling of reaching the bridge over the missing meaning of sounds. Listening therapy is a grouping of music that has certain frequencies changed. At times my ears listen with no difficulty. Other times, I must really focus to hear and make a bridge of sound to cross into the continuation. That seems to help me hear whole words. Before, I would lose certain sounds and the words seemed as garbage to be thrown out with no use to them. You might say I felt I am training my brain to hear better. It helps me to begin to speak better. Also it sends needed rhythm to my speech. I find the classical music best for me. My brain follows the very thorough and detailed patterns.

So many things were hard for me to learn. I now think it was so foolish to ask me to learn to tie my shoes. My brain moved into hiding the reason for not being able to do it, but yet my school believed it important mostly as a way to tell you that you are now just greatly smart. Why is shoe tying important compared to the fact that you can't speak? Like saying the letters, mostly there was no pattern to follow in my brain for tying my shoelaces. After much practice, as with my words, it seemed a pattern moved into my brain, giving direction to my hands. I think my music therapy gave help with this. Doesn't tying your shoes mean you are now enclaved in the world of pigtails and basketballs? When a kid can't tie shoes, you know they get frustrated with you, and even though those words of "it doesn't matter" and "we will use Velcro" are heard, your heart feels defeated. I screamed silently, "Make my mouth work as my hands; can you idiots not see my struggle to tell you I have so many answers to the questions you place before my face? Isn't tying the speech to my mouth from my brain more critical to life than making a piece of cotton secure?" When I was 15 I tied my shoes and people rejoiced as if I had won an enormous prize in some battle. I laughed at them in my brain. If they knew how ridiculous they seemed. Adults deemed it worthy of such excitement. Mom was happy and dad proud, but my mind believed this excited reaction to tying shoes still foolish.

Security comes from making your choices heard. Choices, even something like selecting a cereal, could be hard. In the morning I was given many silly choices. But as my voice was not a true one, I had to pick the choice I heard. Many times it was not my true choice and both my mom and me were mad if I did not finish the cereal. I mean when you are little and have speech that is only just a few small babyish words, you cannot get yourself unstuck to make a new selection. Like a car that keeps slipping into reverse gear because the track isn't strong enough to move forward. It was impossible to move to a joyful and delicious choice. After I was served, I was furious with myself and mad at mom. Even saying "Do you want something else?" didn't help. The gears refused to move. I think many times it felt better to scream and run, than to feel like gagging on the bitter food. Even as the selections were viewed, my brain made only the same choice every day. Many times I desired pancakes but my lousy hand pointed to the bitter choice.

I believe if I had a moveable brain image as a child it would have been easy. The moveable brain image came as I learned to watch videos in moving order. Moving order means to me the ability to make things move along in order and not get stuck on an image or phrase that captured my attention.

Anxiety comes as a regular visitor, just as breathing. I believe my cells have a nucleus filled with it. I think when I was young I walked in a constant pacing to help my body deal with it and I felt my nerves prickle as if a porcupine shot its quills into me. I think that sensory integration . . . has been like a giant Band-Aid to my body. It wraps up the stingers as a ball of cotton and makes things more comfortable for me. I am now able to handle many situations that would have sent me into man-overboard feeling. One thing that sent me overboard was being asked a question when I felt stressed over the voices asking it. Women have a pitch to their vocal cords that are like vibrato. Sadly, you are expected to respond, but you truly feel as a bird trapped. Fluttering away seems lovely, but the expectation [of others] is a wire cage. Fighting to be appreciated, but longing to escape, I feel I made myself struggle, as this was the way to become competent.

Another time the overboard feeling comes is in tests. I need to focus on the question, work with the difficulty of small print which is black and blurs my eyes. The rustle of papers, pencils, scratching, coughing and scraping chairs, and lights drive me crazy. I do well for the beginning, then it adds up as a bank balance ready to be withdrawn. I am a man overboard awaiting my rescue. But you can't leave, can you, or I will fail. Failing is fundamental, but only for those who aren't in special education designation.

I now think it was a big effort for those who smiled . . . and said, "I know you will speak some day." They did not really believe what they said to my face. I knew their smile hid what they really believed and that sympathy and not belief filled them. Why do all those who have said they are educated in the ways of teaching not know that hope and desire must be moved into place as the pillars of strength first before the floors can be built?

The idea of school inclusion can be as a lousy or lovely happening. It's really all in the hands of the teachers along with the permission from the big boss, the superintendent. Teachers must be willing to not just give me a desk and then leave me to fill the chair. I need to be asked questions, and given time for my thoughtful answers. Teachers need to become as a conductor, and guide me through the many places I may get lost.

■　■　■　■　■　■　■　■　■

II. The Myth of the Person Alone

Douglas Biklen

This interpretive chapter begins with an analysis of the more general themes that the contributing authors raise, flows to the more particular, and then comes back to the middle ground that therapists, teachers, parents, and others occupy as people interested in supporting people who live under the umbrella term *autism*. In regard to any of my interpretations and representations, I emphasize two things: first, these are my interpretations, not *the* (i.e., not definitive) explanations of the social construct of autism; second, whatever comments I make in describing or interpreting one person's account, just as in describing any person who has no disability label, do not necessarily apply to all the contributing authors or to most people who have been classified on the autism spectrum. There is enormous variation among people with this classification, as there is within any group.

Guiding Principles

Disability Consciousness

Nearly every study of autism seeks answers, whether about its nature and cause, about educational and therapeutic interventions, or simply about how to interact with the labeled person. I suppose this was the gist of my request to Jamie Burke to describe his vision of an ideal school. To the extent that Burke or the other authors provide ideas about strategy, these are more about approaches they have employed personally than methods that therapists or teachers could or should apply for everyone with the classification of autism. Also, the authors reflect on their development in the context of being acutely aware of how others view them, and of how they are often marginalized within society. In short, they engage in a social justice narrative that is reminiscent of disability rights and the field of Disability Studies (see, e.g., Charlton 1998; Thomson 1997; Linton 1998) but that is disturbingly absent in most professional research and practitioner literature, let alone in popular culture. This is essentially the point that Rubin makes when she says that society has not yet been able to accept people labeled autistic "as being normal."

When I requested he describe *his* ideal school, Mukhopadhyay wrote instead of being marginalized. He asked me why he should imagine the improved look of an institution that had excluded him. He rejects the idea of an ideal school. After all, he reasons, students are not jigsaw pieces—if they were, he says, educators would surely cast him as a "stray piece from another picture"! His analogy is a stark reflection on societal prejudice. Mukhopadhyay points out that his schooling comes from diverse and unplanned directions, for example, from looking at the doubt in others' eyes, and from his fascination with a dust grain that he sees disappear from sight as it moves into a shadow. Burke describes himself as "a mostly invisible being" who had to find a way for people to see and acknowledge him. Do other people regard him as valuable? Do they see him as a learner? Are their expressions of enthusiasm reflective of genuine admiration or cover-ups for their pessimism about the likelihood of him learning? Do people think of him as someone who wants friendships and who can feel loneliness? Is he recognized as a person who evaluates how his peers think about him? Will people think about how the culture can change in ways such that he can be appreciated? Burke ponders these questions. And Attfield calls for schools that put justice and equality at the center.

Blackman, like Mukhopadhyay and Burke, is hardly any more accommodating to what she perceives as my interest in how-to strategies. "'How to' for what?" she asks. When I requested that she write about her experiences with autism so that others might benefit from her analysis, she told me she found it annoying to be approached about such matters and not about her ideas on non-autism-related topics. She felt my agenda assumed she might be "wanting to be normal." She does not. Blackman reminds me that my agenda might not be her agenda, and that if someone feels it valuable for her to be heard, she would rather discuss her "pure intellectual thought." She is not about to unveil a series of "remedies" or "practices."

Wanting to Participate

None of the contributing authors fulfill the stereotype of the "person with autism alone." Through education, through writing, through art, through friendships, and through dialogue, each is a forceful presence. When I discussed their chapters with them, as we went back and forth and I asked for clarifications and elaborations in the editing process, and as I read their accounts, the notion of their being somehow disconnected from society made no sense at all, except as a misperception of appearance.

Ironically, this was especially well illustrated in an instance where I seem to have forgotten the ethnographic dictum to listen rather than impose. Richard Attfield and I were talking about the topic of participation. Here is an abbreviated account of our conversation:

> Richard: At a conference where I was invited to speak on a voluntary basis, I wrote my speech and I wanted to type all of it out [for the audience]. I timed a pre-run and the quickest I could type it was an hour and a half. This left 20 minutes for questions. I did not want to cut it but the afternoon session started 30 minutes late. What would you have done, Doug?
>
> Doug: Have the speech in the computer [and let the] speech synthesizer read the speech. And then answer questions extemporaneously, typing and reading aloud. I would get the speech projected onto a screen so that the audience can read it.
>
> Richard: I typed it out at the conference. I wanted people to see me type it, for themselves. [He explained that his words were projected on a screen, but he did type out the talk on the spot, referring to his notes.]

Doug: What we've been doing [i.e., at conferences in the United States] is for people to have prepared speeches [which they scroll through and have projected on a large screen] and then to demonstrate independent typing in the questions and answers portion of the presentation. So it's quicker and it still allows for more audience participation.

Richard: I am sure you know what works but I refuse to do it that way. I would rather sit and type and be part of the ethos of it all.

Doug: Yes, the ethos of it all. I understand.

Richard: I want to participate in the most fulfilling way I can.

Doug: And that is the way?

Richard: Yes. Otherwise they might just as well leave me home and just tape the machine [i.e., a recording of the voice synthesizer reading his paper which he would have prepared on his typing device].

Doug: [Laughter.]

Richard: Well it is true.

Doug: I totally disagree because you are there and can make comments [i.e., when responding to audience questions].

Richard: But, but, but, it is not enough. It is richness of the experience.

I have to admit that I cringed when I first looked at the above transcript, for it seemed like I was almost bullying, at least awfully rigid, in saying "I totally disagree. . . . " However, Richard more than held his ground. We were arguing like the friends we had become.

At a subsequent public address, upon noticing the serious demeanor of his audience, Richard inserted jokes into his presentation. Writing to me about what happened, he explained how much he values his own participation:

Richard: I cracked a joke but people were scared to react. I stopped my speech, grinned at them and said "That was a joke. You are allowed to laugh." They all relaxed after that and I put in several more jokes. We all enjoyed ourselves. We had to be thrown out of the hall because everyone crowded around at the end and wanted to speak to me. It was the best talk I have given. I felt alive and part of the whole.

Doug: Yes I see what you are saying.

Richard: That to me is what it is all about, the participation.

Richard Attfield's declaration about how he likes to give his public presentations contrasts starkly with the age-old notion of the person classified as autistic being aloof and disinterested in social engagement.

Presuming Competence

Being recognized as a participant relates to whether someone is seen as competent. Without having your intellect taken as a given, participation is easily denied. Mukhopadhyay, for example, is magnanimous in his recollection of the psychologist who labeled him retarded but says that today's special educators should be "more open" in their assessments of individual possibility. They should begin, he writes, with the assumption that the child understands the teacher. They should talk to children with the expectation that they can hear, and not as "hearing impaired" persons. And they should treat students in accordance with their age and not infantilize them. His is a call to what I have previously termed the *presumption of competence* (see Biklen and Cardinal 1997).

The idea here is simple. It favors optimism over pessimism. Like Mukhopadhyay, though perhaps with a bit more exasperation, Rubin says to the world, look harder, "stop being lazy," "peel more layers," and see what is plainly evident. She argues that people who do not yet communicate through speech may reveal multiple other ways of showing their intellect. She notes that a careful observer should see—as many of the parents in Kanner's 1943 study did, and as Kanner did himself—for example, that art and music are nonverbal forms of expression, and that these may be present and obvious when conventional communication is not. In effect, both Mukhopadhyay and Rubin seem to be saying: Give the person the benefit of the doubt, presume competence, then work hard at looking for the evidence, and also support the person in finding new ways of expression.

The opposite stance is a pessimistic one. It says to the person with a disability, "Prove yourself before you will be given opportunity." It equates difficulties in conventional expression and other forms of performance with failed thinking. As Rubin observes, the combined challenge of requiring assistance to communicate and of being tested as to the ability to think is a "difficult hole to have to climb out of." Hence, from an interventionist point of view, presuming competence is the more practical as well as more optimistic stance for the people around her to adopt. My use of the term *presuming competence* is similar to Goode's emic perspective, where intimate contact with the person and an openness to the person allows one to dispense with the fault-finding, deficit-seeking framework of the professional diagnostician and to learn about the person through engagement (Goode 1992). It is what Linneman calls mindedness (2001), where, once a mind has been obliterated in the observer's imagination through a declaration that the person is mentally retarded, "mind can only persist" or reemerge "to the extent that it is experientially preserved" (p. 65). In the circumstance where one person has accepted that the other person has been authoritatively declared and is intellectually incompetent, interacting with the person in a way that requires the person to have understanding is something that "requires some kind of intimate contact" (p. 103). Linneman argues, "The specter of mental retardation creates an altered set of expectations" (p. 183). Thus, if a person is deemed to have "autism but not mental retardation, it is likely that his or her interpretive community will consider 'mind' as present but hidden. If mental retardation is detected [i.e., believed to exist and treated as real], then mind will become contested territory" (p. 183).

Considerations That May Affect Performance: Mind and Body

In this section, I synthesize factors that several authors in this book say affect their performance of a range of actions, even of thinking. Their texts belie the very idea of lacking mindedness.

Sensory Experience

Alberto Frugone opens his essay by speaking of "sensory distortions." He describes being overwhelmed at times by the visual and the auditory and needing to shut down his openness to multiple sensory experiences, allowing in only one sense at a time. He can pay attention to what he hears, he explains, but only if he simultaneously closes out the visual. Thus, watching television in a conventional way proved difficult. If he struggled to pay attention to what he could see, he would lose the meaning that might be given through spoken words. If he focused solely on the spoken words, he would lose the emotional impact of the program. An integrated sense of a television program's message would come to him only as he replayed the piece in his mind, or possibly subconsciously, long after the show had left the screen. If he tried to attend to both pictures and auditory text, his "attention would go." It would be like watching a film in a foreign language, without knowing that language. You would be forced to make meaning through the visual and perhaps through sounds, with the meaning of words remaining unavailable. If you did stop and try to translate the words, you would be unable to keep your focus on the visual action. Tito Mukhopadhyay has referred to this predicament as being "mono-channeled"; he can do one thing at a time, focus on one kind of stimulation at a time. Like Frugone, if he attends to seeing, he cannot also attend to hearing. Sue Rubin shares their dilemma. In her case, she prefers to watch captioned television, rendering television a mainly visual medium. She finds that the written text enables her to make sense of the programs, to get the picture as a whole rather than in pieces.

Forays into public places, particularly new and unstructured ones, can be as disorienting as or more than a television program. The market in Bangalore, India, that Mukhopadhyay's mother took him to, or the village center in Rapallo, Italy, that Alberto's mother took him to, are what Rubin refers to as the "often unpredictable and sometimes unforgiving" real world. The uncertainty of such settings can take time or help to accommodate. Frugone speaks of needing to have his hand held by his mother, especially when he was young; otherwise the sounds, colors, movement, and visual display, including people, would overwhelm him. At home, where he was familiar with the layout and where the setting was by-and-large predictable, with objects remaining in their places, he could manage more independently, not needing his hand held. He could replay the various rooms of his home in his mind, building a memory of them, of his own movements in them, and of sequences of events that occurred in them, much as he might replay a television program. In contrast to the serenity of home, where reference points could be relied on and even memorized, Frugone characterizes the rules by which the outside world operates as a "syllogism" that does not allow him the luxury of repeating settings and events in his mind. Everything keeps changing, as if in a sensory jumble. Routes taken, faces of people, locations of objects, different smells—all would shift, leaving Frugone "too scared to look around." Mukhopadhyay calls this the "chaos" of the open situation, where managing according to normate standards would require paying attention to what you can see, what you can hear, and also to movement, your own as well as others'. If attention to these multiple sensory inputs is attempted simultaneously, venturing into public spaces could be overwhelming. Mukhopadhyay likens this situation to a person in the audience who is suddenly placed on stage; he or she would be out of place, without the benefit of a script, not knowing what to do, what role to assume.

If faced with a room of people or objects, with rules and expectations undefined and shifting and many options open, Mukhopadhyay finds himself wanting to try everything, in effect unable to focus on any one thing. Ironically, such situations can call forth a response that is escapist rather than engaging. Actually stopping and focusing on doing one thing, for example, something repetitive, could provide respite from the "total scattering experience" of being overwhelmed with too many stimuli. Another self-protective strategy for Mukhopadhyay is to make a sound serve as a blocking filter; it cuts away the competing sounds of the world, in effect pushing them to the background. But he can find himself making a sound over and over, unable to stop himself, to the point of becoming immobilized and helpless. In a subsequent section of this chapter, I return to Mukhopadhyay's suggestions on how he and others can move beyond this state of helplessness.

Even within a particular sensory area, such as hearing or seeing, there may be multiple sensory experiences. Consequently, the person must make choices about what aspect of a sense to engage. For example, Mukhopadhyay points out that the word *cat,* as simple a word as one can imagine, can sound different depending on the voice that speaks it. If one is focused on the sound, and on differentiating the sound depending on the type of voice from which it comes or the sound of the voice in a particular location, for example, a cavernous room in contrast to a small study, the meaning could easily become secondary. Frugone explains that he may focus on the rhythm of speech rather than what an individual word sounds like, or on the sound but not the meaning of the word that the sound signals. He proudly describes his ears as being "resilient" in the face of sounds that seem bent on disorienting him. Yet he could become lost in his play with sounds. He gives the example of the word *icon,* where he repeats it in a singsong fashion, *feeling* rather than intellectually *learning* its meaning; in doing this, he develops his own, private meanings for words, such that *icon* means "Madonna"—an icon to be sure, but a particular icon.

Rubin describes her reading of words as looking at fragments and then piecing together meaning. Frugone describes his past practice of playing with the shapes of letters and words, and not concentrating on the meaning of those shapes. A particular word was a "motif inside a blob"; observing the shapes became more important than that the word was *letta,* and that this sequence of letters had a specific mean.

Imagine the difficulties of formal testing and the misunderstandings that could arise from it if the person being tested is focused on some non-test-related element of the multitudinous sensory experiences that the test situation, like any situation, offers. Rubin points out that when tested, she might be focusing on nearly anything else. What if she becomes fascinated by the button on the test-giver's shirt, wanting ever so insistently to examine it? Or what if she is listening to clanging pipes in another part of the building, or looking at the wind rustle leaves on a tree outside the window of the examining room? What would a low test score signify under such circumstances?

Similarly, how should the outsider interpret Rubin's practice of standing at a sink to observe running water? She explains her fascination with water, how it falls, its speed, the glint it may give off, and its gracefulness—an observer would likely not be able to intuit these perceptions. Reading her accounts, I cannot help but think about how artists typically see the world in a way that others do not; this is often taken as an attractive quality. Why, then, not Rubin's perspective this way?

Mukhopadhyay says that he sorts voices into male voices, female voices, and radio voices, for example; but if making sense of the different sounds becomes too daunting, he can escape into his own imaginings. As he aptly notes, anyone can have such experiences, though he describes himself as having been "perturbed" with the confusion of trying to classify such different sounds. Happily, Frugone points out that, over time, as he went through his personal processes of shutting sound off and on, of practicing the matching of words to the sounds he was hearing, of working within his own memory of words and meanings, he eventually developed the ability to hear words without having to focus directly on deriving meaning by consciously retrieving memory.

Sensory Systems and Social Interaction

Given sensory experiences such as those just described, a number of the contributing authors speak about the special challenge posed by the requirements of interacting with other people. Mukhopadhyay declares a "general discomfort" with people in comparison to, say, books. Books are predictable; he can handle them in accordance with his own rules. People, by contrast, expect and require interaction. They are more unpredictable. Books are simpler; they are there to be used. Thus, he explains, in his autobiography *Beyond the Silence,* on a school visit it was more comfortable to spend time at the bookshelf than with people. Interacting with other boys in the school would require being able to adapt to the timing of interaction, managing the sounds, the meaning of sounds, competing voices, and the visual stimuli in an unfamiliar setting. All this is far more complicated than burying one's face in an unmoving book. Rubin explains that, autistic or not, anyone who is self-conscious upon entering a room of unfamiliar people will likely give in to the need to look down at her or his own shoes. Similar to what Mukhopadhyay reports about himself, she says such a reaction, of focusing on objects before people, can be her most frequent first response to a social situation. She notes that for her this is nearly a mandated response, for it is so difficult to do anything else, except with supportive prompting.

Rubin says looking at a person's eyes can be painful. Mukhopadhyay, too, says that he is uncomfortable looking directly at faces, trying to sort them out. He finds faces more unpredictable than many other things. He locates people in his own mind by the sounds of their voices and by the locations where he first met them. Mukhopadhyay would rather stare at an object, even at a dust grain, and listen for recognition than look someone in the eyes as a way of connecting with them. So, Mukhopadhyay explains, if he hears a familiar voice in an unfamiliar or new location, it is a bit disorienting; it may take him a few moments to sort out the disjuncture. His initial response is to think why a person would be greeting him, until he is then able to sort out that the person greeting him is someone he is used to encountering in a different location—he gives the example of his speech therapist, who might greet him on a bus instead of in the therapy room where he is used to seeing her.

With dialogue, one person may interrupt the other. With dialogue, each person is expected to produce thoughts that connect in some way to what the other person has said; in effect, to respond as well as lead. Thus, it is not surprising that Mukhopadhyay says he finds "one-way communication better than dialogue"; it is easier to get his ideas out; it is easier to manage. At the same time, choosing mono-modal communication over dialogue is not the same as turning his back on the world. Writing can create a kind of time-delayed dialogue, where readers give a "payback," reflecting on the author's content and style—Mukhopadhyay explains that the responses his writing generates motivate him to keep improving on his words.

Connecting Mind and Body

Mukhopadhyay says that as a child he had little sensation of his body. He describes his difficulty with feeling his body, noting that he can begin to get a sense of his body and its location when he wraps himself in a favorite sheet, or when he climbs stairs and feels the pull of gravity, when he rides on an escalator or in a car with all their vibrations, and when he rocks in place or spins his body around like a fan. He explains that sometimes he will have more awareness of one part of his body, for example, his legs, than another part, for example, his arms. Even though he knew the meaning of body parts, he could not necessarily demonstrate that knowledge on command. When he recalls going to a swimming pool, he describes himself feeling his legs in the water distinct from his above-water part of the body, the aquatic and aerial parts separated. In this state, he found himself unsure of his footing, "disbalanced." His mother told me that he has a better awareness of his body when he lies down on a mat. This recalls Grandin's description of the relief she derived from getting into her self-made squeeze machine and applying gentle pressure to her body, creating in effect a cocoon that allowed her to feel her body in space (Grandin and Scariano 1986). Frugone explains that he could see other people's movements but then had difficulty locating his own body parts and moving them in similar steps; he could not just "naturally" imitate others. If you have to locate your own body and body parts in space in order to activate them, and if you have to think about putting one step in front of another, or of where you are placing your foot and whether you have good balance, it could become quite difficult to pay attention to other things happening around you.

Take away the feeling of the body, and nearly any physical action involving the body, particularly anything that requires a modicum of motor planning, becomes nearly impossible. There are many ways to simulate this lack of body awareness. It can occur when extremities begin to freeze. It can also occur when the person has been in bed for a long period of time and attempts to walk; balance and depth perception may be off and it may be hard to know where one's legs are. Other strategies for simulating impairment of body awareness that people can try are these: (1) cross the arms and position the palms to face each other, then intertwine the fingers and move the intertwined hands down and then back under the arms and up toward the chest—in this position it may be difficult to locate particular fingers on command; and (2) in a seated position, with both feet on the ground, move the left foot counterclockwise in a perfect circle while simultaneously attempting to write your name or a sentence on a piece of paper—in this condition, either the writing or the leg movement will suffer, for the ability to locate and effectively manage both at once becomes impossible. I do not want to suggest that these activities actually simulate an aspect of autism, only that the sense of body location can be altered.

Several of the contributing authors describe having bodies that often leave them feeling stymied. They say that at times it seems almost as if their bodies have lives of their own. Rubin identifies the recalcitrant body as one of the things that makes autism so hard to explain to people who do not experience it; the non-autistic person has the luxury of being able to do things, to act, when he or she wants (i.e., intentionally), and of being able to "turn off" unwanted movements or actions that seem so determined at times to impose themselves on him or her. At times Rubin does things she would rather not, while at other times she cannot seem to do things that she wishes she could.

Frugone describes the disconnect between understanding and doing. When faced with a multiple-step task, he might be able to conceive of the separate steps involved, and of the sequence in which they must occur, but then, even after reviewing the steps, he is frequently unable to commence with the very first step, no matter how simple that one step might be. It is as if the contemplation of multiple steps makes the first step more than a single step, and thereby impossible. He recalls what it was like as a young student when he had difficulty following a teacher's instructions to place blocks in a container; his inaction made him look like an "idler." Yet the problem he faced was not one of attitude, or even of understanding. Rather, even if he knew what was expected, even if he had observed others doing the very same set of actions, even if he had an image in his own mind of the steps entailed, he might still be unable to initiate or carry through a series of actions.

To the extent that tasks can be kept simple, even single-action (e.g., point to the toothbrush, point to the stove, point to the letter Z), they become less likely to invoke anxiety. Yet most games are highly complex. They involve multiple steps and require linking an action to timing (e.g., catching a fly ball). Also, in a game, each player often must respond to the actions of other players, and frequently these are purposefully hard to predict. Such complexity can create anxiety and can leave the person immobilized. Hence, Mukhopadhyay suggests exercise may be more doable than most games. (See Shore 2003, for a similar analysis.) In exercise, the boundaries of movement and the requirements of timing are narrowed.

Seemingly simple actions—at least they might be thought of as simple from a normate perspective—such as tying shoelaces, setting a table, putting on clothing, taking off a coat and hanging it up, become, for Frugone, Rubin, and others, what Frugone calls "mountains of practical moments." His image is a useful one, for it reveals his understanding of the irony that everyone else's mundane tasks are truly heights to scale for him. To make matters worse, not being able successfully to accomplish a particular task, or even to start it, he will lapse into stereotyped actions, such as flapping his hands or flicking his fingers in front of his eyes. It is the seeming contradiction between difficulty with everyday tasks and evidence of agile thinking that makes for confusion on the part of the outside observer. Frugone says he becomes wooden immediately upon thinking about the act of touching something; it is as if the thought of the action renders him a statue. Intellectually and even practically, the action is possible, but in the attempting to do it, he may freeze up or dissemble. Rubin explains how she could probably learn to string beads or do other such tasks that she now finds daunting, but it would take a great deal of practice.

Rubin often requires a prompt, such as a hand on her back and a verbal cue (i.e., say hello to so-and-so) from a friend or personal-care attendant, to achieve a seemingly simple task such as making a greeting. Carrying out that act, even though she has done it hundreds of times, still does not come naturally. She says she still needs help focusing and initiating. Blackman describes a similar phenomenon; on some occasions, if particularly relaxed, she might say hello and the person's name, but most often she needs to be supported with a reminder, to focus on the greeting. As with other actions, the problem is not one of understanding but of doing. Rubin cautions that for herself and many (not all) people classified as autistic, it is best not to count on them initiating interactions;[1] she says she can initiate communication with another person only if she feels very strongly about it, but she truly has to work at it. And even then, her ability to act can vary from day to day.

Variations in the sensory signals given off by different settings may also affect a person's ability to perform. Blackman, for instance, says that certain settings are not predictable and may not emit sounds to which she can easily orient herself. She cites supermarkets and many streets as such settings. The busier the setting, the more whirring noises it has—for example, from fans or forced-air heating and cooling systems—the more her own behavior can become disoriented. In these contexts, she absolutely requires a personal assistant who can act as a partner to help her negotiate whatever actions are required.

Mukhopadhyay explains such difficulties as relating to his having little sensation of his own body. For each new activity, he says, he needed someone to touch him; he could not act without gaining a sense of his own body. He could fully understand an action, for example, what it meant to throw a ball, and even how to do it. But he could not actually do it unless he would also have awareness of his body. Even something as seemingly simple as taking food with a spoon and bringing it to the mouth had to be learned consciously. He found he needed to be helped, and then, with practice, he could eventually take on the task himself. As Rubin explains, actions that other people would find simple are not necessarily simple for her. When asked to point to an answer from several options, she may will her body to point to the answer she knows is correct, but the body may do something else. A variation of this would be the one Burke describes, where his selection of breakfast always came out cereal, as if it were an automatic response, even when he knew he wanted pancakes.

Blackman's occasional solution to the problem of walking along in public is to latch onto another person's movements as her cue, and simply to walk with them or in cadence with them, thus giving up the need herself to orchestrate her walking. Following the cue of another's steps, she could, in effect, operate on automatic pilot. But then, as she explains, if the person she has hitched onto goes in another direction or for one reason or another stops, Blackman may find herself adrift and "really terrified," even to the point of screaming and of biting her hand below the thumb.

Attfield does not experience such movement problems. Rather, he attributes any difficulties he may encounter to ataxic cerebral palsy. He describes a difficult type of situation, a busy store where he wanted to purchase several post cards. He was standing at the edge of the store, picking out the cards, but then, noticing how crowded it was, prevailed on his mother to venture into the store to actually purchase them. For him, trying to get to the cash register would involve ducking and dodging, being jostled, and possibly ending up "twisted and bent out of shape." He describes it much like a stealthy military campaign, one he has learned not to take on heedlessly. It is a task requiring good balance and agility. Yet, over time, this too he has accomplished. When he first described this and other situations of physical performance, I was ready to interpret them as evidence of movement disturbance, similar to what Rubin, Mukhopadhyay, and Frugone had explained, but Attfield explained that he had none of the body-awareness or even body-control difficulties. This was a good reminder that the outsider may tend to impose available diagnostic narratives, but it is impossible to know how the other person experiences an event unless he or she explains it.

Strategies for Praxis, Implications for Intervention

In Blackman's picking up on and mirroring the cadence of another person's walking, or in Mukhopadhyay's suggestions about the value of practice and the usefulness of games that have discrete steps, can be seen hints for interventionists. In this section, I attempt to catalog some of these strategies. While these themes do not imply exactly what interventionists should do in their own practice, they do provide a context within which interventionists might conceptualize their work.

Escape to Imagination: A Beginning Strategy

A prevailing image of the person labeled autistic is of a person alone, cut off from the rest of the world, *uninterested* in the real world. The first-hand accounts in this book would seem both to support and to contradict this picture. A few of the authors *do* report being alone, even losing themselves in private fantasies. But seeking the imaginary is not, for them, evidence of disinterest; rather, they characterize it as a strategy for managing what initially seems hopelessly overwhelming. In this sense, imagining within oneself seems absolutely rational and ordinary. For others it may be a refuge from rejection. Thus, being alone is never presented as the essence of autism, and certainly not a permanent or single condition of the labeled person. If anything, it is a holding strategy, while the person figures out how to participate in ever-broader social situations.

Frugone describes himself as finding security through flight from the world. He was, in his own words, a person "who let his imagination run riot." He granted himself special power, such as the illusion that he could make a stack of books rise from the floor simply if he willed them to. Mukhopadhyay found similar escape in his "mirror travel." Whereas the real world was too complex at times to manage, his private, silent mirror world was a place where he could build his "own little stories." It was an escape from the confusion of diverse voices or the radio, and from "expectations and worried conversations" around him. Frugone says he had felt "safe" within his fantasies; they acted as a refuge against the chaos of the world, which, somewhat sardonically, he refers to as the Pandora's box of the real world, there to test whether a person is human, whether able to live with uncertainty. He even came to imagine himself "omnipotent"—only when his mother "managed" him by asking "quibbling questions" about his supposed abilities did he find his fantasies "denuded." Yet, clearly, fantasies were more than mere refuge.

They also became strategies for handling chaos or discomfort, a way of being in the world. Mukhopadhyay describes an imaginary gentleman on the train as reassuring; he is eventually replaced by real people. Like Frugone, who had to face his mother's quibbling questions, Mukhopadhyay became determined to use logic to begin to grow and not to "hold on to a dream." Similarly, Frugone played with pictures in his head, of his own invention, to achieve a kind of "private learning inside myself." He also imagined what teaching methods might enable him to do something practical, such as catching a ball or throwing it. Bleakly, he refers to his practical imaginings as "irrational," for typically they did not work. At the same time, such efforts do reflect how imagination was a way of responding to the real world, even of connecting to it, and certainly not indicative of disinterest.

It is ironic that contributing authors should write about their rich imaginations when the current, prevailing definition of autism speaks of a "lack of varied, spontaneous make-believe play . . . appropriate to developmental level" (American Psychiatric Association 2000, p. 75). The imaginary worlds the contributing authors create in their lives are often not visible to outside observers, but they are nevertheless present and rich. They become visible only when the authors can write about them and speak about them.

Conscious Reflection on What Works

Finding strategies by which to become successful in actions—whether it is to pick up cues from another person walking in order to walk oneself, as Blackman described, or to look at television with subtitles, as Rubin does—probably occurs somewhat unconsciously. People find things that work and then rely on them. Knowing this at a conscious level calls for careful self-monitoring and reflection. If I asked myself how I move my hand to pick up a cup, I suspect I would not immediately know. I might think, "I just do it," or "It's automatic, I don't have to think about it." In short, anyone can self-report, but not all self-reporting will be instructive either about the individual who is speaking or for others who may want help themselves.

Some actions may prove to be persistently difficult and continue to evade practical strategies for acquiring independent ability. Rubin says she needs reminders from her staff that not every Lexus car that passes is her mother's car. She knows it intellectually, but somehow she still yells out her mother Rita's name when a Lexus passes. She would like to harness these outbursts but has not yet done so. Blackman says she needs help turning a book to a particular page and that she feels "terror" if she has to search for a book in the library stacks. Mukhopadhyay describes how his mother would sit next to him and hand a ball to him and he would hand it back. As she moved further away from him, instead of throwing it, which he knew he was expected to do but could not, he would stand and walk it back to where she was now located. His mother's method might have worked for someone else, but it did not for him at that point. These are all examples of types of performance that have thus far proven elusive for some of the contributing authors. I share them to acknowledge that certain types of performance can be exceedingly hard to learn; or, to be fair and not put the burden on the student to discover each new path to achievement, educators have not come up with successful strategies for all skills.

One type of performance that Rubin would like to control is one that can be dangerous to her well-being. She describes herself as vulnerable to having some cue in the environment set her off into a bout of head banging. It could be the sight of a car or watching traffic, but her response is a violent banging of her own head on the car window. She says she cannot control the spinning sensation she gets in her head. Her support staff and family members can sometimes intuit what might have set her off, but often they cannot. The best strategy, she explains, is physically to remove her from the situation so that she can be kept from hurting herself. A nondangerous version of this kind of situation is when she gets caught up in repeating echolalic phrases. To stop her repetitions, she needs someone to acknowledge that she is speaking or to tell her, pointedly, "Turn it off."

Mukhopadhyay explains that his lack of awareness of his body, of being able to feel his body, may explain in part his difficulty with doing different activities. To overcome his clumsiness or immobility, he needs to feel his body and body parts. He says touch is always useful, particularly with new tasks. He may need to be touched at the shoulder in order to have the sensation of his shoulder, so he can locate and move it, for example, to soap himself or to pick up a spoon and eat. Whether he needs touch or not depends, he says, on his own awareness of his body and its parts on a given day. Again, tasks that require multiple steps and various parts of the body in coordination can be more difficult and therefore require longer periods of practice; this was the case with learning to ride a tricycle. He needed someone to hold his hands and required repetition to learn tying shoes. Touch was even helpful for his speech. His mother would push his back, enabling him to express "sudden breath" and to bring out sound.

Modeling and Filming Actions

Modeling was another useful strategy. Mukhopadhyay's mother would put out objects and have him point to them. At first she would put them close by, and later farther away. With practice, he developed the ability to point reliably.

Another strategy for gaining success with performance includes simply thinking through the steps. So, at the achievement celebration where he was to be given an award, Richard Attfield went through the situation in his mind. Then, when his name was called, his mother helped by jabbing him in the side, but he had already mentally rehearsed getting up from his seat, walking to the steps, climbing the steps, grasping the award, shaking hands with the presiding official, having his picture taken, returning to the stairs and then to his seat, and sitting back down. It went reasonably well, except for stumbling on a step and for the photographer having problems with the flash. As I reflected on Richard's humorous, self-deprecating account, I had to admit that were I in the same situation, I would have done much the same, mapping out in my mind the scenario of hearing my name called, climbing the steps, receiving the award, saying a few words, and so on.

Frugone's situation seems different. He produced films in his head to prepare himself for things that he was about to do, so that they would feel familiar. In general, he found that the films could ready him for action and that over time he could tolerate how reality often required variations from his imagined versions of it. Eventually he found himself needing such visual preparation less and less, except if the anticipated situation evoked anxiety, such as meeting a girl. Who has not engaged in such mental rehearsals?

Making the World More Predictable

Routine is probably the most obvious way of giving structure to the often unstructured, turbulent-seeming world—for anyone. Sue Rubin says she "absolutely" needs routine in her life. The longer she has lived in her own home as an adult, with support staff, she says she has become less demanding about her insistence on routine; her routines are now looser than in years past. Mainly, she finds it easier to manage life if she is prepared for some of the aberrations from routine that come with living a life. At the same time, she credits her support staff for how they remind her about learning to be patient with unanticipated variations on the routine. So routines can be useful, but Rubin also finds it helpful to learn to live with them as a loose structure, not a guaranteed template of each day.

Intellectually Rehearsing an Anticipated Action

Mukhopadhyay's mother talks to Tito about actions he will be doing and hopes that by talking about them, he will then be better able to initiate and carry them through. She says that it is her dream that he will be able to talk about picking up a cup, for example, and then do it. Ultimately, she hopes that he might be able to say to himself that he will control his behavior, for example, that he will remain calm, and then actually do it. Similarly, writing about actions to be attempted, or having actual pictures of them, could prove calming and focusing. Frugone seems to be describing a somewhat similar phenomenon when he says that knowing the logic of something, such as why one needs to go outside and into town, makes the doing easier. Without having discussed the reason for an action or set of actions, he is reduced to needing to be led by the hand.

Of course, life in the everyday, ordinary world outside the home often calls for more spontaneous and unplanned action. Here the unpredictable can take over, and as noted earlier, the person can become stymied by too many options. A familiar voice talking about what is happening can be helpful. Repeating another's words can assist with attention shifting, as can pictures that describe events. Mukhopadhyay mentions his difficulty in recognizing even familiar people—his speech therapist, for example—if they are out of the usual contexts where he has seen them, thus making it hard for him to assimilate what they are saying to him; the confusion arises when he works on locating them even as they are expecting him to respond to their greeting. A quick prompt from his mother can solve this difficulty. When meeting a stranger who has an altogether different-sounding voice, his mother will repeat what the other person is saying, thus giving Mukhopadhyay time to acclimate to the voice. She can then fade out her support as Mukhopadhyay becomes familiar with the voice. This strategy of repetition resembles a Rogerian therapist's playing back the client's words. It could have the additional benefit of granting the person time to reflect on the ideas being discussed.

Learning in Small Doses

Another strategy for accommodating the unpredictable world is to continually expand one's sphere of experience. Mukhopadhyay calls this a "main struggle," to acquire the essential abilities to manage in the world. These abilities might include tolerance of diverse foods, braving crowded public settings such as buses, and willingness to try new clothing. He recommends exposure, in measured doses. Over time, for example, by practicing again and again, he became "desensitized to the crowd of the market." Again, this sounds like a version of what anyone experiences with something new or unfamiliar and complex.

One way to conceptualize this kind of learning is to think of it occurring in such doses, similar to what Stacey describes in *The Boy Who Loved Windows* (2003), and also in single-channel formats that accommodate the need to focus on the visual or auditory, but not both. Frugone instructed his mother, for example, to make sounds of birds, water, bells, and other elements in the environment, which he would then name on the typewriter. He later progressed to deciphering spoken words. He found that he could better take in a spoken text if he could first read it. So he began practicing that, and thereby built his skills at comprehending spoken speech. Like any other reader, when he now encounters an unfamiliar word, he works at deciphering its meaning by studying is root parts and by examining its relationship to other words in the text.

Mukhopadhyay's mother started him off with blocks and puzzles, taking to heart the professional advice to "keep him busy." Next, she turned him to copying letters and numbers, and then progressed to having him answer specific questions. She would read out his answers, reciting them to anyone within earshot and to herself. Studying, and the ways of studying, thus became habits, and as Mukhopadhyay suggests, habit became an essential part of his life, a kind of guide.

Expanding from Obsessions

On the other side of habit lies compulsion or rigid rule making. Several of the authors mention rules as a functional strategy to manage unpredictability. Yet, as Frugone suggests, they can become a trap; they can become escapism from uncertainty. Mukhopadhyay refers to escapism as doom, and Rubin calls it "giving in" to autism or a relief from the "crazy world." In most situations, it likely will take a teacher or other helper to assist the person to move from fascination and obsession to a broadening of interests. Mukhopadhyay says that as a young child he was better at understanding designs than larger scenery. When his mother found him arranging matchsticks in designs, she seized on his imaginative play as evidence of his learning. And so he and his mother moved to numbers. To him, numbers looked like his designs. She kept the work physically visible, telling him that he had a name and so did accumulations of things, one, two, and so on. She moved on to the calendar, where he learned addition and subtraction.

Finding Kinds of Play That Are Possible

Many kinds of play could prove difficult to a person with movement differences. How can a person kick a ball to a partner if he or she must think about where the foot is, and then where the ball is, and then how to maneuver the leg, and then the direction the ball must take? As the person thinks of these actions, he or she considers how to begin, and it may all seem overwhelming. By that time, someone else may have kicked the ball. When Mukhopadhyay's mother invited children over to his house for play, he found he did not know how to play. He could not plan his moves and at the same time follow the moves of the other children, or the rationales behind their moves, or their banter with each other. There were so many moves to choose from; how could he know which one to do at a particular moment? Thus it is not surprising that walking, weight-lifting, and other forms of exercise might be preferred over group sports.

Firm and Observant Teachers

Alberto Frugone credits his mother with helping him find his "balance" in life. In his words, she could "provide logic to a dull son." She was not afraid to confront his fantasies, but also, during his growing-up years, she was forever looking out for ways that he might come to communicate and participate in everyday life. He credits her for the painstaking way she would describe the steps to carry out an action, and her insistence that he practice the steps over and over again. In this way he learned to eat, to walk, and to type independently. Some things remain too difficult and so she gives him help. At the dinner table, she or her husband will cut Alberto's meat, for example. Now that he can communicate, she looks to Alberto to comment on her ideas about possible strategies for his education, and she converses with him about his ideas. This was apparent in the example I gave in the first chapter, where they discussed a way for Alberto to seek help in an emergency if he were to stay at home alone when she went out.

Each of the authors in this book has this kind of relationship with a mother, other family member, or caregiver. All the contributors point to these individuals as crucial to their degree of independence and self-direction. And all jokingly refer to supporters/teachers in one way or another as kind battle-axes or most trusted allies. Blackman on occasion calls her mother "the Old Hag" but does so in reference to her being, in Blackman's mind, "long suffering." Blackman characterizes her relationship with her mother as one of adult-to-adult cooperation, rather than one of adult-child. Blackman was constantly encouraged to write about how she experienced the world; this process, she explains, helped her see her own relationship to the world and better understand how she learned.

Richard Attfield recalls his mother's early efforts to have him included in school as heroic. He refers to her as his "partner in crime" (personal communication). She enrolled him in a mainstream playschool and found a movement specialist to teach both him and her how to work on his ataxic condition, on walking, balance, co-ordination, "and all aspects of movement"—in addition to a diagnosis of autism, he also had been diagnosed with cerebral palsy. She then assisted him with the movement exercises daily. Over the years, she was also his careful observer, for example, watching how food might affect his health. Further, Attfield's mother improvised methods for him to communicate, first with plastic letters, then with a children's toy, and later with communication devices on which he could type. When I observed him reading aloud his written essays, at the few points where he hesitated on a multi-syllable word, she prompted him by stating the first syllable—this was no problem of understanding, for as he told me, "they were words that I could pronounce clearly in my thoughts."

Often the participation that a parent or caregiver makes possible is partial. Rubin explains that she enjoys sharing in lawn care or kitchen work but seeks assistance to use sharp objects or appliances. For many daily activities, she says, she needs constant prompting from the staff at her home. But clearly this is different than if she had everything done for her. I have often felt that it is somewhat ironic that Rubin interviews and hires her own care workers, who then have as an important part of their responsibilities prompting and coaxing her into action and helping her perform the actions she has said she wants to be able to perform. Yet she also retains and sometimes uses her authority to fire staff. I suppose this is not unlike the position that executive assistants hold. They are interviewed and hired to be assistants; once in the position, executive assistants are expected to remind, prompt, and nag their employers. In Rubin's case, her personal assistants remind her of agreed-upon agendas (i.e., she tells them to help her to initiate some action or, conversely, not get caught up in certain obsessive actions).

Mukhopadhyay gives one answer to the question of how he was educated: "a very firm teacher." He says that his mother would bargain with him, getting him to hold his pencil correctly before they would have lunch, holding him down in a chair until he finished a chapter. I can vouch for the fact that his mother teaches him in a most loving, if determined, way. When Mukhopadhyay said, "Eat, eat, eat," right in the middle of a conversation we were having, his mother reminded him, "Let it be one o'clock." As I have mentioned earlier, in the midst of our talking he might get up and move out onto the rooftop porch next to their apartment, with his mother calling after him, "Tito, Tito, come back and finish." She would then give him a few minutes to wander about looking for an object that might have become an obsession, before calling him again to return. Like many parents, me included, she would hold out the promise of an afternoon stroll in a park or of an ice-cream cone to get him to finish a bit of work.

One of her main strategies as a teacher was to keep him involved. Starting with blocks, then colorful bowls, jigsaws, and numbers, Mukhopadhyay learned in bits, moving quickly from topic to topic. He would suggest topics for study. When I visited, he had just finished Chaucer and was proceeding to work his way through an anthology of English literature; he was twelve at the time. His mother explained to me that in the absence of a set curriculum, she permitted him to have a large role in pursuing topics that met his "fancy."

Another crucial aspect of each contributor's learning seems to have been the teacher's or parent's careful attention to observation. Blackman's mother learned that when Lucy said "Ho'" for "Hot," it was her way of describing the fact that the shower water had run cold. Mukhopadhyay's mother noticed that as a young child he would memorize the words of songs and would give off signs that he was listening to them. He says his first advances in learning English came from listening to his mother recite poetry. His mother did what many parents often do: as soon as she saw that he was paying attention to the words of a song, she would sing as she played with him and would intentionally mix up the words so that he might correct her. Frugone recalls his mother reading fairy tales that had pictures. He was six years old at the time and would occupy himself studying the relationships of what he was observing, even though he had no way to tell his mother of this internal intellectual life.

Resisting the Nexus of Clumsiness and Competence

All through their growing up, the contributing authors found themselves being judged by what they could and could not do, and by how they looked in comparison to others' expectations. Performance was imposed as a proxy for intellect. To borrow from the title of Bogdan and Taylor's classic article on labeling, they were "the judged, not the judges" (1976). Tito Mukhopadhyay has written, "You know that your intelligence or stupidity would be measured by that performance of yours. You tend to get very clumsy. . . . The person says, 'Come on, I am waiting,' which means 'You are a stupid person.'"

Of course, being made an outsider had, as Mukhopadhyay put it when describing his rejection from various schools without ever having been given a chance to participate, a "sting." "Yes, I was hurt," he wrote. Later, in the park one day, it was such memories that likely caused him to remark on girls giggling and playing as being "too happy." In a breath of sarcasm, he told me that people with disabilities were a form of entertainment for other people; they could be watched to see how they would perform, and to see how helpless they could be. Frugone says that for a while during his development, he more or less gave up on trying to perform in accordance with the world's standards rather than feel its "strong and . . . unacceptable silence." Yet, having said that he might retreat, Frugone did not.

It is instructive that in railing against being cast as clumsy outcasts—Mukhopadhyay calls himself "intelligent junk"—the contributing authors prove the error of equating understanding and action. The term *retardation* is, according to Mukhopadhyay, a disgusting label. If his or another person's mind cannot get the body to perform as desired, this does not prove incapacity to think. With much disdain, he chides anyone who would equate inability to "follow basic commands" with an inability to understand them. The problem, according to Attfield, was the complete injustice and insensitivity of expecting children with movement or communication difficulties to have their thinking judged on the basis of dexterity or whether they could speak in a certain way. Not being able to "vocalize thoughts" was not the same as not having any. Yet that was precisely the impression he got when a doctor-in-training would not address him directly and showed no interest in his ideas.

Rubin knows that people often have a hard time squaring her appearance with her intellect. She may *look* uninterested and *look* disengaged, but meanwhile she maintains a 3.67 average at her college. She explains that she understands that by socially prescribed rules she cannot, or at least should not enter a room full of people and immediately immerse herself in an object that is drawing her attention, or commence to run around the room; she must work at engaging with the people present—it is a way she will prove to them that she is intelligent. If she does not select interaction with people in favor of immersion in an object, her "irregular behaviors" can lead people to make "poor assumptions" that she has little or no intellect. Given the myriad ways to observe intellect, Rubin finds it ironic that the frames often chosen for application to her are "most incapable" of highlighting competence. All one would have to do would be to observe ability with patterns or details, as well as other capacities, she explains, to see that those who so often stare at her and others have no reason to be smug.

Concluding Note

Curiously, none of the contributing authors cites behavior modification as a key to his or her own development. They all describe a more open-ended process. Certainly, each often mentions the importance of practice as a key element for success. Each had a parent who believed most of all that children should have all the experiences of a child growing up, including full participation in family life but also participation with peers in school. Their parents sought equal opportunity. Several of the authors, including Frugone, Mukhopadhyay, Rubin, and Blackman, had parents and teachers who gave them support in the form of prompting, hand-over-hand modeling, and similar strategies, and yet the principal element of each person's emergence into social participation has not been behavioral training; it has been inclusion.

Each author speaks of a give-and-take relationship with a parent or others that led to advances, with a high degree of self-reflection and self-direction at each turn. In sum, when they describe their favored teachers and parents, they seem to be describing Goode's idea of the emic relationship. Goode (1992), a longtime observer of people who are deaf/blind, borrows from anthropology to describe two contradictory approaches to understanding the observed person. The etic perspective refers to "objective, analytic, or clinical approaches to understanding culture and human behavior" (1992, p. 198). He notes that clinical perspectives generally operate from the etic frame and tend to be fault-finding; that is, they are "explicitly oriented to finding and eradicating flaws through therapy, treatment, or training of some sort" (p. 198).[2] The emic viewpoint, by contrast, focuses on "native insider reality" by looking at how people in a setting understand their situations. Where the etic approach yields "descriptions of behavior" that "find no value in deviation from accepted behavioral norms," the emic frame "emphasizes . . . the value and creativity of deviant behaviors" (p. 198). Central to the emic perspective, the observer must learn to listen and to hear, which in turn may require a shifting of perspective and, especially, critical awareness of one's own location.

This book was begun with assumption that people who have been labeled autistic have their own subjective understandings about how they experience the world, and that these perspectives are important. From this optimistic beginning point, it has been possible to see how their accounts sometimes complement or, alternatively, dramatically contradict findings from other research traditions. In one central way, their accounts diverge dramatically from the prevailing clinical literature. This has to do with the disability-rights or critical disability perspective that the authors project. These autobiographical accounts reinforce the critical Disability Studies literature's (e.g., Thomson 1997; MacKay 2003; Michalko 2001) insistence on defining all knowledge about ability/disability, even the concept of difference itself, as temporally and contextually situated and as socially constructed. Their richness suggests the danger of privileging other forms of research about autism as more deserving of authority or as being in some way uncontestable. Their forcefulness and consistency should signal clinical researchers to question every assumption brought to the topic of autism.

The value of appreciating the labeled person's subjective knowledge can also be seen in the very specific examples illustrating how the contributing authors encounter the world. Frugone sought out his mother's hand when he felt overwhelmed by uncertainty at entering the world outside his home. Mukhopadhyay found security in a book, rather than engaging the unpredictability of human interaction at a school his mother and he visited; his pursuit of a book, like Rubin's immersion in an object, was no rejection of people, only admission that engaging with people was significantly more challenging. Blackman threw a cup of coffee in a wastebasket when she was excited to see someone. While this was not necessarily intentional or particularly effective in communicating her feelings of welcome, from Blackman's perspective it had meaning; it reflected her excitement. In keeping with what Linneman refers to as belief in a person's "mindedness" (2001), with what Goode refers to as the "emic" perspective (1992), and what I have referred to as "presuming competence" (1997), the observer's obligation is thus not to assume the meaning of something another person does but rather to presume there must be a rationale and then to try and discover it, always from the other person's perspective, listening carefully.

Notes

1. It is important to remember that the concept of autism comprises a list of factors, and that others with the autism label do not necessarily experience such difficulties with sequenced actions.
2. Disability literature often suggests that all behavior is communicative. This may be true, but exactly what particular behavior means cannot be known to the outside observer unless the person observed has a way of explaining him- or herself. Thus it is wrong to impose normate assumptions about behavior, for example, to assume that a person's walking away means disinterest or a person's laughter when others are crying means happiness and insensitivity.

References

American Psychiatric Association (2000). *Diagnostic and statistical manual of mental disorders.* 4th ed. Washington, DC: American Psychiatric Association.

Biklen, D., and Cardinal, D. N. (1997). Reframing the issue: Presuming competence. In D. Biklen and D. N. Cardinal (eds.) *Contested words, contested science* (pp. 187–198). New York: Teachers College Press.

Bogdan, R., and Taylor, S. (1976). The judged not the judges: An insider's view of mental retardation. *American psychologist, 31,* pp. 47–52.

Charlton, J. I. (1998). *Nothing about us without us.* Berkeley: University of California Press.

Goode, D. A. (1992). Who is Bobby? Ideology and method in the discovery of a Down syndrome person's competence. In P. M. Ferguson, D. L. Ferguson, and S. J. Taylor (eds.), *Interpreting disability: A qualitative reader* (pp. 197–212). New York: Teachers College Press.

Grandin, T., and Scariano, M. (1986). *Emergence: Labeled autistic.* Novato, CA: Arena.

Linneman, R. D. (2001). *Idiots: Stories about mindedness and mental retardation.* New York: Peter Lang.

Linton, S. (1998). *Claiming disability.* New York: New York University Press.

Mackay, R. (2003). "Tell them who I was": The social construction of aphasia. *Disability and society, 16,* pp. 811–826.

Michalko, R. (2001). Blindness enters the classroom. *Disability and society, 16,* pp. 349–360.

Shore, S. (2003). *Beyond the wall.* 2nd ed. Shawnee Mission, KS: Autism and Asperger Publishing.

Stacey, P. (2003). *The boy who loved windows.* Boston: DeCapo Press.

Thomson, R. G. (1997). *Extraordinary bodies: Figuring physical disability in American culture and literature.* New York: Columbia University Press.

Whale, J. (director) (1933). *The invisible man.* Motion picture. Hollywood: Universal Studios.

Bibliography

A boy, a mother, and a rare map of autism's world (2002). *New York Times*, November 19, pp. D1 and D4.

American Psychiatric Association (2000). *Diagnostic and statistical manual of mental disorders*. 4th ed. Washington, DC: American Psychiatric Association.

Appiah, K. A., and Gates, H. L. Jr. (1995). *Identities*. Chicago: University of Chicago Press.

Asperger, H. (1944/1991). "Autistic psychopathy" in childhood. In U. Frith (ed. and trans.), *Autism and Asperger syndrome* (pp. 37–21). Cambridge: Cambridge University Press.

Atkinson, P. (1990). *The ethnographic imagination: Textual constructions of reality*. London: Routledge.

Atkinson, P., Coffey, A., and Delamont, S. (2003). *Key themes in qualitative research*. Walnut Creek, CA: AltaMira Press.

Attwood, T. (1998). *Asperger's syndrome: A guide for parents and professionals*. London: Jessica Kingsley Publishers.

——— (1999). Foreword. In L. Blackman, *Lucy's story: Autism and other adventures* (p. vii). Redcliffe, Queensland, Australia: Book in Hand.

Bara, B. G., Bucciarelli, M., and Colle, L. (2001). Communicative abilities in autism: Evidence for attentional deficits. *Brain and language, 77*, pp. 216–240.

Baron-Cohen, S. (1996). *Mindblindness: An essay on autism and theory of mind*. Cambridge: MIT Press.

Barron, J., and Barron, S. (1992). *There's a boy in here*. New York: Simon and Schuster.

Bauman, M., and Kemper, T. L. (1986). Developmental cerebellar abnormalities: A consistent finding in early infantile autism. *Neurology, 36* (suppl. 1), p. 190.

———— (1990). Limbic and cerebellar abnormalities are also present in an autistic child of normal intelligence. *Neurology, 40* (suppl. 1), p. 359.

———— (1995). Neuroanatomic observations of the brain in autism. In M. Bauman and T. L. Kemper (eds.), *The neurobiology of autism* (pp. 119–145). Baltimore: Johns Hopkins University Press.

Bauman, M., Filipek, P. A., and Kemper, T. L. (1997). Early infantile autism. *International review of neurobiology, 41,* pp. 367–386.

Bebko, J., Perry, A., and Bryson, S. (1996). Multiple method validation study of facilitated communication: Individual differences and subgroup results. *Journal of autism and developmental disabilities, 26,* pp. 43–58.

Belmonte, M. K., Cook, E. H. Jr., Anderson, B. M., Rubenstein, J. L. R., Greenough, W. T., Beckel-Mitchener, A., Courchesne, E., Boulanger, L. B., Powell, S. B., Levitt, P. R., Perry, E. K., Jiang, Y. H., DeLorey, T. M., and Tierney, E. (2004). Autism as a disorder of neural information processing: Directions for research and targets for therapy. *Molecular psychiatry, 1,* pp. 1–18.

Belmonte, M. K., and Yurgelun-Todd, D. A. (2003). Functional anatomy of impaired selective attention and compensatory processing in autism. *Cognitive brain research, 17,* pp. 651–664.

Bettelheim, B. (1967). *The empty fortress: Infantile autism and the birth of the self.* New York: Free Press.

Beukelman, D. and Mirenda, P. (1998). Augmentative and alternative communication: Management of severe communication disorders in children and adults. Baltimore: Paul H. Brooks.

Biklen, D. (1988). The myth of clinical judgment. *Journal of social issues, 44,* pp. 127–140.

———— (1990). Communication unbound: Autism and praxis. *Harvard educational review, 60,* pp. 291–314.

———— (2002). Experiencing autism: An interview with Donna Williams. *TASH Connections, 28* (June), pp. 15–21.

Biklen, D., and Cardinal, D. N. (1997). Reframing the issue: Presuming competence. In D. Biklen and D. N. Cardinal (eds.), *Contested words, contested science* (pp. 187–198). New York: Teachers College Press.

Biklen, D., and Rossetti, Z. (producers) (2005). *My classic life as an artist: A portrait of Larry Bissonnette.* Video documentary. Available from Syracuse University, 370 Huntington Hall, Syracuse, New York.

Bissonnette, L. (2002a). Letters ordered through typing produce the story of an artist stranded on the island of autism. Paper presented at the Narrating dis/Ability Conference, Syracuse University, Syracuse, New York.

———— (2002b). Things that matter. Paper presented at the 2002 Autism National Committee Conference, Nashua, New Hampshire.

———— (n.d.). *Constructions and personal insights.* West Glover, VT: G.R.A.C.E. (RFD Box 49, West Glover, VT 05875).

Blackburn, J., Gottschewski, K. McElroy, K., and Niki, L. (2000). A discussion about theory of mind: From an autistic perspective. *Proceedings of Autism Europe's Sixth International Congress,* Glasgow, Scotland.

Blackman, L. (1999). *Lucy's story: Autism and other adventures.* Redcliffe, Queensland, Australia: Book in Hand.

Bogdan, R., and Biklen, S. (1998). *Introduction to qualitative research in education.* Boston: Allyn and Bacon.

———— (2003). *Qualitative research for education.* 4th ed. Boston: Allyn and Bacon.

Bogdan, R., and Taylor, S. (1976). The judged not the judges: An insider's view of mental retardation. *American psychologist, 31,* pp. 47–52.

Bomba, C., O'Donnell, L., Markowitz, C., and Holmes, D. (1996). Evaluating the impact of facilitated communication on the communicative competence of fourteen students with autism. *Journal of autism and developmental disorders, 26,* pp. 43–58.

Borthwick, C., and Crossley, R. (1999). Language and retardation. *Psycholoquy, 10,* #38. Viewed on July 13, 2004, http://psycprints.ecs.soton.ac.uk/archive/00000673/.

Broderick, A., and Kasa-Hendrickson, C. (2001). "Say just one word at first": The emergence of reliable speech in a student labeled with autism. *Journal of the Association for Persons with Severe Handicaps, 26,* pp. 13–24.

Bunting, S. M. (2001). Sustaining the relationship: Women's caregiving in the context of HIV disease. *Health care for women international, 22,* pp. 131–148.

Cabay, M. (1994). A controlled evaluation of facilitated communication with four autistic children. *Journal of autism and developmental disorders, 24,* pp. 517–527.

Calculator, S., and Singer, K. (1992). Preliminary validation of facilitated communication. *Topics in language disorders, 12,* p. ix.

Cardinal D. N., Hanson, D., and Wakeham, J. (1996). An investigation of authorship in facilitated communication. *Mental retardation, 34,* pp. 231–242

Carpentieri, S., and Morgan, S. B. (1996). Adaptive and intellectual functioning in autistic and nonautistic retarded children. *Journal of autism and developmental disorders, 26,* pp. 611–620.

Charlton, J. I. (1998). *Nothing about us without us.* Berkeley: University of California Press.

Cherryholmes, C. (1988). *Power and criticism.* New York: Teachers College Press.

Cohen, S. (1998). *Targeting autism.* Berkeley: University of California Press.

Cole, A. L., and Knowles, J. G. (2001). *Lives in context: The art of life history research.* Walnut Creek, CA: AltaMira Press.

Courchesne, E. (1995). New evidence of cerebellar and brainstem hypoplasia in autistic infants, children and adolescents: The MR imaging study by Hashimoto and colleagues. *Journal of autism and developmental disorders, 25,* pp. 19–22.

———— (2002). Deciphering the puzzle: Unusual patterns of brain development in autism. Paper presented at the World Autism Congress, November, Melbourne, Australia.

Courchesne, E., Lincoln, A. J., Townsend, J. P., James, H. E., Akshoomoff, N. A., Saitoh, O., and Yeung Courchesne, R. (1994). A new finding: Impairment in shifting attention in autistic and cerebellar patients. In S. H. Broman and J. Grafman (eds.), *Atypical cognitive deficits in developmental disorders: Implications for brain function* (pp. 101–137). Hillsdale, NJ: Erlbaum.

Crews, W., Sanders, E., Hensley, L., Johnson, Y., Bonaventura, S., and Rhodes, R. (1995). An evaluation of facilitated communication in a group of nonverbal individuals with mental retardation. *Journal of autism and developmental disorders, 25,* pp. 205–213.

Crossley, R. (1994). *Facilitated communication training.* New York: Teachers College Press.

Damasio, A. R., and Maurer, R. G. (1978). A neurological model for childhood autism. *Archives of neurology, 35,* pp. 777–786.

Des Lauriers, A. M. (1978). The cognitive-affective dilemma in early infantile autism: The case of Clarence. *Journal of autism and childhood schizophrenia, 8,* pp. 219–232.

Duchan, J. F. (1998). Describing the unusual behavior of children with autism. *Journal of communication disorders, 31,* pp. 93–112.

Duchan, J., Calculator, S., Sonnenmeier, R., Diehl, S., and Cumley, G. (2001). A framework for managing controversial practices. *Language speech and hearing services in schools, 32,* pp. 133–141.

Eberlin, M., McConnachie, G., Ibel, S., and Volpe, L. (1993). "Facilitated communication": A failure to replicate the phenomenon. *Journal of autism and developmental disorders, 23,* pp. 507–529.

Emerson, A., Grayson, A., and Griffiths, A. (2001). Can't or won't? Evidence relating to authorship in facilitated communication. *International journal of language and communication disorders, 36* (suppl.), pp. 98–103.

Ferguson, P. (1994). *Abandoned to their fate.* Philadelphia: Temple University Press.

Fine, M. (1991). *Framing dropouts.* Albany: State University of New York Press.

Frith, U. (1989). *Autism: Explaining the enigma.* Cambridge, MA: Blackwell Publishers.

Frith, U. (1991). Asperger and his syndrome. In Uta Frith (ed.), *Autism and Asperger syndrome* (pp. 1–36). Cambridge: Cambridge University Press.

Gallagher, S. (1999). An exchange of gazes. In J. L. Kincheloe, S. R. Steinberg, and L. E. Villaverde (eds.), *Rethinking intelligence* (pp. 69–83). New York: Routledge.

Glaser, B., and Strauss, A. L. (1967). *The discovery of grounded theory.* Chicago: Aldine.

Goode, D. A. (1992). Who is Bobby?: Ideology and method in the discovery of a Down syndrome person's competence. In P.M. Ferguson, D. L. Ferguson, and S. J. Taylor (eds.), *Interpreting disability: A qualitative reader* (pp. 197–212). New York: Teachers College Press.

——— (1994). *World without words.* Philadelphia: Temple University Press.

Grandin, T. (1995). *Thinking in pictures, and other reports from my life with autism.* New York: Doubleday.

Grandin, T., and Scariano, M. (1986). *Emergence: Labeled autistic.* Novato, CA: Arena.

Griffith, E. M., Pennington, B. F., Wehner, E. A., and Rogers, S. J. (1999). Executive functions in young children with autism. *Child development, 70,* pp. 817–832.

Happé, F. G. E. (1991) The autobiographical writings of three Asperger syndrome adults: Problems of interpretation and implications for theory. In U. Frith (ed.), *Autism and Asperger syndrome* (pp. 207–242). Cambridge: Cambridge University Press.

Harris, P. (2003). "Mom will do it." The organization and implementation of friendship work for children with disabilities. Unpublished doctoral diss., Syracuse University, Syracuse, New York.

Hashimoto, T., Tayama, M., Murakawa, K., Yoshimoto, T., Miyazaki, M., and Harada, M. (1995). Development of the brainstem and cerebellum in autistic patients. *Journal of autism and developmental disorders, 25,* pp. 1–18.

Hayman, R. L. (1998). *Smart culture.* New York: New York University Press.

Heimann, M., Nelson, K. E., Tjus, T., and Gillberg, C. (1995). Increasing reading and communication skills in children with autism through an interactive multimedia computer program. *Journal of autism and developmental disorders, 25,* pp. 459–480.

Jacobson, J. W., Mulick, J. A., and Schwartz, A. A. (1995). A history of facilitated communication: Science, pseudoscience, and antiscience. *American psychologist,* pp. 750–765.

Janzen-Wilde, M., Duchan, J., and Higginbotham, D. (1995). Successful use of facilitated communication with an oral child. *Journal of speech and hearing research, 38,* pp. 658–676.

Jolliffe, T., and Baron-Cohen, S. (1999). A test of central coherence theory: Linguistic processing in high-functioning adults with autism or Asperger syndrome: Is local coherence impaired? *Cognition, 71,* pp. 149–185.

Joseph, R. M., and Tager-Flusberg, H. (2004). The relationship of theory of mind and executive functions to symptom type and severity in children with autism. *Development and psychopathology, 16,* pp. 137–155.

Kanner, L. (1943/1985). Autistic disturbances of affective contact. In A. M.

Donnellan (ed.), *Classic readings in autism* (pp. 11–50). New York: Teachers College Press.

Kasa-Hendrickson, C., Broderick, A., Biklen, D. (producers), and Gambell, J. (director) (2002). *Inside the edge*. Video documentary. Available from Syracuse University, 370 Huntington Hall, Syracuse, New York.

Klewe, L. (1993). An empirical evaluation of spelling boards as a means of communication for the multihandicapped. *Journal of autism and developmental disorders, 23,* pp. 559–566.

Kliewer, C. (1998). *Schooling children with Down syndrome*. New York: Teachers College Press.

Kliewer, C., and Biklen, D. (2001). "School's not really a place for reading": A research synthesis of the literate lives of students with severe disabilities. *JASH, 26,* pp. 1–12.

Kvale, S. (1995). The social construction of validity. *Qualitative inquiry, 1,* pp. 19–40.

Linneman, R. D. (2001). *Idiots: Stories about mindedness and mental retardation*. New York: Peter Lang.

Linton, S. (1998). *Claiming disability*. New York: New York University Press.

Lippard, L. R. (1998). *States of grace*. Hardwick, VT: G.R.A.C.E. (P.O. Box 960, Hardwick, VT 05843).

Mackay, R. (2003). "Tell them who I was": The social construction of aphasia. *Disability and society, 16,* pp. 811–826.

Mabrey, V. (producer/director) (2003). *Breaking the silence*. Documentary. *60 Minutes II* (United States).

Marsiglio, W. (2004). When stepfathers claim stepchildren: A conceptual analysis. *Journal of marriage and family, 66,* pp. 22–39.

Matsuo, H. Garrow, S., and Koric, A. (2002). Resettlement process of refugee immigrants from Bosnia and Herzegovina in St. Louis: Finding material and emotional niches. Conference paper, International Sociological Association (ISA), Brisbane, Australia.

Michalko, R. (2001). Blindness enters the classroom. *Disability and society, 16,* pp. 349–360.

Mirenda, P. (2003). "He's not really a reader . . . ": Perspectives on supporting literacy development in individuals with autism. *Topics in language disorders, 23,* pp. 271–282.

Miyake, A., Friedman, N. P., Emerson, M. J., Witzki, A. H., Howerter, A., and Wager, T. D. (2000). The unity and diversity of executive function and their contributions to complex "frontal lobe" tasks: A latent variable analysis. *Cognitive psychology, 41,* pp. 49–100.

Montee, B., Miltenberger, R., and Wittrock, D. (1995). An experimental analysis of facilitated communication. *Journal of applied behaviour analysis, 28,* pp. 189–200.

Moore, S., Donovan, B., Hudson, A., Dykstra, J., and Lawrence, J. (1993). Brief report: Evaluation of eight case studies of facilitated communication. *Journal of autism and developmental disorders, 23,* pp. 541–552.

Morris, J. (1991). *Pride against prejudice.* Philadelphia: New Society Publishers.

Mostert, M. P. (2001). Facilitated communication since 1995: A review of published studies. *Journal of autism and developmental disorders, 31,* pp. 287–313.

Mukhopadhyay, T. R. (2000). *Beyond the silence: My life, the world and autism.* London: National Autistic Society.

Niemi, J., and Kärnä-Lin, E. (2002). Grammar and lexicon in facilitated communication: A linguistic authorship analysis of a Finnish case. *Mental retardation, 40,* pp. 347–357.

Oakes, M., and Lucas, F. (2001). How war affects daily life: Adjustments in Salvadoran social networks. *Journal of social work research and evaluation, 2,* pp. 143–155.

Oppenheim, R. (1974). *Effective teaching methods for autistic children.* Springfield, IL: Thomas.

Ozick, C. (2003). Doubting Helen Keller. *New Yorker,* June 16 and 23, pp. 188–196.

Park, C. C. (2001). *Exiting nirvana: A daughter's life with autism.* Boston: Little, Brown and Company.

Prusley-Crotteau, S. (2001). Perinatal crack users becoming temperant: The social psychological processes. *Health care for women international, 22,* pp. 1–2.

Rapin, I. (1997). Current concepts: Autism. *New England journal of medicine. 337,* pp. 97–104.

Regal, R., Rooney, J., and Wandas, T. (1994). Facilitated communication: An experimental evaluation. *Journal of autism and developmental disorders, 24,* pp. 345–355.

Rubin, S., Biklen, D., Kasa-Hendrickson, C., Kluth, P., Cardinal, D. N., and Broderick, A. (2001). Independence, participation, and the meaning of intellectual ability, *Disability and society, 16,* pp. 425–429.

Sacks, O. (1995) Foreword. In T. Grandin, *Thinking in pictures, and other reports from my life with autism* (pp. 11–16). New York: Doubleday.

Schwartz, S. (1964). *Gilligan's island.* Television series (United States).

Sellen, B. (with Johanson, C. J.) (2000). *Outsider, self taught, and folk art annotated bibliography.* Jefferson, NC: McFarland.

Shakespeare, Tom. (1996). Rules of engagement. *Disability and society, 11,* pp. 115–119.

Shane, H., and Kearns, K. (1994). An examination of the role of the facilitator in "facilitated communication." *American journal of speech-language pathology,* (September), pp. 48–54.

Sheehan, C., and Matuozzi, R. (1996). Investigation of the validity of facilitated communication through the disclosure of unknown information. *Mental retardation, 34,* pp. 94–107.

Shore, S. (2003). *Beyond the wall.* 2nd ed. Shawnee Mission, KS: Autism and Asperger Publishing.

Smith, M., and Belcher, R. (1993). Brief report: Facilitated communication with adults with autism. *Journal of autism and developmental disorders, 23,* p. 175.

Spielberg, S. (producer/director) (1998). *Saving private Ryan.* Motion picture. Dreamworks (United States).

Spradley, J. P. (1980). *Participant observation.* Orlando, FL: Harcourt.

Stacey, P. (2003). *The boy who loved windows.* Boston: DeCapo Press.

Strauss, A. and Corbin, J. (1998) *Basics of qualitative research techniques and procedures for developing grounded theory.* 2nd ed. London: Sage Publications.

Szempruch, J., and Jacobson, J. (1993). Evaluating facilitated communications of people with developmental disabilities. *Research in developmental disabilities, 14,* pp. 253–264.

Terrill, C. (producer/director). (2000). *Inside story: Tito's story.* Documentary. London: BBC.

Thomson, R. G. (1997). *Extraordinary bodies: Figuring physical disability in American culture and literature.* New York: Columbia University Press.

Traustadottir, R. (1991a). The meaning of care in the lives of mothers of children with disabilities. In S. J. Taylor, R. Bogdan, and J. A. Racino (eds.), *Life in the community: Case studies of organizations supporting people with disabilities* (pp. 185–194). Baltimore: Paul H. Brookes.

——— (1991b). Mothers who care: Gender, disability, and family life. *Journal of family issues, 12,* pp. 211–228.

Trevarthen, C., Aitken, K., Papoudi, D., and Robarts, J. (1998). *Children with autism.* 2nd ed. London: Jessica Kingsley Publishers.

Tuzzi, A., Cemin, M., and Castagna, M. (2004) "Moved deeply I am": Autistic language in texts produced with FC. *Journées internationals d'analyse statistique des données textuelles, 7,* pp. 1–9.

Volkmar, F. R., and Cohen, D. J. (1985). The experience of infantile autism: A first-person account by Tony W. *Journal of autism and developmental disabilities, 15,* pp. 47–54.

Vryan, K. D., Adler, P. A., and Adler, P. (2003). Identity. In L. T. Reynolds and N. J. Herman-Kinney (eds.), *Handbook of symbolic interactionism* (pp. 367–390). Walnut Creek, CA: AltaMira.

Weiss, M., Wagner, S., and Bauman, M. (1996). A validated case study of facilitated communication. *Mental retardation, 34,* pp. 220–230.

Wells, H. G. (1911/1997). *Country of the blind and other science fiction stories.* Edited by M. Gardner. New York: Dover.

Welsh, M. C., and Pennington, B. F. (1988). Assessing frontal lobe functioning in children: Views from developmental psychology. *Developmental neuropsychology, 4,* pp. 199–230.

Whale, J. (director) (1933). *The invisible man.* Motion picture. Hollywood: Universal Studios.

Wheeler, D., Jacobson, J., Paglieri, R., and Schwartz, A. (1993). An experimental assessment of facilitated communication. *Mental retardation, 31,* pp. 49–60.

Williams, D. (1989). *Nobody nowhere.* Garden City, NY: Doubleday.

————— (1994). *Somebody somewhere.* New York: Times Books.

Willis, P. (2000). *The ethnographic imagination.* Malden, MA: Blackwell Publishers.

Wing, L. (2000). Foreword. In T. R. Mukhopadhyay, *Beyond the silence: My life, the world and autism* (pp. 1–3). London: National Autistic Society.

————— (2001). *The autistic spectrum.* Berkeley, CA: Ulysses Press.

Wing, L., and Gould, J. (1979). Severe impairments of social interaction and associated abnormalities in children: Epidemiology and classification. *Journal of autism and childhood schizophrenia, 9,* pp. 11–29.

Wolff, T. (1989). *This boy's life: A memoir.* Boston: Atlantic Monthly Books.

Wordsworth, W. (1991). The prelude, book 1. In J. Wilson (ed.), *Lakeland poets* (p. 30). London: Grange Books.

Wurzburg, G. (producer/director) (2004). *Autism is a world.* Documentary. Atlanta: CNN.

Zanobini, M., and Scopesi, A. (2001). La comunicazione facilitata in un bambino autistico. *Psicologia clinica dello Sviluppo, 5,* pp. 395–421.

Index

■ ■ ■ ■ ■ ■ ■ ■ ■

About the Authors

Douglas Biklen is Professor of Cultural Foundations of Education and Teaching and Leadership and coordinates the Inclusive Education Program at Syracuse University. He is a senior faculty member in the Center on Disability Studies, Law and Human Policy. He has authored or co-authored numerous books, including *Access to Academics, Schooling without Labels, Achieving the Complete School, Communication Unbound,* and *Contested Words, Contested Science.* News accounts of his work have appeared in the *New York Times Magazine, Newsweek, U.S. News and World Report,* the *Washington Post Magazine,* and on the *CBS Evening News, NOW, Frontline,* and ABC's *Primetime Live.* He was Educational Advisor for the Academy Award–winning documentary *Education Peter* (HBO) and is co-producer of the CNN documentary *Autism Is a World* (2004).

Richard Attfield lives in England, where he writes and has had several articles published. At the age of fifteen, he won his first writing award in the Young Writers Competition (1993) from among thirty thousand entries. He later attended mainstream college; there he received awards for his writing and for Personal Achievement and Outstanding Commitment.

Larry Bissonnette is an artist who lives with his sister in Vermont. His work has been exhibited at art shows and in galleries in New York City, Europe, and the state of Vermont, where he resides.

Lucy Blackman lives in Queensland, Australia, where she is a graduate student and writer. Among her publications is a book-length autobiography, *Lucy's Story, Autism and Other Adventures* (1999).

Jamie Burke lives in Syracuse, New York, where he attends high school. He was the subject of a research report published in 2001 and has written and narrated a video documentary, *Inside the Edge*, about how, as a teenager, he emerged from typing to speaking.

Alberto Frugone lives with his mother and stepfather in Zoagli, Italy, on the coast of the Mediterranean. After attending inclusive secondary school, he recently passed Italy's postsecondary qualifying exams and became the first nonspeaking Italian classified as autistic to attend a university.

Tito Rajarshi Mukhopadhyay was born in India and learned to speak and write after much intense support from his mother, from a speech therapist, and from others. By the age of eleven, he had written a book, *Beyond the Silence,* and was the subject of a BBC documentary.

Sue Rubin grew up in southern California and is now a college student. Until the age of thirteen, she was diagnosed as both autistic and severely retarded and was thought incapable of academic work. She is featured in and was the writer for an autobiographical documentary titled *Autism Is a World* on *CNN Presents.*

Printed in the United States
By Bookmasters